ANCIENTS AND M

General Editor: Phiroze Vasunia, Reader in Classics, University of Reading

How can antiquity illuminate critical issues in the modern world? How does the ancient world help us address contemporary problems and issues? In what ways do modern insights and theories shed new light on the interpretation of ancient texts, monuments, artefacts and cultures? The central aim of this exciting new series is to show how antiquity is relevant to life today. The series also points towards the ways in which the modern and ancient worlds are mutually connected and interrelated. Lively, engaging, and historically informed, *Ancients and Moderns* examines key ideas and practices in context. It shows how societies and cultures have been shaped by ideas and debates that recur. With a strong appeal to students and teachers in a variety of disciplines, including classics and ancient history, each book is written for non-specialists in a clear and accessible manner.

JÖRG RÜPKE is Professor of Comparative Religion at the University of Erfurt. His previous books include *Religion of the Romans, A Companion to Roman Religion* and *Fasti Sacerdotum: A Prosopography of Pagan, Jewish, and Christian Religious Officials in the City of Rome, 300 BC to AD 499*.

ANCIENTS AND MODERNS SERIES

THE ART OF THE BODY: ANTIQUITY AND ITS LEGACY • MICHAEL SQUIRE

DEATH: ANTIQUITY AND ITS LEGACY • MARIO ERASMO

DRAMA: ANTIQUITY AND ITS LEGACY • DAVID ROSENBLOOM

GENDER: ANTIQUITY AND ITS LEGACY • BROOKE HOLMES

LUCK, FATE AND FORTUNE: ANTIQUITY AND ITS LEGACY • ESTHER EIDINOW

MEDICINE: ANTIQUITY AND ITS LEGACY • CAROLINE PETIT

POLITICS: ANTIQUITY AND ITS LEGACY • KOSTAS VLASSOPOULOS

RACE: ANTIQUITY AND ITS LEGACY • DENISE EILEEN McCOSKEY

RELIGION: ANTIQUITY AND ITS LEGACY • JÖRG RÜPKE

SEX: ANTIQUITY AND ITS LEGACY • DANIEL ORRELLS

SLAVERY: ANTIQUITY AND ITS LEGACY • PAGE DUBOIS

SPORT: ANTIQUITY AND ITS LEGACY • TO BE ANNOUNCED

WAR: ANTIQUITY AND ITS LEGACY • ALFRED S. BRADFORD

ANCIENTS AND MODERNS

RELIGION
ANTIQVITY AND ITS LEGACY

JÖRG RÜPKE

Oxford University Press is a department of the University of Oxford. It furthers the University's objective of excellence in research, scholarship, and education by publishing worldwide.

Oxford New York
Auckland Cape Town Dar es Salaam Hong Kong Karachi
Kuala Lumpur Madrid Melbourne Mexico City Nairobi
New Delhi Shanghai Taipei Toronto

With offices in
Argentina Austria Brazil Chile Czech Republic France Greece
Guatemala Hungary Italy Japan Poland Portugal Singapore
South Korea Switzerland Thailand Turkey Ukraine Vietnam

Oxford is a registered trademark of Oxford University Press in the UK
and certain other countries.

Published in the United States of America by
Oxford University Press
198 Madison Avenue, New York, New York 10016

www.oup.com

First published by I.B.Tauris & Co. Ltd in the United Kingdom

Copyright © Jörg Rüpke, 2013.

All rights reserved. No part of this publication may be reproduced,
stored in a retrieval system, or transmitted, in any form or by any means,
electronic, mechanical, photocopying, recording, or otherwise,
without the prior permission of Oxford University Press.

The right of Jörg Rüpke to be identified as the author of this work has been asserted
by the author in accordance with the Copyright, Designs and Patents Act 1988.

Library of Congress Cataloging-in-Publication Data

Rüpke, Jörg.
Religion : antiquity and its legacy / by Jörg Rüpke.
pages cm. — (Ancients and moderns series)
ISBN 978-0-19-538076-7 (alk. paper) — ISBN 978-0-19-538077-4 (alk. paper)
1. Rome—Religion. I. Title.
BL803.R85 2013
292.07—dc23   2012046502

ISBN (HB): 978-0-19-538076-7
ISBN (PB): 978-0-19-538077-4

Typeset in Garamond Pro by Ellipsis Digital Limited, Glasgow
Printed and bound in Great Britain by CPI Group (UK) Ltd, Croydon, CR0 4YY

CONTENTS

ACKNOWLEDGEMENTS   vii

FOREWORD (*by Phiroze Vasunia*)   ix

INTRODUCTION   1
    Overview   3
    What is religion?   7
    A paradigmatic example: religion of the late Roman Republic   8

CHAPTER I: INDIVIDUAL AND CORPORATE RELIGION   22
    From religion to religions   25
    Individualization   28
    Conclusion   33

CHAPTER II: HISTORICIZING RELIGION   35
    History and religion   36
    Beginnings   39
    Varronian history and systematics   43
    Conclusion   48

CHAPTER III: IDOLATRY AND REPRESENTATION   52
    Religion with and without images   53
    Picturing   54
    Using images   56
    Conclusion   60

CHAPTER IV: THEOLOGICAL HERITAGES: ROMAN PRIESTHOOD AND THE NEW TESTAMENT   63
    Determining contexts   65
    Changing concepts of priesthood   67
    Sacerdotology in Hebrews   74
    Conclusion   77

CHAPTER V: COLONIZING TIME ... 80
  Calendars in ancient Italy ... 81
  Calendrical systems in ancient Italy ... 85
  The diffusion of Roman festivals ... 87
  Why were useless *fasti* produced and displayed? ... 91
  Fighting for details? ... 94
  The calendar as a tool to construct history ... 97
  Conclusion ... 99

CHAPTER VI: DEALING WITH THE FUTURE: DIVINATION BY CALENDARS ... 101
  Reading the calendar ... 105
  Chronomancy: choosing the lucky day ... 108
  Collision of *nundinae* ... 112
  The planetary week ... 115
  Conclusion ... 117

CHAPTER VII: THE PRESENCE OF DEATH IN LIVED RELIGION ... 118
  Lived religion ... 118
  Practical problems ... 120
  Traditions and norms: burial and grief rituals ... 124
  Divinization ... 129
  Life after death ... 130
  Grave monuments ... 131
  Conclusion ... 134

CHAPTER VIII: CONCLUSION ... 137

SOME SUGGESTIONS FOR FURTHER READING ... 141

NOTES ... 143

INDEX ... 171

ACKNOWLEDGEMENTS

I would not have been able to write this book without the conditions of work offered by the University of Erfurt and the Max Weber Centre in the immediate context of the International Research Group 'Religious Individualization in Historical Perspective', financed by the German Science Foundation, and by funding of the 7th European Research Framework Program (agreement 295555). Many fellows and colleagues were involved in talks that gave rise to ideas developed in this book, or criticized interpretations too bold or too restricted. In particular I would like to thank Clifford Ando, Hermann Deuser, Martin Fuchs, Richard Gordon, Bettina Hollstein, Harry O. Maier, Dietmar Mieth, Tessa Rajak, Eric Rebillard, Veit Rosenberger, Sabine Sander, Magnus Schlette, Wolfgang Spickermann, Katharina Waldner, Jula Wildberger and Greg Woolf. Diana Püschel has been helpful as ever. The book is dedicated to my loving wife, Ulrike, who herself has to permanently bridge ancients and moderns.

FOREWORD

Ancients and Moderns comes to fruition at a propitious moment: 'reception studies' is flourishing, and the scholarship that has arisen around it is lively, rigorous, and historically informed; it makes us rethink our own understanding of the relationship between past and present. *Ancients and Moderns* aims to communicate to students and general readers the depth, energy, and excitement of the best work in the field. It seeks to engage, provoke, and stimulate, and to show how, for large parts of the world, Greco-Roman antiquity continues to be relevant to debates in culture, politics, and society.

The series does not merely accept notions such as 'reception' or 'tradition' without question; rather, it treats these concepts as contested categories and calls into question the illusion of an unmediated approach to the ancient world. We have encouraged our authors to take intellectual risks in the development of their ideas. By challenging the assumption of a direct line of continuity between antiquity and modernity, these books explore how discussions in such areas as gender, politics, race, sex, and slavery occur within particular contexts and histories; they demonstrate that no culture is monolithic, that claims to ownership of the past are never pure, and that East and West are often connected together in ways that continue to surprise and disturb many. Thus, *Ancients and Moderns* is intended to stir up debates about and within reception studies and to complicate some of the standard narratives about the 'legacy' of Greece and Rome.

RELIGION: ANTIQVITY AND ITS LEGACY

All the books in *Ancients and Moderns* illustrate that *how* we think about the past bears a necessary relation to *who* we are in the present. At the same time, the series also seeks to persuade scholars of antiquity that their own pursuit is inextricably connected to what many generations have thought, said, and done about the ancient world.

Phiroze Vasunia

INTRODUCTION

To discuss religion in a series called 'Ancients and Moderns' might at first appear to be a straightforward task: today's religions are ancient phenomena. If 'moderns' is a self-description of the Western world, Europe and the Americas, the dominating religions in this part of the world stem from the 'ancients' – whereby the 'ancients' are taken to mean the cultures of the Mediterranean world of Greco-Roman times. This holds true for Judaism, which is present in many cities around the Mediterranean, most prominently in Palestine and Egypt. It certainly holds true for Christianity in its Western (Latin) and Eastern (Greek Orthodox) varieties. And it also holds true for Islam, a religion developed in criticism of ancient polytheisms as well as regional Jewish and Christian thinking. Certainly, the spread of Arabic Islam brought an end to many political structures and cultural traits of the 'ancient' world, as Henri Pirenne formulated nearly a century ago.[1] At the same time, however, the Islamic Empire flourished in assimilating classical material into its intellectual culture.[2] But even if we drop any Eurocentric approach, major religious traditions are classified with 'ancient', Hinduism, Buddhism or Confucianism taking pride of place. 'Ancient', here, is more than a synonym of 'old'. Philosophers such as Karl Jaspers, along with historians and sociologists, have pointed to the temporal coincidence of major 'breakthroughs' in the human grasp of society, driven by the discovery of the transcendent and the resulting possibilities to think about alternatives in ordering one's world. The period from about 500 BC onwards (datings vary dramatically) – the time of Israelite prophets, Buddha and Confucius, as well as Socrates – has been termed an 'axial age', determining the societal and religious condition of modern mankind.[3] Thus, without doubt the 'ancients' are highly relevant for us 'moderns'.

However, does my use of 'ancients' meet all expectations? In terms of the history of religion, 'ancient' frequently refers to pre-axial religions, to animal sacrifice instead of the Eucharist, to the cult of the temple at Jerusalem instead of synagogal meetings on the Sabbath, to polytheism and idolatry instead of prayer without images. Thus, to deal with religion in a series called 'Ancients and Moderns' seems to be, in fact, a rather difficult task. 'Modern' does not simply denote 'younger' or 'less old'. We are far from an age that regarded classical antiquity as an unsurpassable measuring rod, a world in which aesthetic, moral, even institutional values and solutions served as ideals or, at least, gave orientation. The *querelle des anciens et modernes* – the quarrel of the ancient and modern – has long been decided.[4] The notion of 'modernity' includes the idea of a radical break. It questions the value of all historical knowledge. For religion, the key notions are secularization, individualization and privatization of religion, the invisibility of religion, and its plurality.[5] One could also ask if it is adequate to speak of 'religion' when considering pre-modern practices that lack the organizational framework of a church.

Against such a backdrop, a volume on religion can neither simply give an overview of ancient religions nor systematically compare ancient and modern religions. Thus, this book instead looks into the similarities *and* differences of ancient religions as compared to contemporary religions, identifying genealogies into modern religions as well as demarcating the breaks already within antiquity, in order to explore and better understand the religious and cultural matrix of today. Given the complexity of the latter, the sketch of consequential features of ancient religion will not be met by a parallel description of the modern, which is diversified and pluralized to the point where 'religion' as a term is frequently rejected for concepts such as 'spirituality'. Thus, each chapter employs different strategies to relate ancient data to modern concerns. This ranges from the genealogy of classical features of today's Christianities to the invocation of anthropological points of comparison, to pinpointing concerns of major religious traditions as well as religious non-conformists. Rather than confront ancient phenomena with a collection of contemporary anthropological data, each chapter invites reflection on local (or one's own) religious or not-any-longer-religious practices, thus neatly illustrating 'survivals'.

Overview

In order to meet this challenge, the book starts with a brief characterization of ancient religious practices, but this will not be organized as an introduction to ancient religions, which can be found elsewhere.[6] Instead, I address aspects of religion that are crucial for historic as well as contemporary religious practices, beliefs or organizations. Attention will be given to areas in which ancient developments arrived at situations or solutions that are comparable to, or still identical with, institutions or constellations of today.

Chapter I argues that two important phenomena that are characteristic to the image and self-image of religions in and beyond Europe can be traced to Mediterranean antiquity in the Hellenistic and Roman periods. The first is the transformation of religious practices and beliefs that led to the formation of boundary-conscious and knowledge-based religious groups, which could be called 'religions'. At the same time, however, religious individuality is shown to be much more important than is usually admitted in dealing with ancient pre-Christian religion. The first process is clearly gaining in momentum during the period analysed, as is shown by the history of several important terms and organizational developments; the second area does not allow a clear judgement on any progressive individualization. The concept of 'axial' and 'pre-axial' ages is applied to stress the role of empire in these processes.

Writing about changes implies that religion has a history. But how can the eternal change? Chapter II addresses the historicization of religion and the memories transported by religion. What is memory? How does it differ from history? Historicization is usually seen as an achievement of the modern period: everything is historicized, and modern religions take part in the enterprise. In contrast, ancient religion is usually seen as a static system, modified only by additions or oblivion. Nevertheless, ancient religion is characterized by crucial elements of self-historicization. For example, it is the proclamation of some ancient Greek authors to replace the lies of mythical storytelling by critical historiography which has been regarded as the origins of European historiography. For religion, the processes of historicization can be observed by looking at a neighbouring culture confronted with these different types of storytelling: in this case Rome. By the second century BC the growth of cults in the city of Rome is mapped in chronological terms by the combination of calendars and lists of magistrates (*fasti*). By the first century, Varro in his 'Divine Antiquities' seems to have integrated chronological data into a historicizing approach towards religion on a large scale. The chapter will draw these factors together to paint a new image of a historicized religion contemporary to Judaism and early Christianity.

Chapter III looks further at elements that are central to ancient self-historicization, but here the perspective changes. To give a face to the divine is important for religious practices. How did ancient religions solve the problem of making the divine approachable, of making the unseen seen? For that purpose, the ancients employed all the techniques of interhuman communication in their communication with the all-powerful divine. At the same time it was accepted that any representation would be unable to adequately sketch the divine, which always transcends human attempts to grasp it. Images and criticism of images seem to rise contemporarily. The chapter traces the techniques and emotional components of practices of imaging the divine, and reflects on these techniques to deny the validity of the same representation, concentrating on imperial practices, philosophical critique of images and superstitious forms of dealing with them. In using statues and temples, ancient religions had a powerful instrument to construct – or, from a different perspective, represent – the divine in a differentiated, polytheistic form. It enabled ritual access, stimulated reflection, inspired imagination in day or night dreams and visions, and it even informed

INTRODUCTION

critical philosophical thinking. Inquiring into the will of the gods in the many forms of divination drew on this system of representation, too. The gods could be met and addressed in their temples; sacrifices enabled the petitioner to put his question and get an immediate answer via extispicy. Thus basic positions and practices are identified that are still valid for today's popular religious practices – as iconoclastic positions and 'negative' theology. The chapter will sketch this differentiated system and look at how these different strategies relate to each other, as well as addressing the problem of their clashing: what about having the gods destroy their own representations by lightning – melting the bronze statues and destroying the temples? The situation of the first century AD – the singular evidence from the buried site of Pompeii as well as Greek and Latin texts from contemporary writers – offers a unique glimpse into practices and reflections.

Chapter IV starts from the modern notion of clearly demarcated religious traditions. This notion is tested via a text that belongs to the Christian New Testament and which proposes a crucial notion of post-Reformation Christian theology, the priestly role of Jesus. Assuming a Roman origin of 'the letter to the Hebrews' around the end of the first century and the beginning of the second century AD, the implications of a firm contextualization in a religiously plural society are spelled out. The dating implies an audience educated in Flavian times and informed by Roman culture, as expressed in public buildings, images and – even if we think about a Jewish family background – rituals. The text is thus analysed in terms of contemporary urban culture and religion. Special attention is given to priestly roles, which are compared to the prominent role of *pontifex maximus* of the Roman emperors and to the developments of major public priesthoods during the second half of the first century AD. As a result, Christianity appears as a much more 'ancient' religion than is usually assumed, when Christianity itself is identified as the great break with antiquity.

One of the most spectacular, but hardly noticed, survivals from antiquity and ancient religions is the Julian calendar. How could a pagan calendar – with months dedicated to deities such as Janus, Mars, Aphrodite, Maia and Juno, or to divinized emperors such as Julius (Caesar) and Augustus – be accepted as the framework for the Christian year? The Julian calendar was, of course, rejected by Jews and Muslims. Chapter V inquires into the religious framing of time and its modification in situations of religious pluralism, through into the early modern age.

Chapter VI continues the topic of the calendar, but addresses a different use of time. Divination was a large field of practices densely connected to other forms of religion and notions of the gods. In contrast, modern forms of divination have either taken rational, scientific forms (futurology) or have moved to the margins of accepted practices (astrology, cards, folklore). At the same time, divination is a multibillion-pound business integrating modern media as well as forms of legitimization by ancient traditions. The chapter will present ancient divinatory practices related to the calendar and explore their religious and political functions. It will open up a view on a continuous history of contemporary divinatory practices from antiquity onwards – which is still relevant to thinking about the future.

Chapter VII addresses death. It identifies the consequences of individual death, from the problems of the decaying body to social consequences and expectations of a post-mortal existence. What were the solutions found by the ancients? How did they evolve over a time span of half a millennium? Religious rituals are embedded into a social construction of death that embraces familial practices as juridical regulation. From the point of view of an individual of at least moderate means, death could be seen as an individual project of preserving one's position in society and one's social capital accumulated beyond the end of physical life. Ancient monuments still confront us with the same problem of individual and social continuity in the face of death, even if our answers are different and as diverse among contemporaries as they seem to have been among the ancients.

What is this 'antiquity' that this book is talking about? The period concentrates on the Mediterranean basin from around 500 BC to AD 400. Not unlike the moderns, the ancients are of surprising diversity. As Islam differs from Bradford to Islamabad, from Sarajevo to Cairo, and Christianity differs from Nigeria to China and urban England to the American Bible Belt, so Greek religion was different to Roman, and Isis cult on Hadrian's

Wall differed from the cult at Alexandria. Ancient and modern religion does not differ like 'city religions' and 'world religions'. In antiquity, religious exchange connected Italy and India; many forms of modern religion are astonishingly local. In order to contextualize religious practices, time and again the chapters in this book will focus on practices at Rome and open up possibilities of generalization. There is more to the ancients than Roman culture. Greek myth has imbued European literatures and iconography, even if Latin writers and versions – Ovid for instance – were much more widely read (and understood!) than their Greek pretexts. In the field of religion, many an Italian development was shaped by models and symbols of the ancient Near East and Greece. And yet, frequently it was the Etruscan, Latin or 'Roman' form that shaped West European and North African practices more intensively. The impact of the Roman Empire and the Roman assimilation of Christianity might be the two single most important factors.

I hope that this book, in making knowledge about pre-modern cultures accessible, will enable a better understanding and, in this way, encourage readers to more daringly explore the contemporary religious world. Vice versa, our contemporary concerns will help to review ancient, perhaps seemingly exotic, forms of religion. Thus, specialists of antiquity, too, I hope, will find fresh ideas for their studies of cultures that frequently appear to be unnecessarily isolated from today's world.

What is religion?

One cannot talk about an ancient religion in a scholarly context as something that can be either identified in its own right or found hidden beneath other cultural practices. In the late Roman Republic, there were attempts to coin cumulative descriptions such as *sacra et auspicia* (Cicero, *De natura deorum* 3.5), meaning 'cults and divination', yet only Cicero uses *religio* as a generic term encompassing a group's duty towards and care for the gods. Cicero's *religio*, however, encompasses neither the organizational infrastructure and degree of coherence of these activities nor their shared symbolic language, or any related metaphysical reflection. To talk about ancient religion, therefore, is to talk about a range of cultural practices conforming to *our* notion of religion; this notion has, to be sure, grown out of ancient reflection and terminology, but it has been strongly influenced by early modern and nineteenth-century Christian discourses.

It is no improvement to substitute the plural 'religions' for the singular 'religion'.[7] This use of 'religions' (to be treated in Chapter I) goes even further in suggesting the existence of a plurality of self-contained and neatly separated religious traditions or systems on the model of early modern Christian denominations.[8] By contrast, this book aims to demonstrate both the internal pluralism and the characteristic lack of clear borders of Roman religious practices within their ancient Mediterranean context. The coexistence of private or familial religious loyalties to special groups such as Bacchanalian cults is part of a religious 'division of labour', and represents a range of religious options and activities on different social levels. Only the political elite identified such activities as an alternative to a so-called 'religion of the Roman people' (Livy 39.13). The conflict resulting from the Bacchanalian affair of 186 BC, when people engaging in a cult of Dionysus/Bacchus were persecuted as a political conspiracy, neatly illustrates how ancient religion could have a history of its own. Such a 'history of religion' is an idea that will be looked into further in Chapter II.

A paradigmatic example: religion of the late Roman Republic[9]

When Cicero mentions both *sacra* and *auspicia* in his definition of 'religion' (quoted above), he juxtaposes a vast range of diverse cultic practices with a fairly clear-cut ritual, a special set of *divinatory* practices, known as 'the auspices'. However, Cicero's combination of these two Latin terms can hardly be considered an ethnographic inventory, especially since it comes from a member of the augural college, the priesthood entrusted with the supervision of the auspices. If, on the other hand, one concentrates on the interrelationship between religious and political practices or on the prominence of religion in the textual remains of late republican literature, Cicero's description is entirely accurate. 'Augural law' was the most spectacular field for the interlacing of religious and political strategies, and for the religious foundations of the Roman elite's rules governing political decisions.[10] Practices that frequently seem to us to involve manipulation of religion in fact constitute the ingrained religious traditions of a society that simultaneously produced radically sceptical accounts of religion.

Divinatory practices are a universal phenomenon. Techniques for learning about the future, conceptualized as something predefined by the gods or by fate, are manifold and ease the burden of making decisions by indicating their outcome in advance. Divination appears in a variety of forms and was usually an attempt to overcome uncertainty in situations where a difficult decision was to be made. At the same time, risks could also be reduced in other ways. Sometimes it seemed important to relate one's own actions to the cosmic order. Geomancy or astrology, with their purported knowledge about the cosmic order, offered techniques to determine places or times for inoffensive 'intrusion' into the natural order of things. Finally, divination could be a means of seeking the approval of the gods. In Rome, the politically dominant cult practices conform to this latter type. A Roman would, for example, always ask for Jupiter's consent to an action on the very morning of the proposed action. The answer would be sought mostly in the behaviour of birds, known as 'translators' (*interpretes*) of Jupiter's will. Lightning bolts could also demonstrate Jupiter's assent. There are certainly elements of Etruscan traditions present here, but the rich and complicated Etruscan system of lightning types and their directions, interpreted by the professional priesthood of the *haruspices*, was reduced by the Romans to the mere appearance of lightning in the sky.

Roman divination was not restricted to augury performed by magistrates and priests (*augurs*), and the variety of signs, as well as the range of persons taking the auspices (*auspicium privatum*), was said to have been even wider in earlier times.[11] The analysis of entrails continued to be practised as part of ritual sacrifice. It constituted, however, not a technique to learn about the future, but rather a system that expressed the risk of communication between men and gods – and at the same time it overcame such risks. A noticeable interest in astrology started in the late second century BC, and by the end of the first century BC the basic astrological tenets of the planetary week seem to have become common knowledge.[12] The interpretation of dreams is already presupposed in Plautus' comedies *Rudens* and *Miles gloriosus* in the early second century BC. An important and rather underrated phenomenon must have been the *vates*, or prophets, whose memory has been reduced to some derogatory remarks in the surviving texts of the mainstream tradition.[13] But the concept of *vates* in Augustan poetry, in the second half of the first century BC, cannot be understood without a reconstruction of its institutional background, which consisted of figures who addressed the Roman public, although not in any official capacity, on topics concerning both the future and ethics.

By contrast, the auspices were fully integrated into the constitutional framework of the Roman Republic. Their legal basis (namely the *leges Aelia et Fufia*) had been formulated during the latter half of the second century BC, when written 'constitutional guidelines' were first envisaged in Rome. Politically relevant roles were restricted to the highest echelon of magistrates, consuls and praetors, and, in certain functions, to the augurs as a body (to give judgement and advice) or as individuals (for the observation of special signs and advice). In practice, techniques for the interpretation of signs themselves seem to have been fairly easy, despite a rather large body of rules that were apparently no longer applied. When observing the flight and the cries of birds before sunrise, the magistrate used a formula to specify in advance what the relevant signs would be. Even this exercise was frequently replaced by the so-called *tripudium*. A person in charge of caged hens observed whether the animals were greedy or reserved when they picked the fodder offered to them. The reaction of the birds was open to effective manipulation, as contemporary Romans were well aware. Likewise, the observation of a lightning flash was no matter of empirical 'scientific validation': the very announcement that such a sign was anticipated constituted a factor relevant to religion and politics. Hence a political opponent's declaration that he was looking for adverse signs could in itself be taken as the effective realization of the celestial veto for the proceedings at hand.

INTRODUCTION

The obligation for the presiding magistrate to 'take the auspices' before important actions (popular assemblies, voting, elections, departing for warfare) gave divine approval to these actions while at the same time laying them open to auspicial criticism and obstruction. Given the range of legitimate participants and of actions involved, augural law complicated the processes of political decision making.[14] Thus augural practice enabled the formalization of opposition and dissent in a way that overrode majority votes in a consent-oriented elite. However, the effectiveness of the veto should not be overrated. Even augural dissent was usually ignored in legislative decisions. Here, the auspices were just one of the ways to 'opt out' of political decision-making procedures. The augural delegitimization of a newly elected magistrate was, however, decisive. Divine consent of the leading figures in the community, and of their most important actions, was no less important than having the majority of human votes. Augury constituted a system for enforcing societal consent and for temporalizing dissent. Furthermore, prodigies (i.e. supernatural events observed as spontaneous signs of divine anger) enlarged this 'system' by further variants, which were open to interpretation by every Roman citizen, but which were also filtered by priesthoods and magistrates and had to be dealt with by means of special ritual procedures.[15] It is the methodological option of any non-theological approach towards religion to 'explain' religious practices as social practices, without any reference to the existence of (but of course, belief in) superhuman beings (gods) and without any judgement of their existence.

It seems useful, before turning to other types of religious practices, to put divination into a broader context by describing other types of public ritual. From the mid Roman Republic onwards, religion – expressed first in the building of new temples,[16] and then in the financing of games,[17] which developed into an area of primary importance for the public display of wealth and its use to benefit the community as a whole – a practice easily recognizable in modern sponsorship. Obviously, the resulting prestige for the individual and for his descendants reflected and enlarged the prestige of the offices that regulated the access to these opportunities. The ritual of the triumph was the most important. It originated in an honorary procession for Jupiter, which corresponded to the departing ceremonies before a war. In time, the triumphal procession turned more and more into a magnificent presentation of booty and feats of war, ending with donations and spectacles for the populace.[18] The right to wear triumphal dress, to be buried within the city walls, and to erect triumphal arches and statues perpetuated this prestigious moment. I suspect that the list of the triumphators, the *fasti triumphales Barberiniani*, were the first lists of office holders to be publicly displayed in stone.[19]

Despite the fact that a small number of ritual forms dominate the literary record, and probably also the public's perception, it is important to note the varied forms of religious ritual in the areas considered so far. The *supplicationes* (supplications), for instance, were used as a crisis ritual in mid republican Rome. As a reaction to military catastrophe or as preparation for a difficult war, a day could be declared a public holiday and the whole adult population would be encouraged to approach and pray in the temples (all opened up for the event) in order to implore the goddesses and gods of Rome to restore their harmonious relationship with the people.[20] The same ritual of processions to all the temples could be employed to offer thanks. This variant came to be used as an instrument to honour generals, especially in the late Republic. In reaction to a written report about a major victory or about the end of a war, supplications to the immortal gods were declared 'in the name of the general'.[21] The length of the supplications corresponded to the appreciation felt for the victory and for the victor himself: in the third and second centuries BC, supplications could last from three days to an exceptional five days, while in the years from 45 to 43 BC no fewer than three supplications of 50 days each were held.[22]

The major games were developed out of a few ancient horse races (*Equirria, October equus*), athletic competitions (e.g. *ludi Capitolini*, never reaching the broad range of disciplines of the Greek Olympic games), and under the influence of dramatic spectacles of Greek origin as staged in southern Italy. Whereas the first originally involved aristocrats or at least citizens, the latter were from the start a matter for professionals, mostly of foreign provenance. This social division of the practitioners of these arts is

INTRODUCTION

not unknown today: praising aristocratic competition and the amateur sportsman, yet often despising wandering groups of performers. At Rome, the number of games and their length multiplied during the last decades of the third and second century BC. All of these games were staged in rather provisional settings in the valley of the Circus Maximus, as well as on the Campus Martius. By contrast, the first stone theatres, built in the middle of the first century BC, were not intended as permanent structures for specific games but as parts of vast building projects with a significance of their own (e.g. the theatre of Pompeius).

Fortunately, the archaeological record has not only preserved traces of these massive projects but can also supplement the elite-oriented literary discourse on matters of private religion. Thousands of votive objects made of clay illustrate areas of religious activity that have barely left any literary traces, and frequently not even any epigraphic record. For the fourth to first centuries BC, several votive deposits have been found in central Italy (with a remarkable decline or shift towards specifically local types at the end of the period). Typically, a wide range of objects, often miniatures, are included. The distribution of similar or identical types points to the role of manual mass production, but it also indicates the wide range of individual needs catered for by every single cult. In imitation of and in generalizing mainland Greek practices, central Italy especially favoured the use of reproductions of human body parts, imploring gods about health problems far beyond specialized healing cults. Legs and feet are most common, followed by arms, eyes, breasts and genitals. Representations of inner organs (e.g. intestines or the uterus) might even include abnormalities and ulcers, but we must realize that these objects are not intended to document individual anatomical findings, but are the results of mass production that have been chosen as interpretations of a person's own health problems.[23] Many Greek Orthodox and Roman Catholic sanctuaries continue this practice today.

The special areas of individual rather than collective risks and anxieties include illness, economic success or failure, childlessness, the risks of childbirth, and occasionally long-distance travel. Vows (*vota*) thus form an important part of the religious practices of all strata of Roman society, finding archaeological expression both in small-scale objects of everyday use and in temple buildings worth hundreds of thousands of sesterces, promised at the turning point of a battle. For antiquity, as today, 'religion' cannot be thought of but in terms of, on the one hand, individual convictions, and on the other, concerns and public functions, or even massive institutions. At the same time, modern religion cannot be reduced to privatized or even 'invisible' religion,[24] nor can ancient religion be reduced to a collective enterprise best conceptualized as 'polis' or 'civic religion'.[25]

The rituals under discussion, despite the term 'crisis ritual' attributed to them, were part of a sequence rather than isolated events. Biographies of individual Romans reveal sequences of actions, starting with familiarity with the deity concerned (as a result of individual or family tradition), prayers and consultations, the fulfilling of the vow and its documentation, the resulting publicity and the hope of a new engagement of the divine. These sequences, while not restricted to any individual god, would normally be directed towards entities within a pool of divinities familiar to the person's surroundings. However, special tradition, publicity, success, and an inviting local environment (baths, for instance) did favour the growth of certain cults of regional or even supra-regional importance. In Rome, on an island in the Tiber, a sanctuary of the healing god Aesculapius (Greek Asklepios) was established; the date of the cult transfer from Epidauros is given as 293 BC.[26] Together with famous oracular cults (again Lavinium, later on Praeneste with its great sanctuary of Fortuna), such healing cults formed a religious infrastructure that transcended political boundaries.

Other areas of individual worship are less accessible to us. When Cato the Censor wrote *De Agricultura* ('On agriculture') shortly before the middle of the second century BC, he produced a normative text on the investment in, and management of, an Italian farm. Religion was part of the enterprise, a technical and social necessity for the farmer. Cato and some antiquarian writers offer us a glimpse of the minimal daily routine of burning scraps of food in the hearth and praying to the tutelary spirits of the house (*Lares*) or to the head of the family (*Genius*). Rituals

INTRODUCTION

surrounding childbirth, name giving, coming of age, marriage, death and burial are hardly ever described, and then only in texts written several hundred years after the supposed practice was enacted. Archaeology, for example in Ostia, does not encourage the view that any architectural structures such as house altars (let alone sumptuous ones) were common in middle- and lower-'class' homes.[27] Thus it is reasonable to reckon with a broad range of attitudes towards religious traditions and their traditional obligations, even in an ancient society.

It is even more difficult to determine the level of participation of the populace in public ritual. Judging by occasional literary references and institutional features, there must have been a high level of participation in festivals such as the New Year celebrations on 1 January (*kalendae Ianuariae*) and the *Saturnalia* in December, which encouraged local festive activities in families and neighbourhoods. The splendour and the material rewards of watching a triumph must also have produced a huge number of spectators. But for simple reasons of space, nearly all other centrally staged rituals could accommodate only a tiny percentage of the Roman populace as witnesses. A study of reconstructed calendars of religious groups from imperial times typically reveals that only one or two dates from the 'official' calendar have been integrated. The reception of festivals was not a central feature of the diffusion of calendars, as will be seen in Chapter V.

Religious groups existed during the Roman Republic; indeed, the literary and archaeological evidence of the Bacchanalia proves the existence of primarily religiously induced group formation as early as the third century BC.[28] The formation of comparable Orphic circles in Greece and southern Italy antedates this process by around two centuries,[29] and is a regular part of the classical Greek city. Evidence of professional associations, usually united by, and often named after, a common cult, also comes from republican times. For Rome, too, the historiographical tradition attributes their original foundation to Numa, the second king of Rome. Later tradition tended to see all these groups as delegates of a central religious organization,[30] but their actual structures seem to follow the contingencies of local coherence and of individual initiatives and interests. Although only a few names are known from the second and third quarter of the first century BC, they show the range of religious diversity outside the cults cared for directly by the Roman elite: for example, Favonia M. f. and Casponia P. f. Maxima were public priestesses of Ceres, and C. Vergilius C. l. Gentius and A. Calvius Q. l. served as functionaries in the funerary centre of Libentina.

Rome, as a growing commercial and political centre in central Italy, had never been isolated. This circumstance is attested in different ways by the presence of Greek artisans and myths, by oriental motifs and by the fifth-century treaties with Carthage. However, the three Punic Wars dramatically increased the intensity and the scope of external contacts. Apart from commercial, military and political aspects, the encounters also had a cultural dimension. While absorbing (and pillaging) an attractive and in many ways superior culture, the Roman elite had to define and assert its place in an enlarged Mediterranean world (*oikumene*). One way was to find a place within the large and complex mythological framework offered by Hellenistic Greeks, who themselves worked towards the ideological integration of an 'empire' of independent cities and states. The legendary groups that were said to have dispersed in the aftermath of the Trojan War, Aeneas foremost among them, offered numerous genealogical lines and were part of the Greeks' own thinking, transferred to Rome by means of Greek-educated marginal men such as Livius Andronicus, Naevius and Ennius, who produced Latin epics (for the *symposia* of the rich) and Latin drama (for the religious festivals of the citizens).[31]

Yet the transfer of the Greek form of interstate communication, based on the establishment of common mythological links, was not successful in the long run.[32] Mythological epic did not flourish before Virgil, nor did drama after the end of the second century BC (not even in the form of the *fabula praetexta*, which dealt with subjects of Roman history). Even the traditional Roman mechanism of establishing foreign cults, stemming from peaceful transfer (or *evocatio*) from captured towns, came to a definite halt during the later part of the second century. Instead, Roman senators – many of whom were also priests – started to elaborate local Roman traditions, both by writing narrative histories and by organizing and systematizing political and ritual practices. The legislation on augury and its uses (*obnuntiatio*) and on the election of priests (*rogatio Licinia* and *lex Domitia*) are one side of the coin, while antiquarian literature dealing with religious traditions is the other.

Beginning with Varro, the intellectual pressure of Greek philosophy and theology led to the apologetic creation of 'three types of theology'. The idea of a civic theology (*theologia civilis*) was used to give theoretical status to the actual and contingent practices of Roman cult. Hence, the 'documentation' of Roman cult, as given in Varro's *Antiquitates rerum diuinarum*, aimed to align Roman practices with the requirements of a proper system. Rome's multifaceted polytheism had to be organized according to the principle of functional clarity. The *di selecti* and *di certi*, the 'selected' and 'certain deities', were those to whom an explicit function could be attributed, and who could be invoked in prayer and cult. The Romans' concept of the gods clearly tended to multiply deities and their specific attributes instead of integrating different aspects into more and more complex personalities for individual gods. Yet the characteristic dryness of the seemingly limitless Roman 'pantheon', as noted by generations of scholars, is due to the specific intentions felt by the authors of our most important sources, who were writing Roman religion in the face of Greek philosophy and rationality.[33]

There were many priests and priestly groups (*sacerdotes, collegia, sodalitates*) that engaged in some annual rituals. With the exception of the female priestesses *Vestales*, and perhaps the high priest *Flamen Dialis*, for whom religious duties constituted a full-time job, these priests performed their religious duties as merely part-time or even spare-time activities.[34] In historical studies, prosopography serves as a good indicator for the public importance of the various priesthoods.[35] None of the republican Arval brethren or Sodales Titii are known by name. Of about twelve minor *Flaminates*, each of whom cared for the cult of special deities, only two can be tentatively identified for the whole time of the Roman Republic, a *Flamen Carmentalis* of the fourth century, and a *Flamen Floralis* of the third. Of all the Salii, only six are known, and those only due to exceptional events or to numismatic self-advertisement. The first known Lupercus (a priesthood restricted to equestrians under the Empire) entered the college in about 60 BC. By contrast, for most years after the beginning of the second Punic War, between one- and two-thirds (sometimes more) of the members of the augural college are known; the rate for the *pontifices* never drops below one-third.

From the second half of the third century onwards the pontiffs assumed a central position in the organization of Roman public cult. Their duties included supervision of the full-time priesthoods of the Vestal Virgins and of the priests (*flamines*) of Jupiter (*Flamen Dialis*), Mars and Quirinus, and perhaps even included some authority in relation to the augurs. The growing importance of their traditional knowledge of processional law, their judgement in matters of property rights with regard to land, and their right to regulate the calendar by intercalation formed the bulk of their duties and the basis of their increasing prestige.[36] It paralleled the prestige of the augurs; both groups also had monthly meetings, the augurs on the nones (the fifth or seventh day of the month), and the pontiffs on the ides (the thirteenth or fifteenth day). Even the scribes of the pontiffs were accorded, as *pontifices minores*, the prestige of a priesthood. In 196 BC, the task of performing ritual meals at the temple of Jupiter (*epula*) was excluded from the agenda list of the pontiffs and given to the newly founded priesthood of the 'three men for the meals' (*tresviri epulonum*). Enlarged to comprise seven members, then ten during the last years of Caesar, this was the fourth college to be counted among the 'major colleges' by the imperial period. Yet such an equality between the priestly colleges – reflected in the careers, ritual roles and political powerlessness of the priests – was in no way prefigured during the Republic. The partially hierarchical position of the pontiffs contrasted with the operational sphere of the augurs, and with the very special task of the *decemviri sacris faciundis* (ten, later fifteen, men for the performance of rites), whose main function was to inspect the Greek hexameters of the Sibylline books, at the request of the senate. On the basis of the answers found in these books, the ten men proposed ritual remedies against fearful omens. The imperial period diminished differences between the colleges and expanded the position of the supreme pontiff. '*Pontifex*

INTRODUCTION

maximus' became a regular part of the competences and titulature of Roman emperors from late Augustan times onwards and down to the late fourth century AD.

The Roman calendar was characterized by weak astronomy and strong practicability. By the beginning of the third century, it had been developed into an instrument (*fasti*) that effectively controlled the time slots for political and juridical activities outside the senate's meetings. It took account of the sacral allotment of time to certain deities (*feriae*) in the same way in which land was allotted as divine property, but the Roman *fasti* never served as a liturgical timetable. The drive to fix Roman traditions in writing led, however, to the employment of a written format for the annual pattern of the juridical quality of each day. In addition to explanations of the *feriae*, the annual commemorative and festival days of temple foundations were inserted. This initiative took the form of a private calendar painted on a wall, in connection with the building programme of a censor, Marcus Fulvius Nobilior. Nobilior's calendar was copied and used as a complex historical document. However, a conscious calendar policy and calendar religiosity, using the calendar and calendrical dates as a means of propaganda and reflection, did not arise before the last decade of the Republic, with Caesar's introduction of the 'Julian calendar' and the subsequent proliferation under Augustus of decorative calendars carved in marble (which will be discussed in Chapter V).[37]

Finally, attention must be paid to the role of religion in the categories and implementation of property rights with regard to land. Roman law distinguished public and private property. Public property could be allotted to deities and could thus become 'sacred' (*sacer*); private property could at most attain some of the character and protection of 'religious' property – that is, by being used for tombs; walls could attain the special protection of being *sanctus* ('hedged') (Gaius, *Institutiones* 2.3–9). Thus, property law required the senate's involvement each time a new cult was instituted, insofar as the cult intended to build or dedicate a temple or any sacred spot (such as an altar or a grove). No one was allowed to give public property to the gods without the permission of the Roman people or the senate. Generals were free to designate parts of their booty for the building of a temple for a god of their own choice, but in order to find a spot in Rome (and to be assigned the job of formally dedicating the building and its precinct), the general had to obtain the consent of the senate.[38] No master plan of Rome's sacral topography existed; the proliferation of temples followed the pattern of public building in general.

Public law, as far as divine property was concerned, was shaped by the dynamics of social differentiation and by its architectural consequences. Private building and garden projects encroached upon sacred groves, many of which had already become obscured by the time Varro was writing.[39] On the other hand, private architecture imitated sacral buildings. In general, the elite were those most often present at religious rites, and public priesthoods were at the same time private banqueting circles, offering a context for leading Romans to meet, to discuss and to sacrifice on private ground.[40]

Roman religion served the ruling class, and enabled the communication of the elite and the people at games, in supplications and through crisis rituals. Religious rituals sometimes helped to express and to reflect social divisions, as well as to differentiate along lines of gender, age and juridical status. In politics, Roman religion appears as a medium of communication rather than a medium of separation. The ritual of appropriating foreign gods (*evocare deos*) established links with political entities that had been defeated or destroyed.[41] In the area of divination, external specialists (*haruspices*) who came from the leading families of Etruscan cities were used as advisers. The one official oracular collection consulted by the senate, the Sibylline books, was written in a foreign language (Greek) and was of foreign origin. By acknowledging and expiating prodigies beyond the borders of Rome and Latium, religion established links and claimed control over independent Italian communities.[42] At the same time, Roman citizens were not as free as citizens of Greek *poleis* to take part in 'secret cults'. Religion did not have to be indigenous, but it had to be practised in public. No unified 'Roman religion' existed, but there were no independent religions either. To talk about Roman religion is to talk about cultural practices that fit our notion of 'religion'.

INTRODUCTION

The plausibility of all of that, however, rested in the manifold religious activities and beliefs practised and held by primary social groups and individuals – and more and more secondary religious groups also. It was the shared beliefs and practices that made aristocratic and monarchic 'instrumentalization' both possible and successful.

CHAPTER I

INDIVIDUAL AND CORPORATE RELIGION

It is perhaps not necessary, but is at least justifiable, to start by reflecting on beginnings. Within the past 200 years, the status of the ancients has changed from being one of unquestionable norms and unsurpassable masters in nearly every aspect of life to being valuable objects of comparison, oscillating between the fascinating or honorific past to the status of a pre-modern society excelling in complexity – or just the closest 'other'. Throughout this book I will assert the fruitfulness of such comparisons. To begin, in this chapter a genealogical relationship between the ancients and important traits of contemporary European religion is proposed.[1]

To start a genealogy is to make an argument about the present. I narrate a long history in order to make readers aware of its importance today. Such a history of religion does not focus on religion as such, but on its position in – and in relation to – the non-religious, society and culture. Hence, the claim I am going to make is that in the course of the historical phenomenon that we conceptualize as religion and to which we attribute significance in today's Europe, some important changes happened in the Hellenistic and Roman period. My claim will be that translocally organized religions – as individual options and subject to juridical regulation by the state – can be fruitfully traced back to that period. I will consider the formation of such characteristics, not their further development.

Before doing so, another problem must be addressed. If such forms of translocally organized religions are important today – and I do not claim that these are the only forms – one must add that the phenomenon is not restricted to Europe only. Instead, what I am hinting at is very close to the concept of 'world religion'. These 'world religions' are not only to be found outside of Europe today but have acquired genealogies that lead to extra-European and even extra-Mediterranean origins. Here, I briefly refer to the idea of an 'axial age' as already hinted at in the Introduction. The term, not invented but used by Karl Jaspers to initiate the modern debate,[2] denotes the new place given to transcendence (according to Shmuel Eisenstadt[3]) or the appearance of 'theoretic culture' (according to Merlin Donald[4]), both processes leading to a tension between a theoretic or transcendent order and the actual mundane order. Thus, new perspectives on one's own society are possible, a new reflexivity, initiated by intellectuals driving towards institutionalization of alternative models of society.

So far, the discussions about the axial age (or even multiple axialities)[5] have included more and more cultures (or 'civilizational formations')[6] and periods, but have carefully circumvented Rome and the Roman Empire before late antiquity. Greece and ancient Israel, China and India, and perhaps (post-)Zarathustrian Iran, are credited as having witnessed primary 'breakthroughs'; Christianity and Islam (i.e. late and very late antiquity) are seen to be at least secondary breakthroughs. The concept of an axial age – and that is important now – is to be credited with explicitly avoiding Eurocentrism. The lack of a geographical bias, however, is replaced by a certain monotheistic bias, perhaps not so much inherent due to the necessary alterity of the transcendent order, but rather to the search of the genealogies of today's universalistic religions. Neither ancient Hinduism and *bhakti* nor Greek religions – despite the inclusion of Socrates – have been included.

The model of axial civilizations has long been clean of crude causalities. Shmuel Eisenstadt identified a large number of intellectual, political, social, religious and cultural fields of change.[7] Recent studies have stressed the importance of economic factors in a medieval axial period.[8] Based on a reinterpretation of Jaspers' concept of the axial age, and a long exchange with Eisenstadt, Björn Wittrock has tried to conceptualize the idea of axiality as generally as possible. Thus he excludes a large number of culturally specific realizations while at the same time admitting the variety of different realizations and consequently different paths of development. What is not culturally specific is the idea that the axial age is a period of deep change in the fundamental dimensions of human existence, namely radical shifts, as textually manifested, in reflexive consciousness concerning cosmology, historicity, sociality and agency.[9]

This minimal definition stresses an intellectual development while at the same time acknowledging that institutional changes – political and economic – are as important for the identification of axial cultures as they are consequential for their actual formation. However, as Wittrock stresses, he did not solve the historical problem. Instead, 'the most important direction in future research [. . .] is to spell out the links between the set of intellectual and cosmological breakthroughs and sea-changing institutional transformations that a limited sense of the concept of the Axial Age denotes'.[10] One cannot any longer use 'axial age' as an abbreviation for the similarities in ideas of some distant founder figures. The term – if it is used at all – refers to an interaction between religion and political space, not of inherent qualities of belief systems but of complex cultural constellations.

I have been dwelling on the concept of an axial age for two reasons. On the one hand, the term reminds us that explanations have to be looked for on the same scale as the phenomena to be explained, as Greg Woolf has stressed in his pleading for the important role of the formation of empires in the development of axial age religions.[11] On the other hand, the Hellenistic and Roman empires are far from marginal for such a period. Even if the founding figures are not to be found within the temporal limits of these empires, it was the imperial periods that witnessed the emergence of the respective religions. They are crucial to the understanding of early Christianity, Rabbinic Judaism and – last but not least – circum-Mediterranean Islam; they were in cultural exchange with both India and Iran, importing ideas such as dualism, and the 'gymnosophists' (the naked yogi philosophers), and exporting important media – for example, coinage – with religious imagery and the type of statuary spreading the image of Buddha. At the very least, we are focusing on a seedbed of secondary axial civilizations that were fully exposed to the influence of primary axial ideas and institutions.

From religion to religions

Talking about spaces of subcontinental size as places of religious origins is rather misleading: the local character of – not only – ancient religion has to be stressed as a starting point. Religion is rightly seen as being embedded in social and political structures and practices, which usually tend to be centred locally. Speaking of a local character does not mean that religious practices are focused on political identity and dominated by the elite's investments in religious infrastructure, as my criticism of the terms 'polis religion' or 'civic religion' have shown in the Introduction. This criticism makes the notion of – for example – 'an Athenian religion' just as complex as a plural such as 'religions *in* or *of* Athens'. This is as true for Hellenistic as for Roman cities. As a consequence, I will focus for the moment on a single city, Rome, as its role in the formation of terminology and legal frameworks was most consequential for European history.

Due to continuous contact since the early urban phases, Rome, the city on the margins of the Greek world, had no significant difficulty accommodating and acculturating influx from the Greeks, be it 'Mater magna' from Asia Minor or 'Venus Erycina' from Sicily; only by the fourth century AD did Firmicus Maternus look back on a Roman society whose infection had started with the import of the cult of Ceres/Proserpina from Sicilian Henna.[12] According to the testimony of Cicero, by the middle of the first century BC – that is, the end of the Republic – other cultural and religious areas beyond Italy and Greece remained exotic, but not dangerous or adaptable; examples include Syrian fish gods, Egyptian animals and an Indian variety of Jupiter. The existence of Egyptian variants of divine genealogies was noted more frequently, but those were not accorded the status of dangerous knowledge. Such genealogies were perceived as distant local variants, having no importance beyond those localities. As the Romans had their public *religio*, others had theirs also and these might be compared.[13]

Cicero, however, does not employ a plural here. 'Everybody has his own religion, we have ours', he formulates in the speech for Flaccus.[14] In Cicero's time, by the middle of the first century BC, this is an exclamation – a statement of radical differences, not of possible choice or meaningful co-existence. In the long history of the Roman Empire, integrating previous Hellenistic structures and Hellenistic developments, this view had to be changed.[15]

The influx of cults into Rome, their blossoming in the city, and the frequent establishment of a Roman centre of cults that originated in other places (such as Isis or Christianity) has been described in detail in modern research.[16] Rome, the capital, captivates and captivated the interest of modern and ancient intellectuals. That everyone venerates their own gods, and the Romans all of them, is the summary observation of Caecilius, a character in the third-century Christian apologetic dialogue written by Minucius Felix.[17] Such a Rome-centred view is understandable from an immigrant from North Africa. Rome's position, however, is not unique. The image of Rome as the 'temple of the whole world', which is behind these North Africans' views, is spelled out in the hermetic treatise *Asclepius*, where it applies to Egypt.[18] An extraordinary mobility, enabled by the structures, needs and possibilities of the Roman Empire, modified the religious landscape everywhere, as is clearly seen by the same observer with his experiences of Rome and North Africa. Thus, Minucius Felix had his figures looking back to the time 'before the globe was open to commerce and the peoples mixed their rites and behaviours'.[19]

But there was more than ritual. Even the slightly more intellectualist notion of *religio* (and its plural) could hardly reflect the realities of the formation of groups employing religious symbols for their group identities. Within the religious framework of the ancient world, the cult of a specific deity would only occasionally correspond to or constitute group boundaries: it could be a shared sign and an important one, but hardly an exclusive sign – a fact that questions the usual interpretation of epigraphic *corpora*. Other terminological solutions evolved. *Secta*, obviously translating the Greek *hairesis*, was primarily used to differentiate the philosophical schools of the early Hellenistic age, but could also be used for Jewish groups such as Saducees or Pharisees.[20] The term is rare in Cicero, who used it more frequently for political rather than philosophical groups, but it appears frequently from the first century AD onwards and is attested in the so-called tolerance edict of AD 311.[21] Here, the emperor Licinius looked back on his earlier attempt to bring the Christians back to their 'good senses', as they had left 'their parents' sect'. The term is very frequently used for all varieties of sects in the norms collected in the sixteenth book of the *Codex Theodosianus* (in particular 16.5), including a few instances of 'catholic' or 'orthodox sect'. We should not forget that the term *Christianoi/Christiani* (used by administrators and judges much earlier than by the so-called Christians themselves) does not convey the idea of 'venerators of the god Christ', but 'the gang of the man Christ', his followers (*sequentes*).

If a plurality of (and this is important) comparable and reversible choices can be expressed in terms of different philosophical schools, this implies a body of knowledge as a special way of life. By the term *disciplina*, this could be applied to certain types of religious specialists – magicians, *haruspices*, even augurs – by the late Roman Republic. It was extended to include a wider variety of religious practices by Christian apologetics by the end of the second century AD and reached official texts in the fourth century.

In the course of the growth of the Roman Empire, its large-scale dislocation of people and – as Clifford Ando has stressed[22] – its delegitimization of local authorities, this sort of bond-producing religion had become more than the natural consequence of a religious disposition towards a contingent deity. It was subjected to rational interpretation and explanation. In its evaluation, intellectuals appealed to universal standards of humanity. For a growing number of people, it had become a necessary part of one's way of life, to which the division of public and private could not be applied without difficulties. It was an economic and political factor as well as a medium of a functionally non-religious – that is, in particular political – discourse. These elements were neither new nor consistent. They fitted together with terminological changes, with *ratio* and *fides* – rational argument and received belief – controlling *religio*, with an insistence on *vera religio*, 'true religion', with *disciplina*, 'lifestyle and morality',[23] and *secta*, a grouping that is neither public nor private. By its use of inscriptions, images and architecture, religion became one of the most important media of public communication.

The mobility of more densely organized 'venerators' – but by no means of every deity, *religio* and *cultus* – caused the problem of translocal recognizability. The problem was solved by the rather standardized cult image of Mithras, by unusual rituals and Egyptian decoration in the case of Isis, by the exchange of letters and collections of narratives in the case of the Christians, and by the attempt to regulate every aspect of life in the case of the Rabbinic authors of the Mishna in Palestine. To define the place of such a loaded concept of 'religion' and the appearance of boundary-creating 'cults', in particular from the time of Aurelian and Diocletian onwards, the Roman administration employed legislation, and, where necessary, penal law and violent persecutions. Some forms of Judaism, Christianism and Manicheism were among the survivors, but the process involved the formation of many other religious groups – a fact usually overlooked in axial age accounts.

Individualization

Evidently the period from the third century BC to the fourth century AD, politically and culturally characterized as the Hellenistic and imperial period, witnessed the development of a plurality of densely organized, partly professionalized sets of symbols, practices and groups – I slowly approach the term 'religions' – of which the confessional and exclusive character was hardly characteristic before the end of the period. Nevertheless, I am proposing to apply the term 'religionization' or 'religionification' to this process, which involved a far-reaching though not irreversible shift of the social location of religion. Jonathan Smith's dichotomic notion of a shift from locative to utopian religion is helpful here. The fundamental orientation of religious ideas and practices shifts from life, welfare and legitimacy in and of the present order ('locative') to the imagination of a better social and cosmological order beyond contemporarily dominating powers, an order not yet realized ('utopian'), but informing the attempts to improve oneself and society.[24] This differentiation was developed in order to characterize changes in late antiquity, but is intended to be generally applicable for the history of religions. It is helpful to understand some important changes, but we must keep in mind that the Roman as well as the Byzantine forms of Christianity soon came to be locative religions par excellence. Starting with antiquity neither means to narrate progress nor to anachronistically modernize the past.

That said, I dare to introduce a second term, not a neologism, but one even more tainted by the danger of anachronism, namely individualization. The theoretical agenda is related. If 'religionization' is interested in the precarious and contingent character of the systemic and organizational dimension of religion, and its place in – and relationship with – society, 'individualization' directly focuses on the individual person as locus of experience and agency, and his or her interdependency with society and religion. Again, notions of progress and anachronistic modernization must be avoided. It would be hard to find in antiquity the complex notion of de-traditionalization, of a biographical approach to oneself, a permanent reflexivity and narcissistic drive towards authenticity claimed to be typical of contemporary individualization.

How could such a notion be applied to the history of religion? Two steps should be taken. The first is to clarify terminology. In accordance with recent discussions, I propose to restrict the term 'individualization' to large-scale structural or discursive changes. In other words, individualization refers to historical processes that can be identified on the basis of multiple and widespread findings only.[25] Naturally, individualization would refer to growing degrees of individuality. Here, I would like to keep de-traditionalized action as a primary marker, producing differences or distinctiveness with regard to other persons' actions, ranging from perfection to deviance. Such terms imply that individuality is not a purely descriptive term, but must be related to contemporary discourse and practical constraints. In order to map such differences I propose to differentiate five different types of individuality that would ultimately shape the detailed description of any long-term processes. These are: practical individuality, moral individuality, competitive individuality, representative individuality and reflexive individuality.

These types are not necessarily correlated. Practical individuality – the fact that people have to act on their own instead of simply following traditions – points to situations of disembeddedness, due to a temporary rupture of social bonds (as in the case of migrants, travellers, survivors) or a strict division of labour. This could be prepared for by written or learnt instructions, for instance for post-mortal travelling.

Moral individuality involves concepts of law, sin and punishment, and the ascription of people's responsibility for their own behaviour. In antiquity, the standards would normally be those of others and would include judgements about social obligations, often to the point of negating individuality. Specific duties rather than universal rights are stressed in ancient reflections. This thinking hardly displays any notion of individuality in the sense of modern declarations of human rights. We therefore have to look at the details. An obligation to participate in rituals might already be indicative of such a moral individuality that transcends mere bans.

Competitive individuality refers to the widespread aristocratic struggle for distinction, typically aiming to establish lofty goals to which other social groups might aspire. Individual differences would be sharply noticed by contemporary observers, yet evaluated by a discursively constructed common ethos that stressed the commonwealth or family status. Concrete norms would be very much shaped and modified by actual competitive behaviour, and conflict is inherent.[26]

Representative individuality is surely related to the two preceding points. Individuals were meant to strive to become exemplary and would then be remembered as examples. Not individual difference, but perfection in fulfilling a social or religious role – whether, for example, as Roman general, Christian martyr, or male Jew – is the aim, yet fulfilment is a personal feat.

INDIVIDUAL AND CORPORATE RELIGION

Finally, reflexive individuality would demand the formation of an individualistic discourse – an individualist ideology so to speak. Again, such reflections on the self or on individual human nature, for example in the Stoic figure of *oikeiosis*, would frequently be informed by normative concepts of social roles, thus pointing to the type of representative individuality.

All these types are gendered, have particular places in society, will be found in the elite or on the margins in different forms and degrees, are transitory phenomena and give rise to processes of institutionalization. The latter types might easily revise judgements about deviancy. Institutionalized individuality – for example rules on representative individuality – could easily outlaw earlier norms governing competitive individuality. Self-control can be the most effective form of public disciplining, in modern confessional practices as well as in ancient monastic communities.[27] On a large scale, economic security is a precondition for individuality and must be taken into account for any analysis of Mediterranean antiquity or the modern period.[28]

Individuality is to be measured against constraints and discourses. At the same time, it is a result of the relevant person's previous individuation, as an enlargement situational agency is part of such an individuation as an ongoing process. Of course, individuation is inseparably bound up with socialization – the development of a social, individual persona. For ancient thinkers, the concept of individuation, the development of personal self-identity, was hardly ever separated from social interaction and functionality. However, the concept can be used for historical analysis in order to map the possible fields of developing different types and degrees of individuality in religion, to look for opportunities offered by religions for increasing individual differences and spaces of action not defined by traditions, and consequently to ask for the outcome of religious institutions and practices for the persons involved.

Some relevant fields should be pointed out. The increase in religious options has been described as one of the major characteristics of the period under consideration – the third century BC to the fourth century AD – up to the point of comparison with modern religious pluralism.[29] This was primarily due to the mobility of merchants, administrators, soldiers and slaves. A competence to select deities according to situational specifics is fundamental to the Mediterranean types of polytheism. The proliferation of cults that generated religious groups popularized concepts of exclusivity and led to the problem of religious deviance on a mass scale. Within the framework of an additive polytheistic system that is open to extension, the introduction of new gods and veneration options into local temples (by setting up votives to gods not previously venerated) or into 'panthea' (that is, introducing new cults into a locality) was quite frequent and just as frequently subject to individual whims.[30] The most important set of religious symbols, the assembly of local gods called 'pantheon', was a fortuitous result of different people's individual decisions.

Donating a new sanctuary was a complex matter not restricted to the establishment of a new god. Selection of the place, choice of architectural details, regulation of rituals (often hardly visible for us): all of this involved many decisions that would relate to existing traditions, interpreting and – as benchmarks in a competitive society – creating new norms. Normative statements in this sense could also be made in the form of tomb monuments. I am thinking of the tomb of Eurysaces, the Roman baker and contractor, which will be analysed in Chapter VII. Striving for originality, the tomb is representative rather than exceptional in giving expression to a world view that is dominated by Eurysaces' own professional experiences and horizon. In a number of such monuments and even in a religious text such as *The Shepherd of Hermas*, it is professional activity that is given ultimate value.[31] On a societal level, such utterances did not successfully question the dominance of a rather aristocratic system of values. However, they indicate an individual re-evaluation of everyday life that is reminiscent of the importance given by Charles Taylor to the appreciation of everyday life in modern civilizations and in particular North American culture.[32]

For Greek and Roman antiquity, with their traditions of domestic cult, a clash with the authorities might be provoked by domestic rituals that seemed to be mimetic representations of public cult. The extent of such ritual practices and the conflicts they caused with ecclesiastical institutions has been shown for late antiquity.[33] A growing individuality is contemporaneous with growing centralization and standardization.

Personal communication with gods was never restricted to public rituals or temples. Votives probably resulting from personal concerns are widely attested to from the archaic period onwards. Forms and intensity, however, are changing and might be related to a growing concern about one's family and oneself. The rise of the cult of Asklepios could be such an indicator, as healing and the social topography of healing imply statements about the relationship between a person and society;[34] Aelius Aristides' *Hieroi Logoi* (Sacred Discourses) are one of the most important testimonies of religious individuality from antiquity.[35] The imperial reinvigoration and proliferation of oracles is an interesting area of research for the individualization of institutions.[36] Astrology as a mass phenomenon of the personalization of temporal orders would be another one (and will be analysed as such in Chapter VI. It refers a person to a universal natural order that is made compatible with specific, for instance Jewish or Christian, cosmologies at the same time.[37] For some intellectuals in late antiquity, theurgy offered another way of efficacious personal contact.[38] The vast array of practices called 'magic' concludes my list. Apart from individual concerns about health, the attempt to counter results that were to be expected on the basis of social status in social relations or legal conflicts is obvious. In the highly risky area of relationships of and with prostitutes, for example, the lack of traditional regulations is replaced by magic.[39]

Conclusion

If the later Roman Empire is a period characterized by 'religionization', it is not as easy to characterize the period starting after the death of Alexander the Great (323 BC), the Hellenistic age, and the early Roman Empire as a period of 'individualization'. I have argued for the usefulness of the analytical tool of different types of individuality and of looking for the individual in our data of the history of religion. Any judgement about the period as a whole would be premature. And yet, it is obvious that some of the types and degrees of individuality that are characteristic of the period might be positively or negatively related to the formation of the supposedly intellectually coherent and socially bordered institutions called 'religions'.

The phenomenon is not without modern parallels. The Protestant Reformation was critical of the existing ecclesiastical institutions. Sacerdotal power was conceptually replaced by the general priesthood of all Christians. Protesting against a dominating order helped to further develop the notion of individual conscience. Without question, the century of the Reformation saw a major growth of religious individualization. And yet, for Europe, the following century has been rightly characterized as an age of confessionalism.[40] (Chapter II will consider some consequences for the field of calendars and 'church years'.) Religious differences were tightly organized; religious 'options' took the form of confessional discipline and orthodoxy, again leading to more individual reactions such as Pietism. The same dialectical movement could be observed for the following period of Enlightenment, with its phenomena of religious deviance, secret communication, and stress on the individual persona in the form of a bearer of human rights.[41] Again, the subsequent nineteenth century could be described as a second era of confessionalization.[42] The wide range of figures of thought and practices, shifts in institutions and legal frameworks, which might be summarized under the umbrella term of 'individualization', is in a paradoxical way institutionalized (and hence secured) as well as countered by a similarly wide range of processes. Canonization and institutionalization are processes that might be found in many trajectories of religious developments. The same holds true for developments of dogmas and clearer definitions of membership criteria. We must include the ancients in any historical explanation for the complex position of religion and the individual in today's 'modern' culture.

CHAPTER II

HISTORICIZING RELIGION

If 'religionization' and 'individualization' are processes that are important for religion today and began in the ancient world, historicization is no less so. It seems self-evident to speak about 'history of religion' or 'church history'. Protestant Christianity in particular has accorded history paramount importance in theological reflections. Scripture – that is, canonized texts – is read in the light of historical knowledge about the social composition of early Christian groups, modes of communication and mechanisms of tradition. 'Historical Jesus' is only partly the figure described in the gospels; the latter might stem from the first half of the second century, 100 years after the crucifixion.[1] At present, the Qur'an is undergoing a similar process of radical historicization; scholars are dating parts of it to the second or third generation after Muhammad instead of to the prophet's years at Mecca or Medina.[2] This gives rise to a lot of sceptical voices or even outright protest. The relationship of history and religion is far from easy. Thus, I will start with a general reflection on this relationship before I address the role of ancient thinkers in the development of a self-historicizing discourse. The focus will be on the late Roman Republic, a period for which textual evidence and our knowledge about the larger political and religious developments coincide.[3] Against the backdrop of a broad range of historiographical genres developed in Greece, one can observe how Roman authors tried to employ historiographical strategies in their attempts to describe, systematize, preserve and make sense of their own religious traditions. Thus, the achievements of Greek authors (to be seen against the backdrop of older Near Eastern historiographical traditions) are always lurking in the background. Since Herodotus and Thukydides, 'history' has been presented as a critical alternative to 'myth', aggressively introducing the rational criterion of plausibility and occasionally the question of testimonies into narratives of the past.[4]

History and religion

Human action taken in the present is directed towards the future. Occasionally we 'remember' the past (some people more frequently than others) or are struck by the similarity of a person, place or situation to a past event and thus we reflect on the differences (for example, when sitting on a train, surrounded by people on their mobile phones, memories of the good old days of phone booths may come to us). Certain events regularly provoke such a look into the past. Funeral services are a sure bet, graduation ceremonies perhaps less so. In Egypt, biography and autobiography have their origins in the laudatory or even self-laudatory narratives on tombstones. And, generally, conversations with the older generation are more likely to result in 'histories' than conversations with children.

We memorize on occasion and on purpose. Collectively, such awareness of changeability is permanently present, even if this need not take the form of narratives, of organized historiography:

> There is no human culture without a constitutive element of common memory. By remembering, interpreting, and representing the past peoples understand their present-day life and develop a future perspective on themselves and their world. 'History' in this fundamental and anthropologically universal sense is a culture's interpretive recollection of the past serving as a means to orient the group in the present.[5]

The citation needs a supplement. First, to speak of 'a culture' needs differentiation. I started from individual memories: for example, grandfather's history, the story he tells, is so interesting because it is different from the history learnt at school. Whether or not we agree is second to that. Familial or ethnic groups, social movements or religious organizations tell different stories, or 'histories' – for whatever purpose. Others might or might not have a place in these histories; they could, but need not overlap. The orientation towards the future might be explicit or implicit. And sometimes stories are retold that are 'out of date'. The perpetuation of text by multiplication in the form of printing and preservation in libraries lacked the correcting effect of the limited capacity of human memory and suppression by oblivion. They also transmit stories that served past purposes, 'old histories', some of which people may no longer want to hear. The documents we have to deal with can change their meaning over time, and might suddenly reappear in representations of the past that they were never intended to corroborate.

I have not been very precise so far in my use of the terms 'memory' and 'history', terms that have been intensively discussed during the past decades.[6] Without doubt, Roman religion was a repository of memories about the past.[7] Religion, traditionally associated with mythical narratives, offered founding stories for their values and institutions. It could easily comfort non-discursive individual and collective memories. Monuments such as temples (supplemented by building inscriptions) evoked narratives or feelings. The same holds true for rituals. These were connected to specific places associated with stories, such as tombs, which occasionally employed archaic instruments or simply evoked a recollection of a previous ceremony. This, however, is not my concern here. Rather I side with Paul Ricoeur, insofar as I am interested in looking for a discursive, usually narrative reconstruction of the past of religion and in religion. Like any historiography, religious historiography critically engages with individual and collective memory and gains its plausibility and importance by such memories.

A history that cannot appeal, even critically, to individual memory – be it due to direct experience or mediated learning – can hardly be accepted as 'ours': the readers' or hearers' history. In my opinion, this explains the attraction of a historiography dealing with the audience's recent history. If this is a demand factor, the greater liberties offered to historiography in its construction of distant history explain the attraction of such a type of history for historiographers, i.e. the supply side.

Perhaps it is this dialectical recourse to memory that marks a difference to mythical narrative, which in form and function – and often even in the topics covered – is close or identical to memory.[8] In the European tradition, history invents itself in the attempt to critically – not always plausibly – question mythical narrative, as Thukydides did for the Trojan War. Of course, history remains the business of people who are raised with collective and individual memories. Even if history is critical – asking for clarification, more precision, or total revision – it is critical of some particular issues of the past, not of the past as a whole. It is this stress on critical (and of course constructive) dealings with memory that makes me side with the term history, rather than memory, for the rest of the chapter.[9]

Understandably, religious convictions contribute enormously to their adherents' or cultures' conceptualizing and narrating of the past – a past that is predefined by god(s), repeating itself, a period of testing, or the like. While a community's account of its past, and its particular recollections of itself, are not the only means of achieving orientation and constructing a coherent identity, historical narratives generated by a given community are consistently important. Post-Reformation confessional divides have proven to be particularly fruitful. Such historical narratives are furthered by professionals in their historiographic enterprises, popularized by bestselling books, in theatres and by large-scale monuments, memorized in schools and commemorated in public rituals. This also holds true for religious groups that produce a large variety of accounts of their past. They might concentrate on a founding phase or try to integrate as much as they can of the 'history' remembered by a society. Mythology and history are, as mentioned above, not opposites, but variants of historical narratives, perhaps including very different time indicators.

My switch from 'religion' to 'religious convictions' and 'religious groups' is deliberate. Historical narratives from within and about religions have, of course, been used for general history, as well as the history of religion –

both academic disciplines. But if they have been used frequently, they have hardly been analysed as objects with an interest of their own. If we try to differentiate history as a practice that not only narrates a past, but also applies a temporal or even chronological framework to it, the connection between religion and history is not as natural as the one between religion and mythology. By its chronological framework, history allows one story to relate to another. By introducing contingency, it allows stress on the pastness of the past, its distance.

In order to understand how such a history could help to legitimize present claims, we must take into account that conflicts and contesting claims frequently trigger historical narratives. History, then, would never come in the singular, and tends to be contested, endangered. Critical from the very beginning, history – as opposed to memory – introduces contingency in order to question the established truth of others. To introduce competition into the legitimizing past is risky and might endanger traditional order. But we should not forget that 'history' is written by individuals, following their own agenda, even if acting out of a specific collective identity. Some religions and some epochs are more prone to historiography than others. Revolutionary monotheistic religions could seem to be candidates for historicization, questioning the legitimacy of their forerunners. Rather surprisingly, even a religion so utterly traditional as ancient Roman religion started to historicize itself. It will help our understanding of what historicization can do for religion if we take a closer look.

Beginnings

Memory turned into history is traceable in written form from the beginning of the third century onwards. We have evidence of honorific funerary inscriptions, increasing in scale with the sarcophagi and *elogiae* to the Scipiones from the early second century BC onwards. The earliest known funerary oration (*laudatio funebris*), in fragmentary form and thus presumably a speech recorded in writing, dates from 221 BC and concerned the consul and supreme pontiff L. Caecilius Metellus. By the middle of the third century, the *pontifex maximus* Ti. Coruncanius had begun to record changes in membership, prodigies observed and decisions taken. Ascription of agency to the very actors, specific priesthoods within the net of ever more formalized and differentiated authorities, seems to have been the dominant function. Thus we know that in 275 or 274, L. Postumius Albinus was the priest called 'Rex sacrorum' who witnessed the introduction of a new divinatory practice.[10] The *haruspices* started to pay attention to the victim's heart in their scrutiny of entrails.

From the late third century BC onwards, Romans developed a historiography of the rise of their city along the lines of Greek historiography, actually starting by writing in Greek and by the late first century BC leading to the comprehensive account of Roman history by the Augustan writer Titus Livy, a text full of religious data, prodigies, temples, accessions to priesthoods and large rituals performed by magistrates. Religious data were an important element of Roman historiography, a factor in secular history and an argument in secular historiography.[11] An interest in religious change developed on the margins of the historiographic mainstream only.[12] The first traces can be detected in the early second century BC.

In 189, Marcus Fulvius Nobilior was consul with one Manlius Vulso, and assumed military command on the Aetolian front.[13] Tradition records as the most important event of this campaign the siege and capture of the city of Ambracia, north of the Gulf of Actium, and it was in fact the booty from this city in particular that the victor displayed in his triumphal procession after his return to Rome in 187.[14] Fulvius not only brought his treasures home: he put a roof over their head. He transformed a temple of Hercules into a 'museum' in the real sense of the term: a *Museion*, a sanctuary of the Muses, and the first one in Rome. Probably only after becoming reconciled with Aemilius, his former antagonist and fellow censor in 179 BC, Fulvius undertook the extension of an existing temple of Hercules, presumably that of Hercules Custos. He provided it with a columned hall, and then installed the statues of the nine Muses taken from Ambracia. Hercules became Hercules Musarum, signifying powerful protection for cultural production – the newly acquired self-image of parts of the Roman elite.

HISTORICIZING RELIGION

Terminus post quem is the beginning of Fulvius' censorship in 179; completion and dedication would have occurred in the following years.[15]

Fulvius installed a calendar, *fasti*, in the *aedes Herculis Musarum* in the form of a wall painting,[16] adding to the interior of a meeting place for poets, furnished with many statues and Greek paintings. The few quotations from this calendar in later literature indicate a dedication formula in the shape of a heading that might have run like this: 'The consul and censor M. Fulvius Nobilior set up this calendar after the Aeolian War: Romulus had named ten months, the first in honour of his father and foremother; after having divided the people into older and younger, to ensure that one part should defend the state by advice, the other by arms, he named the third and fourth in honour of both parts; the rest was named by numbers.' Numa added two and named them after Ianus and the gods of the netherworld. A thirteenth month was intercalated according to a law by the consul Acilius in the year 562.

This is not a faithful reconstruction, but a basic hypothesis capable of explaining all the quotations of, and references to, Fulvius' calendar.[17] The cultural product of the calendar is given a history. But is this already a history of religion? It is likely that no contemporary encompassing concept of religion existed that would have formed the basis for an answer. The author of the painting added another element, a list of annual consuls and occasional censors, perhaps starting with the Gallic sack of Rome, an event marking a second (or even third) birth of Rome. This clearly was an attempt at 'scholarly' history, also condensing and unifying the most important and eponymous agents – that is, those employed in dating into a coherent list, extracted and reworked from historic narratives.

The combination of these elements proves the historicizing significance of a third element and invention of Fulvius' mural calendar. The calendar records *dies natales templorum* – that is, foundation days of urban temples. In Rome, in the half-century that followed the end of the war against Hannibal, temples financed from war booty were sprouting like mushrooms. They were donations to the gods that had given victory to the Romans in individual battles; they commemorated military success. Romans saw

41

history differently, in much more tangible terms in those temples, after they had seen, heard and smelled the victories in lavish processions and games. This was a new element to a calendar whose purpose was to document the political and juridical year, and which included religious dates only where they affected (or, unexpectedly, did not affect) that purpose. Temple foundations rank highly in the list of those historical events that were the most precisely retained in Rome's collective memory. Temples were, however, also monuments to a god. A temple owned by a deity and usually housing its statue was the most tangible sign of the deity's presence and a testimony to its relationship with the Roman people. A deity might publicly enter the city as a statue, but frequently the temple came first. Within the possibility of a polytheistic system open to additions and multiplications of divine figures, it is the production of statue and temple that brings the god into social life – regardless of their earlier ontology.[18]

The analysis of the introduction of the temple-foundation days into the *fasti*, and the way they were combined with the magistrate lists, has shown that there was a historical perspective to this integration of elements alien to the *fasti*. The timeless character of the dedication days distributed across the year was transferred to the historical phenomenon of successive temple foundations, and the religious reading of those events as embodying the history of divine epiphanies and cult diversification acquired a political dimension. In the history of ideas, this kind of inversion is referred to as Euhemerism. And it is precisely a protégé of Fulvius, a contemporary intellectual and historian, who introduced this type of thinking to Rome.

Quintus Ennius' narrative *Euhemerus* is not merely eponymous for the Latin tradition. In this treatise, probably written before the beginning of the *Annales* in the latter half of the 180s, he concerned himself directly with the origins of temples and – in this order – annual festivals. Ennius followed a Greek model and, according to the surviving fragments, the narrative about some past adventure does not contain any *explicit* history of the origins of *dies natales templorum* in the city of Rome. It is difficult today to arrive at an appropriate assessment of his position. To us, a story telling how figures contemporarily venerated as gods were kings and benefactors in some distant island appears as fundamentally critical, even downright radical, in its seemingly implicit denial of the divine status of these figures. It may, however, not even have occurred to Ennius and his readers that an explanation of the genesis of the gods and the cult necessarily implied atheism and denial, not to mention a call for action in the real world: this would certainly have been the last thing the temple's patron needed. Despite its critical implications, a philosophical treatise like the *Euhemerus* constituted less an attack on religion than the application of historicization to religion. It was a powerful instrument of ordering a quickly changing world. Ennius' *Annales* replaced anecdotal forms of gentilician memory (whether in the form of inscriptions or *laudationes funebres*) with a coherent and sequential history. This is what the Fulvian *fasti* did as well, although in this case the means used was not a narrative, but the chronographic form of the calendar.

Varronian history and systematics

With Varro's *Antiquitates rerum divinarum*, the sixteen books of 'Antiquities of things divine' (dedicated to Julius Caesar in 46 BC), we reach full-blown systematization and – as I will demonstrate – historicization of religion at the end of the Republic. The extent of the latter is difficult to tell: the sixteen volumes of this work survive in the form of frequently isolated quotations by later, mostly polemical authors, Augustine of Hippo taking pride of place, Tertullian being second.[19]

My argument is helped by the existence of chronologically ordered passages at the beginning and end of Varro's work. Fragments 35 to 39 of the first book of Varro's *Antiquitates rerum divinarum* list the introduction of deities and cults into the city of Rome by the earliest kings, starting with Romulus who 'established for the Romans as gods Ianus, Iupiter, Mars, Picus, Faunus, Tiberinus, and Hercules', followed by Titus Tatius and the parsimonious Numa:

> During the reign of Numa, religion did not yet consist of images or temples for the Romans. A parsimonious piety, poor rites, no

Capitol-like splendour, but temporary, turf-made and Samian (i.e. terracotta) vessels, the city of Rome was not yet flooded by the ingenuity of Greeks and Etruscans to form images.

This sequence was longer, as I will show shortly. The second chronological sequence occurs in book 15. Fragments 214 to 221 added further cults, enlarging the chronological realm back to Hercules' visit to Rome.

The few historical data roughly conform to the narratives found in general historiography of the time. In Varro's listing of sacred places in 'On Latin Language' he refers to the introduction of Sabine deities by Titus Tatius to the 'annals'.[20] Such information, too, would agree to the combination of lists of consuls and temple foundations in the *fasti* of the temple of Hercules Musarum, chronologically relating objects and actors and hence suggesting causation and responsibility. But there is more evidence for a historiographic strand, at least in the framing books, than just two lists. The narratives named so far are embedded in a historically sensitive framework. The loss of knowledge about gods, the loss of memory, forms the starting point of the whole enterprise: 'He [Varro] was afraid that the gods might perish, not by attack by enemies, but by the citizens' negligence. He says that they are liberated from the latter like from a ruin by him, and the gods would be stored and preserved in the memory of the good men by books of this kind.' Clearly, radical change is imaginable for a religion in the course of history.

The same acceptance of historical change characterizes Varro's thinking about the earliest stages of Roman religion. Religious institutions are products of historical development. However, such a contingency does not rob them of their obligatory character for all those posterior to the founders' decisions, as Varro acknowledges for the consequences of his own reasoning (fr. 12), as:

> he is not to follow his own judgement concerning the institutions of the Roman polity . . . If he would found a new polity, he will have been dedicating gods and their names according to nature . . . But as

he is living in an old people, he has to clinge to the accepted history of names and surnames, as it has been transmitted . . . and he has written and researched all this to the purpose that the simple people would venerate these gods rather than despise them.

History did not stop at the end of the founding phase. Political and art history mark major steps in the history of religion. The introduction of divine images is such a step, chronologically related to the building of the large Capitoline temples. It is a major step in itself, marking the transition from the regal into the early republican period. Again, such contingent steps are consequential. Images are nice to see but introduce harmful change, as is stated for the ancient Romans, who 'have venerated the gods for more than 170 years without an image. If they would have kept this practice until today, the gods would be observed in a purer manner . . . Those who first put images of the gods in front of peoples have robbed their polities of fear and added error' (fr. 18).

In other contexts, too, Varro applied historical reasoning to ritual change. Jupiter and Summanus were originally deities of equal power, the one responsible for lightning at daytime, the other at night. Due to the contingent factor of the building of the Capitoline temple, Summanus fell into near oblivion (fr. 42).

To an extent unknown to us, Varro might have noticed the foundation of temples down to his own time. At least two fragments survive that are related to foundations in the latter half of the second century BC, dealing with the temples founded by Lucullus and Marcus Aemilius (fr. 43–44). Varro was aware of opposite decisions, too. Thus, he acknowledged the driving out of Liber Pater (or Dionysius) from all of Italy in 186 BC (fr. 45). For the time immediately preceding the publication of the books, he notes the conflict between the senate and the general populace about a ban of Egyptian cults from the Capitoline hill (fr. 46a).

The introduction of cults need not take the form of the erection of temples. Varro was interested in the exact dating of the introduction of festivals. Pliny the Elder, about a century later, refers to the foundation of the Robigalia in the eleventh year of the reign of Numa, and of the Floralia in the year 516 of the city.[21] In both cases, Varro reflected on the differences between seasonal dates and the civic calendar. The introduction of scenic games was of equal interest to him, and in his 'Antiquities' (*Antiquitates rerum divinarum*) he discusses at length their beginnings in Rome by dedicating at least two volumes of his work to the problem, titled 'On the origins of scenic games'.[22]

History frequently takes the form of one's own history. It is religion in the city of Rome that we see being historicized in the *fasti* of Ennius and Fulvius as well as in antiquarian writings of the second and first centuries BC. The painting in the temple of Hercules Musarum might be seen as establishing the histories of the Roman calendar, Roman temples and Roman consuls as subjects worthy of literary elaboration. This would clearly imply a 'we' of Latin-speaking Romans against the backdrop of literature by Greek authors, maybe even of Greek literature in general. The focus is an urban one. Varro's 'Antiquities', however, put Roman religion in a wider context. The 'Antiquities of things divine' must have had, according to the description given by Augustine, a wider scope than the preceding 'Antiquities of things human', 'which do not concern the whole world, but just Rome',[23] which Varro nevertheless, as he said, felt fully justified in writing before the books on divine things. The opposition or paradox implied by Augustine works only if a larger than urban, probably universal orientation of the latter part of the oeuvre is to be assumed. To talk of 'universal' in that period always needs an additional note. The standards of universality were set by Greek thinking, based on the experience of the oikoumene of the Mediterranean world, Greek colonization, international trade and the Hellenistic empires. Beyond that, the *barbaroi* remained, peoples only occasionally acknowledged to have human culture.

Varro's universalistic stance is beyond doubt. Frequently he uses the plural *civitates* or *urbes*. The philosophical foundation of his argument is universalistic. He is at pains to define his three types of theology as a Greek, hence universal, classification.[24] Only on such a basis can we understand Varro's statement that the god who governs everything and is venerated on the Capitoline hill as Jupiter is called by the Jews – literally, by monotheistic venerators obliged to aniconic cult – by another name (fr. 13–15). Read in this perspective, an astonishing number of fragments do not necessarily imply an urban Roman context.

That is not to say that Varro does not speak about Rome. Clearly, he is Roman and includes his readership in a Roman 'we' at the very outset of his work (e.g. fr. 3, 12). As a Roman, he clearly marks out the differences from the Jews (fr. 16), the Chaldaeans (fr. 17), or Greek peoples such as the Spartans (fr. 32) or Eleusinians (fr. 271), or even the Greeks in general (fr. 200). In the introduction to the last book, dedicated to 'special and selected deities', he first dealt with general notions of gods before he addressed those gods who were defined by Roman places of worship and statues.[25] It should not be forgotten that Roman citizenship was extended to most of Italy by the time of Varro's writing. He not only acknowledges the introduction of Italian deities in Rome by the early kings, but deals with a wealth of middle Italian local deities, belittled (and preserved as fr. 33) by Tertullian as 'town council deities'.

The old Romans, even by their wrong decisions, contributed to a very special, and nevertheless binding, history of the urban territory and the society developed in that place. Narrating in such a manner is deliberately distancing. Varro supports Roman religious tradition despite crucial historical mistakes by its agents, right at the start as well as later on in introducing iconic cult. Such a traditional religion might even be embarrassing, whether in their use of images or in the old Romans' invention of divine genealogies – that is, mythical narratives of sexual relationships among gods (fr. 19). Romans would share such a feeling with the Lavinians and their public cult of male genitals (fr. 262).

At the beginning of this chapter I pointed to the use of history for strengthening groups and the boundaries creating these groups. Whose history did Varro write? Which purpose did he serve? The answer is rather surprising. Varro does not use the histories of religions in order to mark boundaries. He seems to be interested in the bridging capital of a shared history rather than in the binding capital. This holds true on different levels. Within a universalistic framework, religious traditions of different peoples offer a heritage that can be shared. Varro names heroes from Africa and Boetia (fr. 31). As already shown, the same god could be venerated under different names. Even a negative trait such as images of the divine is shared by many polities (fr. 18). Roman precepts for ritual action, as well as Greek precepts for ritual abstinence, were resources for the resolution of human problems (fr. 50 and 49).

I have already pointed out the weight given to the introduction of Italian deities in Rome by the first kings as well as the documentation of contemporary local deities of middle-Italian townships. Varro, born in 116 BC, had witnessed the start of the Italian civil war as a military tribune and was very aware of the problem of Italian unity. But in a book published in late 47 or in 46, he shows awareness of internal schisms in Roman society, too. If Caesar, the murderer, is the dedicatee of the *Antiquitates*, his victim, Pompey, is the subject of a laudatory oeuvre at the same time. Varro's programme of three types of theology does not aim to deepen dividing lines, but to hold divergent developments together (fr. 11 and 9). Poetry and its invention of embarrassing stories about the gods serve the theatre and entertainment and still offer something to civic cult. Philosophy, producing physical interpretations of religion, should be confined to smaller circles, but offers something to civic theology, too. Both are universal phenomena and hence shared reservoirs for the many local civic variants of religion.

Conclusion

Varro was not alone in using religion in an attempt to bridge existing gaps in society. Despite all party historiography, there was a strong current in Roman historiography that aimed at creating a history common to Roman families from all parts of Italy and all social strata. Annalistic history, narrating Roman history year by year with ever-changing protagonists, and the introduction of a long line of military victories into the calendar by means of founding dates of votive temples, offered the possibility to level out differences in individual or gentilician contributions, to write history without hierarchy. Cato attempted writing a history without naming individuals. His example, however, was not followed by the history of religion, as attempted in Varro's 'Antiquities'.

Just a few years before, Caesar, in his books on the war in Gaul, described Celtic and Germanic religions. He spoke about the Gallic cult of Mercury.[26] This was, of course, a translation, an *interpretatio Romana*. But it was a translation that presupposed the principal universality of the phenomenon of religion and of the gods. Differences could be acknowledged, easily acknowledged. Being subjected to ethnographic *topoi* or historical explanation, the importance of these differences was diminished – diversity is natural and contingent and does no harm. After all, the Romans were to build an empire. Management of diversity must have been the demand of the day.

Varro wrote historical accounts of religion within a universalistic framework. His intended readers were Roman and his focus was Roman, but his interest was in religion as a universal phenomenon, enabling Italian and imperial communication rather than strengthening mutually exclusive ethnic or urban identities. In this context, Varro is intellectually to be assigned to contemporaries such as Diodorus Siculus or Pompeius Trogus, writers of universal histories. This, of course, is a minority position in the late republican practice of historiography, probably dominated by the highly individualized genre of historical epic. Here is the polemical stance that I postulated earlier for any historiography, when I claimed that history is never written in the singular, but organizes memories in alternative form.

To this purpose Varro had to take a radical step. *Religio* is defined not as a tradition, but as an institution, an *institutum*, something 'set up' by humans. Surely, the Romans had known about earlier religion before, had memories of temples being set up, games being dedicated and continued. Thus, Roman religion could accommodate a lot of Roman history. Varro goes one step further. The whole differentiation of the divine into endless lists of names, he claims, has been contingent, historical – not just some cultic practice. Contingency implies distancing: one could reflect on such decisions; one might even criticize them. But in a contingent world, decisions are necessary, including negative ones, the driving out of cults. Before the age of historicism, such decisions – invested with proper, legitimate authority – would be binding despite a possible critical stance towards them. This is the basis for Varro, the systematizer. Within the historical framework, a recipe book on religion is offered. In Cicero's *De natura deorum*, written one year after the publication of Varro's *Antiquitates*, Cicero accepts Varro's concept of religion as the contingent human reaction to the conviction that the divine exists. Only the latter is subject to philosophical reasoning, but the former definitely needs control.[27] This is not exactly what Varro wrote, but leads back to a rather narrow, 'civic' definition of religion.

The fully fledged Varronian history of religion, dimly visible through the scattered 260 fragments of the *Antiquitates rerum divinarum*, tries to construct not a Roman but a universal history of religion, applicable for a Roman polity extending all over Italy, certainly into Greece and beyond, an incipient *Imperium Romanum*. In this respect, Varro and his dedicatee, Caesar, share the same perspective.

This was no unilinear development. New gods were to arrive who demanded stories about the shrinking of diversity, about resistance to unity and about differentiation being of secondary concern. In such narratives, conspirators such as Sextus Tarquinius and Judas replaced Numa and Fulvius Nobilior.[28]

As I stressed at the beginning of this chapter, history is a powerful instrument even today. By retelling and celebrating the memory of the murdering of Ali, the Shi'a stabilize their specific identity in contrast to Sunni Islam. Protestants retell Martin Luther's publication of *95 Theses*, at Saxonian Wittenberg, as a founding event of Protestantism as a critical and better alternative to Roman Catholicism. The history and diffusion of Buddhism has been described by tracing 'schools' dominated by heads of monasteries who were prolific writers, and at the same time interpreters of earlier texts and objects of serial biography. Shinto has cast Japanese history in the form of divine genealogies, again countered by a 'critical historiography' since the seventeenth century.[29] Legitimacy is based on correct or imagined genealogy; differences are memorized by the evocation of critical events. Here, the processes described in this and the preceding chapter interact. On a global scale, the concept of 'religion' and the self-organization of social groups as 'religions' have proven to be highly successful formats for establishing oneself as a national or international agent. This proliferation of a Western concept of 'religion' (as a parasite construct riding on the back of national identity) has brought with it the construction (or continuous cultivation) of an interpretive account of such groups and their history, whether this is done to create boundaries by pointing to old feuds and differences or to forge alliances on the basis of a common ancestry. Talking of 'Abrahamitic religions' by pointing to the veneration of Abraham in Judaism, Christianity and Islam is a strategy for using narratives of the past in order to transcend divisions. Varro's example demonstrates that such a use of historiography is not without parallel. Historical narratives start as individual attempts to deal with a situation, but in order to get canonized, to become the blueprint of ritualized retelling or even public celebration, these narratives need a congenial audience and shared interests. Chapter V will take a closer look at such processes. First, however, concepts of gods and the media of their representations must be addressed.

CHAPTER III

IDOLATRY AND REPRESENTATION

The ancient polytheist religions around the Mediterranean had simply been called 'idolatry' for centuries by Jewish or Christian polemicists and observers.[1] Not every religion conceptualizing itself as 'monotheist' does without images, but there seems to be a widespread tendency to stress the alterity of the one and only deity by avoiding images or falling back on aniconic symbols. In contrast to an anthropomorphic sign, such signs could more easily underline the transcendent, inconceivable, maybe even unfathomable character of the divine. In order to keep such a deity present, however, a lot of energy must be devoted to making such symbols visible and attractive – in art and architecture, for instance – and to compensate the lack of visible presence by verbal or ritual presentification. The frequency of rituals or simple repetition of narratives about the deity tends to be much higher than the average for the ancient gods; the development of daily cult and monotheistic tendencies went hand in hand. In fact, in using statues housed in temples, ancient religions had a powerful instrument to construct – or, from a different perspective, represent – the divine in a differentiated, polytheistic form. Such techniques enabled ritual access, stimulated reflection, and inspired imagination in day or night dreams and visions. It even informed critical philosophical thinking. The gods could be met and addressed in their temple; sacrifices enabled the petitioners to put their questions and get an immediate answer via extispicy. The inquiry into the will of the gods in the many forms of divination frequently draws on this system of representation, too.

'Idolatry' seems to be a much less derogatory term today. Or at least, it should be. In an age of media innovation, we have rediscovered images as a major source of inspiration, artistic stimulation and also religious resource. The combination of suspicion and attraction invites us to consider ancient practices of dealing with the problem of how to handle the transcendent. Did they represent their gods and, if so, how?

Religion with and without images

In Cicero's (106–43 BC) speech to the pontiffs, he protests that Clodius had robbed him of his house without sufficient legal basis for turning it into a sanctuary – that is, having consecrated his house, having made a monument in the place of his house, having dedicated a statue.[2] Clearly, this is an intensification of religious quality. It is the use of the statue (of which we will learn further details later on in Cicero's speech and this chapter) which seals the sacralization of previously private property, and which, I suppose, created unambiguity. As we have seen in the previous chapter, Varro (116–27 BC), Cicero's contemporary, claims that the use of statues is an old but secondary development, after 170 years of cult without images, even if temples – Varro speaks more precisely of 'roofed structures' – had already been in use earlier.[3] Varro probably rightly points to Greek and Etruscan influence in these matters and to the fact that statuary is intimately related to architectural decor. In Tuscan temples and their Roman variants, it is not the images in the temple's interior but the many images put on the roof that would have been the more striking innovation and remained the hallmark of this and later periods.[4]

Varro makes a philosophically motivated statement that postulates the absence of large images in a locality before the start of urban monumentalization. I do not intend to discuss the historical significance of this (because I do not see how Varro could possibly have clear evidence for the lack of images). And yet, Varro was probably right. With the exception of Egypt and some peculiar local developments, the rise of anthropomorphic images in the mainlands and on the margins of the Near Eastern and Greek cultures, according to recent research, is dateable to the end of the first half of the first millennium BC.[5] Central features of Greek and Roman religion could function without reference to images. Even prayers and sacrifices could be performed without directly addressing an image. Beside anthropomorphic imagery, a tradition of barely shaped wooden posts or slabs (*xoana*) continued to function as venerable signs of the divine even in fully mythologized Greek religion, down into late antiquity.[6] A temporarily raised altar of grass sods and simple earthenware for the vessels would do, as Varro points out in the context of his criticism of temple luxury.[7] But this is no adequate description of the period under consideration.

Picturing

A Roman of that time did not need to go to a temple in order to know about images. For a brief moment I enter or pass some Pompeian houses. In the doorway of the Casa dei Vettii (VI.15.a/b in the archaeological grid of Pompeii) a visitor encountered an image of Priapus. It is famous for his penis being balanced against a bag of money, but it is representative of Priapus being frequently encountered near an entrance, probably indicating sexual punishment for thieves and badly behaving guests rather than sexual lust.[8] The complex position of the doors enabled the gatekeeper to force certain guests into a direct confrontation with Priapus through a smaller entrance or to let them pass the image through a wider doorway – only to encounter Priapus again in statuary form on a fountain in the peristyle.[9]

In a house at VI.7, famous for the so-called 'carpenters' procession' (that shows common people, perhaps the proprietors, carrying an image of Minerva), doorway 9 (now faded) greeted a visitor with paintings of Mercury and Fortuna to his left and right. John Clarke's interpretation is confirmed in many instances: 'The owner was, as it were, doubling his luck, since Mercury was the god who made tradesmen and shopkeepers prosper. Fortuna brought wealth and prosperity as well.' Outside, a painting of Minerva completed the combination of protective deities.[10] A third example can be added. Over the entrance to the Shop of the Procession to

IDOLATRY AND REPRESENTATION

Cybele (IX.7.1 in the archaeological grid) was a row of four busts, showing Sol, Jupiter, Mercury and Luna. Again, I follow Clarke and expand on his interpretation: Sun and Moon put the shop into a cosmic framework, inside of which the bearded Jupiter points to the political Roman framework, Mercury to the wealth accumulated by trade.[11] Obviously, such a form of communication between owner and visitor or client presupposes a standardization of the 'medium' and its meaning – to use a first classification. It is a restricted number of items – that is, deities – which are combined. The stabilization of meaning is produced by the iconographic practice.

This mechanism had been recognized by Varro. In his introduction to 'On special and selected gods', the sixteenth book of *Antiquitates rerum divinarum*, he defined these as being those gods who received temples and who were 'distinguished by many signs' (fr. 228). A single god could be venerated without image, but for further differentiation temples and images are necessary. The dedication of a statue by a number of women enables the creation of a Fortuna Muliebris at Rome; Fortuna and Felicitas were differentiated first of all by having different temples (fr. 192).

It should be pointed out that narratives are not referred to in these contexts – huge differences between religious knowledge encoded in texts and knowledge encoded in images are a frequent phenomenon. An important confirmation of this interpretation of the Varronian fragments is given by the pontiff Cotta's account in Cicero's treatise 'On the nature of the gods': 'From childhood onwards we know Jupiter, Juno, Minerva, Neptune, Vulcanus, Apollo, and the other gods in that appearance, that was intended by painters and sculptors, not only in facial appearance, but also in paraphernalia, age, and clothing.'[12] Of course, this very fact is a problem, as the philosophical debate points out, in that images and attributes are arbitrary and contingent, not firm facts on which one could build a concept of anthropomorphic gods, as the Epicureans did. But the occasional criticism of intellectuals – naturally shared by Varro – did not endanger the actual functioning of the semantic system, and intellectuals knew to account for practical usage, too. After all, Varro passes over his earlier criticism: the statues and their paraphernalia, he says elsewhere, were intended to help the initiated to see the real significance of the gods, the soul pervading the world (fr. 225).

In a historical perspective, other advantages were more important. The dominance of the iconographic system enabled an easy generation of new gods – Fortuna Muliebris has already been mentioned. The cult of divine qualities or personifications that seems so awkward to modern accounts of ancient religion loses all exceptionality if approached from the visual angle. Temples and statues made them an integral part of the system. Judged by the number of prodigies reported for their Roman temples, Salus, Fortuna and Concordia were no different from Juno or Mars; about one-third of the prodigies reported for temples relate to such deities.[13] It is from the temple of such a goddess, Fortuna huiusce diei, that we have fragments of one of the largest statues. The statue of probably more than eight metres heigh stood on a base of more than two metres and must have filled the small space of the circular temple B in the Largo Argentina in the centre of Rome.[14] The recently popularized concept of 'picturing', of transforming a world by making pictures of it, seems to catch this process neatly.[15]

The previous remarks seem to imply an unlimited proliferation of new gods and statues. The opposite is true. The same Ciceronian Cotta already noted that the number of gods named in Roman pontifical rituals and texts was rather limited.[16] Inflation of signs would have endangered the working of the semantic system, as described before. New cults were subjected to a complex senatorial procedure, and a second potential source of inflation was curbed, too. A lot of trouble was taken to distinguish divine and human images,[17] with the latter proliferating from the fourth century BC onwards.

Using images

It is a truism of the iconic turn that images are created by seeing, that by being seen they are perceived as looking at the observer, thus focusing the analysis on the interaction of object and observer rather than on inherent qualities of the object and a semiotic approach only. The gaze of the temple visitor changes the image, creates a new social fact. Varro might be right in stating that images made of bronze, earthenware, plaster or marble do not feel and do not demand anything, thus producing neither guilt nor gratitude (*Antiquitates rerum diuinarum*, fr. 22), but from today's point of view the visitor praying to the image makes the god hear, even if the deity refuses to grant the wish. There is negative evidence, too. In reflecting on the limits of appropriate religion, practices related to statues are included in the criticism of superstition. One of the few fragments known from Seneca's treatise 'On superstition' deals with such practices – for instance, people who from a distance wash or comb a statue. There is hardly a livelier description of religious experiences and articulations made in the public space of large sanctuaries:

> But if ever you go up on the Capitol, it will make you feel ashamed just to see the crazy performances put on for the public's benefit, all represented as duties by light-hearted lunacy. So Jupiter has a special attendant to announce callers and another one to tell him the time; one to wash him and another to oil him, who in fact only mimes the movements with his hands. Juno and Minerva have special women hairdressers, who operate some distance away, not just from the statue, but from the mirrors ... There used to be an old, decrepit but very experienced pantomime artist who put on his act every day on the Capitol as if the gods were enjoying the show of a man, who those human spectators have deserted. Every type of artisanship has settled down there working for the immortal gods.[18]

These are acid remarks, addressed at traditional cult as well as individual radicalization. At the same time, it is precious evidence for the embodiment of ancient religion, hard to swallow for sublime philosophical concepts of the divine. The Greek Plutarchos, writing around AD 70, therefore concentrates his criticism of *deisidaimonia* (fear of the gods) on human behaviour in temples, too. Plutarch's text 'On superstition' is prominent for his contrasting of *deisidaimonia* on the one hand and atheism on the other, as the two main forms of an incorrect position against the gods (*Peri desidaimonia* 1). This antithesis structures the whole text, leading to a comparison that – surprisingly – prefers atheism, which never leads to superstition, whereas superstition frequently results in atheism (10a–12). The dominant characteristic is the fear of the gods, clearly displaying an incorrect concept of the gods, a mistaken theology.[19]

In his treatise Plutarch concentrates on the resultant ambiguity of piety, if tainted by unwarranted fear. It is his choice of examples, his observations, that give an insight into pragmatic concerns with regard to contemporary religion. His analysis starts in the private realm, in sleep or at home (3c–d), but quickly arrives at temples. Instead of places of salvation in crisis, sanctuaries become places of punishment (4a). This logic of hate and fear and seeking the vicinity of the gods (11) permeates the whole treatise. Proskynesis in front of the images instead of a realistic conception of transcendent deities, combining criticism and refuge (6b), is characteristic. To stay at home is a rather mild form of *deisidaimonia* (7d); the most severe forms are realized in the temples of the gods (9b). It is the image of the Carthaginians sacrificing their own children that forms the final climax (13) of the concluding analysis of *deisidaimonia* as emotional disorder (14), leading to atheism rather than – the final word – *eusebeia*, piety (14).

Even if certain reactions to images and anthropomorphic images – to images of humans in particular – have an anthropological foundation,[20] such reactions and even a mere glance are culturally informed and potentially a matter of conflict.

Obviously, many Roman users interpreted the confrontation with the statue as a personal encounter. I should like to come back to Cicero's speech to the pontiffs. For about five paragraphs Cicero dwells on the deity to whom his house had been dedicated:

> Did that beautiful Liberty of yours turn out my Penates and the Lares of my family, in order to be established there herself by you, as if in a conquered country? . . . And what goddess is she whom you have established there? She ought indeed to be the good goddess; since

she has been consecrated by you. 'She is Liberty', says he. Have you then established her in my house whom you have driven out of the whole city? Did you . . . then place the image of Liberty in that house, which was of itself a proof of your most cruel tyranny and of the miserable slavery of the Roman people? Ought Liberty drive him, of all men in the world, from his house, whose existence was the only thing that prevented the whole city from coming under the power of slaves? . . . But from whence was that Liberty brought? For I sought for her diligently. She is said to have been a prostitute at Tanagra. At no great distance from Tanagra a marble image of her was placed on her tomb. A certain man of noble birth, not altogether unconnected with this holy priest of Liberty, carried off this statue to decorate his aedileship . . . He gave the statue which he had taken from the prostitute's tomb to that fellow, because it was much more suited to such people as he is than to Public Liberty. Can any one dare to profane this goddess, the statue of a prostitute, the ornament of a tomb, carried off by a thief, and consecrated by a sacrilegious infidel? Is it she who is to drive me from my house? Is she the avenger of this afflicted city? Is she to be adorned with the spoils of the republic? Is she to be a part of that monument which has been erected so as to be a token of the oppression of the senate, and to keep alive for ever the recollection of this man's infamy?[21]

The passage starts and ends with personifications. Libertas is acting, is expelling Cicero from his house. In between, the history of the actual statue is told, a funeral statue of a prostitute, object of a sequence of illegitimate translocations. However, Cicero does not discriminate between goddess and material form. 'Your special type of Liberty' is not a benevolent address of a deity, and it is perverse that the arch-enemy of civil liberty entertains such a goddess. But it is a deity. Semantically and syntactically, the conceptual and the material form of the deity are treated strictly in parallel, stressing identity. The goddess is present in her image; she is acting as image. The deity is as negative as her statue and vice versa.

This sense of presence converges with archaeological findings. Paralleling a development that is visible in the restoration of some Greek temples in Hellenistic and imperial times,[22] but which was prevalent in Sicily and southern Italy, Roman temples seem to have staged this sense of presence in order to enable corresponding experiences. Indicators are the lavish interiors of temples, complex architectonical regulations of access and a very careful presentation of the cult statue. Doors and doorways gained in importance; floor mosaics or curtains could articulate the structure of the temple interior and the temporal dimension of the process of access to the statue.[23] Positioning the statue directly onto a mosaic floor stressed its mobility. The combination of different materials heightened the impression of vividness.[24] This hardly goes well with the Greek tradition of awe-inspiring aesthetic beauty displayed by a magnificent and large image towards the back wall of the innermost chamber.

Anecdotal evidence agrees. According to later historiographical tradition, P. Cornelius Scipio Africanus spent every night before a major decision was to be made sitting by himself in the *cella* of the Capitoline Jupiter, as if in dialogue with the god.[25] Temples offered space for individual religious experience, even if not everybody dared to demonstrate this.

Conclusion

How can we conceptualize the ancient findings and make them compatible with modern thinking on images? The concept of representation might serve as a starting point. If we give priority to the notion of the metaphysical existence of the gods, this concept is useful. The statue is a sign or symbol for something else: it is 'showing the invisible'.[26] Such an interpretation is communicable with ancient philosophical and theological thinking. One could discuss the suitability and adequacy of the semiotic material, in the sense of metaphors as of actual matter.[27] For statues of emperors, beginning with Caesar, this was a veritable political discourse.[28]

The usual indexicality of signs implied an advantage already pointed out by Hans-Georg Gadamer, whose position can be summarized like this: 'A

IDOLATRY AND REPRESENTATION

representation enhances the ontological reality of what is represented.'[29] Or more specifically, if images refer to gods, gods must exist. Discussions about the iconicity, the likeness, of the sign might ensue, as we have seen in the controversy between the Epicurean Velleius and the sceptic Cotta as imagined by Cicero in his dialogue *De natura deorum*.

For the Roman habit, which we have briefly gazed at in the form of widespread practices, 'representation' does not work, and neither does casual presence. The opportunity to admit or negate the presence of the god when confronting his or her image does not work along the lines of inhabiting, finding a temporary place or the like,[30] concepts that all suppose the metaphysical distinction between god and image. But simply opting for presence would be too easy,[31] even if we restrict ourselves to a sort of mainstream observer. Roman gods are not just present in their images.

When regarding non-statuary Roman images of gods, they are frequently not veristic, and do not intend to catch the deity in all its vividness. Instead, these images refer to statues; they are representations of statues and are iconographically marked as such. This holds true for different genres. Roman coins frequently enabled an (unrealistic) gaze into a temple's interior onto a statuesque or living god; lamps depicted gods (as humans) in a statuesque way.[32] Idyllic landscapes in wall paintings present statues of gods that made the depicted observers inside the painting aware of the presence of these gods.[33] That presence is not arbitrary, but it is statuesque. It draws its plausibility not from a specific form or material, but from an emotional experience, produced by the specific context of temples, perhaps heightened by rituals.[34] The many gods of Roman polytheism came into existence by picturing them and by experiencing these statues. Prodigies related to these statues formed a necessary element of their appraisal. They demonstrated the uncontrollable aspect of gods who were – with a few exceptions of images fallen from heaven[35] – artefacts and were known and presented to be artefacts, thus giving legitimacy to their existence.

The lesson thus learnt is important for the reading of cultic scenes with which I started. The wall painting of the procession to Cybele on the outside of the shop of the same name (IX.7.1 in the archaeological grid of

Pompeii) probably does not only depict the shopkeeper and his wife (together with other colleagues) with some ritual paraphernalia. Cybele is in the image, clearly displayed as a sitting statue but twice life sized, placed on a litter, and she is actually interacting with all the people gazing at her. We will not be able to repeat the experience of the original observers, not being part of their religious individuations. But we can try to imagine their previous experiences and their habits, their inner imagination and cultural stabilization, thus seeing references to a presence that is not anthropologically inherent in the image, but is due to the historical circumstances that I have reconstructed.

Neither 'idolatry' as a polemical critique nor 'representation' as a central problem of religion was confined to antiquity. The use of images remains a major topic of inter-religious criticism. It was applied by Christian colonial entrepreneurs and missionaries in the phase of European expansion to the peoples of the Americas and Africa, but it was also a topos of Protestant criticism of Catholicism. From this point of view, the 'fetish' (the man-'made' image of the divine) and the image of a saint differ only in details. Protestant imagery has tried to replace Catholic iconography with symbols, among which the Bible holds a prominent place. Much earlier, Islam had developed a similar strategy. Based on a strand of criticism of images of Jahwe in the Hebrew Bible, the Islamic tradition, from early hadiths (traditions about the prophet) onwards, has developed a sharp opposition to the representation of Allah in the form of images, later argued by some as concerning even images of humans (despite a large development of pictorial art).[36] For the representation of the divine, architecture and ornament – in particular ornamental writing of the names of Allah and Qur'anic texts – replace images. Evidently, it is much easier for a strictly monotheistic religion to shift the balance to the vetoing of anthropomorphic imagery than for traditions allowing for different superhuman figures (angels for instance) or the importance of a multitude of individual human intermediaries as in Catholic or certain Buddhist traditions.

CHAPTER IV

THEOLOGICAL HERITAGES: ROMAN PRIESTHOOD AND THE NEW TESTAMENT

Ancient temples witnessed changes other than the shifting modes of individual religious experiences and articulations. One of the most important developments of the history of religion in the imperial Roman period is the substitution of sacrificial religious practices with reading practices.[1] By concentrating on reading rather than sacrificing, for us a religion appears to be modern rather than ancient. Like other rituals, ancient Christian cult had developed towards miniaturization and towards replacing actual sacrifice by the memory of sacrifice.[2] In such a constellation it could only function through the possibility of reference to sacrifice in texts. One could easily refer to narratives of sacrifice in the Septuagint, the Greek translation and the enlargement of the Hebrew Bible. In addition, new texts were composed which included much more than replacement, spiritualization or memory of biblical sacrifice. Across religious boundaries – which appear to have been much less rigid and clearly defined than is usually supposed – such texts engaged with contemporary religious practices, cross-fertilizing different traditions and thus leading to surprising innovations.

By accepting the *communis opinio* of the Italian or even Roman origin of the tractate or sermon to the Hebrews (which figures at the end of Paul's letters in the New Testament, but is not explicitly ascribed to him) at the end of the first or beginning of the second century AD,[3] this chapter argues for such an innovation of and engagement with contemporary practices across textual traditions. It will do so with regard to a text that came to be included in the inner canon of Christian writings, a process that privileged certain types of reading against others. If the dating is correct, it implies a Jewish audience educated in late Neronian or Flavian times and shaped by Roman culture as expressed in public buildings, images and rituals. 'Hebrews' is thus analysed in terms of its immediate context: contemporary urban religion.

Even if the sacrificial metaphors ('to bring offerings', 'animal sacrifice') are very important for the sermon, my special attention is given to the priestly roles involved in the transcendental sacrificial scenario. Shaped by Christian traditions, the modern concept of 'religion' entails the notion of 'priests' as an important structural element of religious practices and organizations. In Christian thinking, the priesthood of every believer is an important notion for the justification as for the critique of priestly institutions. Hebrews is the single most important text for this line of thinking and a showpiece of the complexity of the connecting lines between antiquity and the contemporary religion. Thus, I will compare the sacerdotal imagery of the text to the prominent role of the Roman emperors as *pontifices maximi* and to the developments of major public priesthoods around the turn of the first to the second century AD. This promises a deepened understanding of the cultural setting of the text and the interaction of its audience with the institutional setting of Rome, of which any audience in the Roman Empire would be part in institutional and cultural terms. Despite the fact that the tractate is one of the fundamental texts responsible for the shape of late ancient Christianities and its further history of reception, I regard the genesis of the text as much as a date in the history of Roman Judaism as in the history of Christianity. Its analysis opens up a window into the pitfalls of a scholarship that projects modern thinking about religious boundaries into antiquity.

Determining contexts

Obviously, New Testament as well as classical scholars are struck by the massive presence of sacerdotal semantics in the anonymous text called *Ad Hebraeos*. We are confronted with a Jesuology focused on the figure of a heavenly high priest. The results of *Quellenforschung* – research into the (lost) literary sources of a literary text – could be summed up like this: using the Pentateuchal descriptions of priestly services in the pentateuchal books Exodus and Numbers (especially focusing on atonement rituals) and Psalm 110 (109 in the counting of the Greek translation in the Septuagint),[4] as well as perhaps barely traceable elements of Qumranic Melchizedek traditions,[5] early Christ-as-intercessor motives,[6] and first-century spiritualizations of priesthood and cult as witnessed by the Alexandrinian Jewish thinker Philo,[7] the unknown author of the text developed a fully fledged theory of the elevated Crucified as high priest and son. Originality can be taken for granted in comparison to the traditions used. The intellectual and scriptural network thus established offers neither an explanation nor even a motif.

With only a few obvious clues given in the text, hypotheses about its setting and the presuppositions for any interpretation move in hermeneutic circles. Our placing of the text influences our reconstruction of possible associations of contemporary readers, or better: hearers. Given the few clues in the text regarding the place and time of its production or addressees, I must rely on hypotheses. The time of Domitian is an obvious, though – I repeat – hypothetical choice;[8] I extend this period to include the early Trajan period, too. The most reliable evidence for a *terminus ante quem* is the quotation, or rather direct borrowing, by 1 Clement 36.2–6, most probably dating to between 90 and 120 AD,[9] but in fact we cannot rule out that Hebrews used the first letter of Clement. I must stress that some of my arguments depend on this decision in dating. Rome or Italy are the most probable among the few feeble possibilities as far as place is concerned; in the final line (13.24) the audience is addressed as people 'who are from Italy' – the ideas shared with the letter of Clement written at Rome likewise suggest geographical vicinity.[10] My argument does not depend on this choice, but is helped by it very much.

Rome was the oppressing reality of the imperial Mediterranean, even if mitigated by distance or Greek language. Given even the slightest chance that the text derives from the city of Rome or heavily romanized urban centres, we should pay as much attention to local Roman traditions as to the Alexandrian or Jerusalem ones quoted above. Roman context and the dating have two corollaries: the question of persecution and the destruction of the temple. From a historical point of view, the evidence for any persecution of Christians under Domitian is feeble.[11] For Rome, Xiphilinos' excerpt from the third-century historian Cassius Dio (the sources of Dio's negative version of Domitian are difficult to identify[12]) points to religious arguments employing the concept of 'Jewish traditions' in the persecution of members of the senatorial class and possibly beyond. This, however, relates to the very last year of Domitius' reign, as would John's Apocalypsis, more probably a second-century text. But even admitting a Domitian date does not attest to more than some local conflicts in Asia Minor. Despite the negative portrait of the emperor in senatorial and later Christian historiography and by Pliny,[13] it is most probable that the enthusiastic image conveyed by the poets Martial (who, however, never had direct access to the emperor[14]) and Statius was much more representative of popular feeling, even if the poets' readership has to be looked for in the ranks of an upper class rather than the larger populace, which was directly addressed by Domitian with the help of games and military spectacles rather than the employment of poets.[15]

Vespasianus' and Titus' destruction of the temple of Jerusalem are of great importance. The Romans' ending of centralized Jewish sacrificial ritual and the factual disappearance of the priesthood offered a powerful incentive to reflect on these kinds of religious practices and to convert them into resources of powerful symbols and imagination. Evidently, that would have been an important precondition for thinking about related developments in Roman religion. A Jewish audience would have been used – and opposed – to ruler cult from Hellenistic times onwards. The Flavian innovations and intensifications in this area would have been noticed,[16] even if not welcomed in the manner reflected in, for example, Statius' poems. Yet the image of the emperor was shaped by many aspects; being god-like was just one element. Other roles – political, patronage, military, cultural – were fundamental, even through the lens and perspective offered by emperor worship. Religious roles, and in particular sacerdotal roles, were among them.[17] People were able to react differently to changes in these roles, as I hope to make clear.

My reference to the image of Domitian has already paved the way for my argument that the conceptualization of Jesus in Hebrews must be seen as engaging with the contemporary conceptualization of the Roman emperor. In taking up traditions from the Tenakh, the author of Hebrews, employing brilliant rhetoric, paints the image of heavenly Jesus – or more precisely *Iesus Dei filius*, to translate the Greek formulation at the start of the central part of the sermon (Hebrews 4.14: *Iêsoûn tòn uíou toû theoû*) – as a priest in competition with the supreme priest embodied by the earthly emperor – and, of course, winning. The emperor cannot challenge transcendent sacrifice and priestly honours.

My argument will be developed in three steps. First, I demonstrate the plausibility that the priestly role of the second and third Flavian emperors was a threat to the eagerness of the Jewish group following Jesus. Second, I demonstrate how Hebrews' sacerdotology tackled this problem. Third, I explain a few corollaries of my argument.

Changing concepts of priesthood

As was usual for princes and indeed many nobles, the sons of the emperors Vespasianus, Titus and Domitian became members of public priesthoods at a comparatively young age. Titus was co-opted into, as it was known, 'all colleges' in AD 71, implying membership in the colleges of the pontiffs, augurs, *Quindecimviri sacris faciundis*, responsible for the Sibyline Books, and the *Septemviri Epulones* as a minimum.[18] At perhaps the same time, certainly by the year AD 73, Domitian was co-opted into the same colleges and into the Arval brotherhood.[19] Such a membership demanded occasional presence; the formal dress was identical to the *toga praetexta* worn by magistrates in office. Visibility of the priestly role was hence restricted to a few ritual events.

From Augustus onwards, the acclamation as emperor had led to an additional honour: election to the office of *pontifex maximus*,[20] the only one of the many religious offices that became an element of full imperial titulature. Formally, this was just the head of the large pontifical college,[21] but the office entailed certain prerogatives towards other priests and was opened to plebeians and made subject to a specific sort of popular election from the third century BC onwards. Caesar entered into this office four years before his first consulship; Augustus did without it for the first quarter of a century of his reign. Even if it afterwards became a standard component of the extended form of imperial nomenclature, it is extremely difficult to relate specific actions to this office. Nearly everything we associate with the religious policy of the emperors had nothing to do with the office of supreme pontiff, transliterated to Greek as *pontiphex maximos* or translated as *archiereus* or *archiereus megistos*. This holds true down to the reinterpretation of the office by the emperor Julian in the 360s.[22]

There were, however, exceptions. As Suetonius relates in an astonishing phrase in his biography on the emperor Titus, written by the 120s,[23] Titus was the first to make a declaration that he would keep his hands pure while in office. Probably suffering from bad press, on entering the supreme pontificate (probably a few months after his accession to the throne) he promised that he would rather die himself than kill anyone:

> Having declared that he would accept the office of *pontifex maximus* for the purpose of keeping his hands unstained, he was true to his promise; for after that he neither caused nor connived at the death of any man, although he sometimes had no lack of reasons for taking vengeance; but he swore that he would rather be killed than kill.[24]

Magistrates had to swear an oath on the laws within five days of entering office; there is no evidence for elected priests having to perform the same thing. The connection of priestly offices to ethics is not a new one in Roman culture; Livy in his history of Rome relates an event of the year 209 BC, when an unwilling noble, Gaius Valerius Flaccus, was forced into the office of *Flamen Dialis* by the *pontifex maximus* – and changed his way of life as a consequence.[25] Yet 'clean' (*purus*) is rarely – and only in association with the Vestal Virgins – a priestly quality.[26] As far as purity is concerned, Roman religious practices differed markedly from Greek practice and Greek concerns about the avoidance of pollution and corresponding rituals of cleansing.[27] Vesta and the rites connected with her – and hence her priestesses, the Vestal Virgins – deal with *purgamina* ('instruments for cleaning') and hence the concept of *purus*.[28] Given this background, Titus' initiative should be judged as innovative, not simply fitting to the office.[29]

In a similar manner, Domitian, following his brother into office in AD 81, stressed the dignity of the office of *pontifex maximus*. Like earlier emperors, his taking up of the office was announced on coins and on many inscriptions.[30] Evidence of a particular importance given to the office is provided by Suetonius' detailed account of his multiple prosecutions of Vestals, a task intimately connected with the office of *pontifex maximus*: 'He punished the cases of sexual misbehaviour of the Vestal virgins, that had been neglected by his father and brother, in different and severe ways, first by capital punishment, later in the old manner [of burying alive] . . .'[31] The first case must have occurred around AD 83 – that is, early in his reign; the second might belong to the year AD 89.[32] It had wide repercussions that transcended historiography; a reference to his personal role in the investigation as an explorer might be found in Statius' *Silvae*.[33]

Another incidence that would be most easily related to the office of the supreme pontiff concerned the dealing with a member of the pontifical college, the *Flamen Dialis*, the priest of Jupiter. Witness is born by the contemporary Plutarch's fiftieth of the 'Roman Questions':

> Why did the priest of Jupiter resign his office if his wife died, as Ateius has recorded? Is it because . . . Or is it because the wife assists her husband in the rites, so that many of them cannot be performed

without the wife's presence, and for a man who has lost his wife to marry again immediately is neither possible perhaps nor otherwise seemly? Wherefore it was formerly illegal for the *flamen* to divorce his wife; and it is still, as it seems, illegal, but in my day Domitian once permitted it on petition. The priests were present at that ceremony of divorce and performed many horrible, strange, and gloomy rites.

Further evidence, overlooked so far, is given by the inscription of an altar dedicated to Volcanus. The regulation of the altar presents itself as the reinvigoration of an annual vote instituted at the time of the Neronian fire of Rome. Here, the wording of the inscription clearly differentiates between the emperor Domitian who dedicated the altar, the annually changing official who has to perform the rite, and the *pontifex maximus* Domitian, who constituted the sacral regulation. It is the supreme pontiff who sets the regulations.[34]

Other activities cannot be related to the office of *pontifex maximus*, but attest to a degree of religious activities that was unknown to earlier emperors since Augustus. Suetonius mentions the founding of a new priestly college related to the cult of Minerva and a new dress for the *Sodales Flaviales* and the *Flamen Dialis*.[35] The founding of a new Capitolian competitive game is to be related to the year 86; in 88 Domitian had secular games organized, again using coinage to broadcast his religious activities. The series with different ritual details is truly exceptional.[36]

Domitian is to be credited with not only the number of newly founded games or temples,[37] – the rebuilding of the Capitol, the so-called Forum Transitorium, the completion of the Domus Aurea and the Flavian amphitheatre ('Colosseum')[38] – but also the visibility of religious offices that must be seen as characteristic of his reign and the time immediately preceding. Not only did he survive the civil war of 69 in the guise of an Isiac priest, he also published an edict prohibiting the sacrifice of cattle during the absence of Vespasianus:[39] whatever the exact content and circumstances, Suetonius' anecdote points to a very particular public image of Domitian, giving him a specific religious aura as a religious actor, not only as a recipient of ruler cult.

In analysing the religion of the Flavian period, historical research has not stressed the emperors' priestly offices, but the veneration of the emperor imperial cult. For the latter 'the Flavian era is... the most significant period since its origins under Augustus', now including the living emperor from the start.[40] This holds true on a global scale. Without a noble or urban background, the new dynasty stressed ruler cult as a vehicle for legitimacy and authority. That included Titus' new *Sodales Flaviales* and the temple of the deified Vespasianus as well as Domitian's initiative to include his brother, the deified Titus, in these projects.[41]

I do not wish even to sketch Flavian ruler cult, but rather to highlight a few motifs that might be relevant for our understanding of Hebrews. Much stress is laid on presence, the closeness of the divine emperor in comparison to other gods. Statius characterizes Domitian as the one who 'nearer than Jove directs the doings of mankind' or talks about the 'genius of the lord who is present'.[42] The 'lord and god' is a present god.[43] His throne of gold and ivory is put up among the gods – that is, his gold statue is set up in a temple. A radiant crown is included. Domitian is son and father of the gods.[44]

In the context of imperial Judaeo-Christian history, 'ruler cult' tends to immediately produce mental images of stone effigies being venerated by sacrifice; in other words, an unacceptable veneration of humans – rituals that any reasonable human being must abhor. This is very much a provincial perspective, in that the presence of the emperor is being reduced to statues. These played an important role in Rome, too, but they served to enforce the presence of an emperor personally visible on many occasions to the few as well as to the populace. Domitian's contemporaries Statius and Martial,[45] flatterers, maybe, but highly valued poets at the same time, in their poems paint the image of a popular emperor – maybe charismatic more by office than personality – constructing his imperial authority also by use of religious media. Religious language and devotion is a genuine means of answering this call, the top of rhetorical flattery and genuine admiration, grateful and awesome at the same time. Honouring somebody as above average – meant to fall into the cultural inventory of honouring the gods – is to replace bronze statues by gold, to move the statue into a temple, to compare actions not with those of other humans but with those of the gods. Glamour and eccentricity, visibility and arrogance might have put off members of the old elite and some intellectuals: criticism and executions are attested and elite historiographers such as Tacitus indulged in such opposition and made us love their narratives and insinuations. But why should researchers living in today's society doubt the attraction of such phenomena to a majority of contemporaries?

On such a perspective, imperial cult must not be seen in isolation. For the emperors, receiving cult and performing cult are necessary compliments. Piety and religious activities mark out the importance of the religious field and invite activity in this area by others. Filling religious roles was, as I have shown at the beginning of this chapter, part of the stock of public political roles, even before the imperial age. Competition with precursors and possible co-runners led to modification, intensification and innovation. Augustus filled and stressed a wide range of religious roles, not all related to priestly functions: the important role of the emperor as performer of sacrifice was not usually dependent on a sacerdotal office. Titus' and Domitian's stress on the supreme pontificate must be seen as such an innovation.

Whereas the other priestly colleges stressed equality – and hence forced the emperors to communicate by letters and reduce their presence to rare occasions such as the secular games (e.g. in the case of the *Quindecimviri sacris faciundis*) – the supreme pontiff could act on his own on many occasions. A century of principate rule had made this office the prerogative of the emperor and the only religious role, as has been pointed out above, spoken of in standard titulature. Severe problems remained: the visibility of the role was, as I have shown, restricted and had to be expressed by actions both cruel and spectacular, such as punishing Vestals.

In contrast to being augur, pontiff, a *vir epulonum*, fetial or *sodalis*, the office of *pontifex maximus* was an office without rivals. The potential of the office is demonstrated by the words of the contemporary Pliny the Younger in his panegyric to Trajan (AD 98–117), a speech held on 1 September 100 and published in a considerably enlarged form the following year. Very few passages in Pliny's speech name the pontificate of the emperor (who is gratefully addressed for the transferral of the consulate), but the three passages that do are highly significant.[46] Stressing the modesty of the emperor,[47] Pliny employs the titulature to contrast the sitting consul with the emperor standing before him:

> I am surprised, senators, and neither believe my eyes or ears, and again and again ask myself, whether I see or hear: For the Imperator and Caesar and the august supreme pontiff stand before the lap of the consul, and the consul sat while the *princeps* was standing before him and he sat untroubled and without fear and as if that was usual.

The phrase *Augustus pontifex maximus* expresses the climactic structure, giving the highest possible qualification of the *princeps*, 'the first man', a religious ring, implicated as much in *Augustus* as in *pontifex*. It is the priestly office that removes the emperor from the world of ordinary man more than anything else.

Equally important is that the reflection about the fittingness of Trajan's wife is conceptualized with reference to this priesthood (83.5). 'Your wife brings you decorum and fame. What could be more blameless than her, what more having the virtues of old? If the supreme pontiff had to choose a wife, he would have elected her or a similar.' The religious ring of the context is visible in the term *sanctius* ('holier') and even *antiquius* ('more ancient'). Pliny implies that among all offices held by Trajan, it is the supreme pontificate that involves the highest standards and hence is suitable to judge whether the wife is matching the qualities of the emperor.

These observations are confirmed in the final prayer to Iuppiter (c. 94). Referring to the adoption by Nerva (AD 96–98), Pliny formulates (94.4): 'You have spoken with the voice of Nerva, what you thought; you have made his son a father for us and a supreme pontiff for yourself.' It is in the role of the supreme pontiff that Trajan engages in direct contact with the polity's highest deity. Avoiding functional political terms, it is the concept of being a son that describes the most intimate relationship to the predecessor, the concept of fatherhood – of course referring to the official title of *pater patriae* – that describes the most intimate relationship with the people, and the concept of the supreme pontiff that describes the most intimate relationship between man and god of somebody who already equals the gods in his ability to answer prayers.[48] On the basis of our knowledge of the Flavian period and their strategies of legitimacy sketched above, Pliny, writing at the very beginning of a new reign, might have modified some points, but based his speech on patterns established before.[49]

Sacerdotology in Hebrews

My attempt to read Hebrews as a reaction to developments starting in the Flavian period – as we are used to reading Pliny – is justified not only from the originality of the canonical sermon's priestly images, but from a peculiar observation. The development of the high priest theory in Hebrews starts with an expression that is quite unusual (4.14): 'Therefore, since we have a great high priest who has passed through the heavens, Jesus the son of God, let us hold fast the confession.' The expression *archiereus megas* is not the title of the high priest used in the Septuagint, the Greek version used elsewhere,[50] that normally uses *hiereus megas*. Biblically used only in 1 Maccabee 13.42, the phrase 'great high priest' must be judged exceptional.[51] As *archiereus megistos* is the standard expression for *pontifex maximus* – *archiereus* being used for local or provincial chief priests – a reference or, better, a semantic signal asking for reflection on one of the most commonly known offices of the time must be inferred.

Such a reference would not be exceptional. There are a number of instances that point to differences from contemporary Roman practices or claim comparable status for Jesus. In fact, the sermon 'To the Hebrews' starts with 'titulature', *onoma* (1.4).[52] It stresses the divine transferral of the office instead of a possible self-arrogation of it (5.4 f.):[53] 'And one does not take the honour for himself, but is called by God, just as Aaron was. (5) So also Christ did not glorify himself so as to become high priest; rather it was he who said to him, *You are my Son, I have begotten you today.* The uniqueness of the priestly office (7.11–19) may be contrasted with the plurality of Roman priesthoods, even if held by the same emperor. Jesus makes new ways metaphorically just as Domitian (especially in his last years) did literally (10.20). The heavenly sanctuary (*tes skenes tes alethines*, 8.2) is not manmade like the many urban temples.[54] Perhaps even the *testamenti sponsor* – to quote the Latin of the Vulgata (7.22) – could have a contemporary reference, as Suetonius transmitted Domitian's excessive demand for herediites in the context of his dealing with the Jews (Suetonius, *Domit.* 12.2). In Pliny's panegyric on the successor Trajan, he refers to Domitian's avaricious and illegal dealing with others' testaments and contrasts the new Trajanic practice of respecting testaments (Pliny, *Paneg.* 39–40). There is no Tenakh parallel for this latter phrase, as there is no oath-taking of the high priest in Exodus 28: the image of Jesus' priesthood is informed by contemporary institutions as much as by Scripture.[55]

To develop a Jesuology of a heavenly priestly office responds to a recent political development in the conception of Roman rulership, but concentrates on an aspect that would allow the framing of the comparison of Jesus, which is derogatory, to the emperor – a potentially capital crime – in strictly religious language. Focusing on the supreme pontificate of the emperor (recently stressed by Vespasian's sons) does not just potentially reinterpret the Flavian destruction of the Jerusalem temple perhaps commemorated on the occasion of the homily (see below). This recent religious development in the city of Rome enabled the author of Hebrews to counter the attractiveness of the towering figure of the emperor on like terms. Priestly offices are compared. Given the complex composition of Domitian's (like other emperors') earthly and divine status, the argument grew complex and led to inconsistencies: the shift between earthly and heavenly high priest was necessary to locate the argument within the Jewish tradition and to establish the high priest of the Pentateuch as the competing office. The fact that the dim tradition of Melchizedek already combined a priestly office with kingship may have invited that choice. At the same time this office, temporarily obliterated by Titus, had to be transgressed towards an incomparable heavenly office, held by the son of god, *Iesus dei filius*.

'Son of god' was, however, just as valid for Domitian, and thus the author of the sermon specified: 'And when, again, he brings the firstborn into the world, he says, *And let all the angels of God bow down before him*' (Hebrews 1.6). The Greek term πρωτότοκον, 'firstborn', not only takes up a Christological title of the Pauline tradition,[56] but gives it a political ring. Domitian, by all means, was born only in second place.

Contrasting Jesus and the living emperor (of course for reasons of criminal law never referred to explicitly or even by name), however, need not and could not lead to a competition in megalomania. Rhetorically, just the opposite could be useful. Hebrews stresses the humanity, the compassion of the son (e.g. 2.11–18) even in relationship to the office: 'For we do not have a high priest who is unable to sympathize with our weakness, but one who has been tested in every respect, in these same ways, without sin' (4.15). This again strikingly compares with Pliny's strategy early in his speech: 'Never shall we flatter him as a god, never as a divinity. We do not speak of a tyrant, but of a citizen, not of a lord, but of a father. "I am one of you" (did he say) . . .' (2.3 f.). Again, this is a reference to Domitian's having himself addressed as *dominus et deus* (see above), but again it implies expectations of an audience that might have been shared by the addressees of Hebrews: legitimacy by sonship is important, but a follower of Jesus cannot hope to have the crucified win a competition in mere divinity. On the contrary, compassion and closeness was the better argument.[57] The role of the highest priest must have been a standard set by Domitian – one of which he failed by the judgement of at least the upper class. Otherwise, Pliny would not have dwelled on it in crucial passages of his speech. Hebrews followed the same path in opening the eyes of his audience to the competitive character of their own standard. It might be noted that the earliest parallel text, *1 Clemens*, uses the high priest title of Jesus Christus in the phrase *archiereus kai prostates*, in Latin *pontifex et patronus* (*1 Clemens* 36.1; 61.3), associating military structures in the following chapter (37). In using the title of high priest, Clemens Romanus obviously associated the combination of contemporary roles envisaged by the emperor.

Conclusion

It is evident that the destruction of the second temple looms in the background of the tractate's audience.[58] This would help to bring out differences between the group addressed and its politically as well as geographically Roman environment. The group constituted an audience that was in danger of losing enthusiasm – if it has been rightly observed that Hebrews addresses 'a certain weariness in pursuing the Christian goal'[59] – rather than in fear under the impact of persecution; even apostasy was considered a real danger by the author.[60] The rhetorical strategy aimed not for radical dichotomy and incompatibility, but for competition on equal terms, taking seriously the religious dimension of the non-Jewish environment. The message was: we have a sort of *pontifex maximus*, too (*echein archierea*, Hebrews 8.1), but he is a better one, as is sworn by god, he is eternal and present[61] – the son remains the son and will not be replaced by his brother, as Titus was by Domitian. The implication of this rhetoric need not be spelled out: sacrificial cult monopolized in heaven renders earthly sacrifice superfluous. This is cult criticism in cultic language.[62] Jewish, Christ-related and other ancient religious practices and traditions did not live in separate worlds, as the modern division of labour of academic disciplines frequently suggests. The very Roman text of the 'tractate to the Hebrews' is an instance of the intensive interaction and open boundaries in the complex religious ecology of the Roman Empire.[63] Individuals had to deal with the complexity of their situation and to appropriate whatever religious resource was available to them. These contingent developments form part of antiquity's heritage to modernity, even where this heritage seems to distance itself from those ancients, who were the religious 'other'.

Accommodation is a perennial and paramount problem and challenge of segments of culture defining themselves by reference to tradition. This is particularly true for religion, as the treatment of historicization has demonstrated. Islamic Salafism, now frequently taken as a synonym for fundamentalist traditionalism, had been a movement openly taking account of cultural and political changes in the nineteenth century and trying to implement traditional virtues and bodies of knowledge into a changed environment. After centuries of open hostility to many forms of modernization, the Roman Catholic Church had initiated a process of balancing tradition and modernity in the Second Vatican Council (1962–5), making accommodation ('aggiornamento') one of its aims. As can be seen with the development of Salafism, as with immediate and recent reaction to the Council's outcomes, such processes are rarely integrated by the whole of a religious organization. Quite frequently, such reform movements might result in partial movements or even the splitting of groups. The integration of the sermon 'To the Hebrews' into the canon of the New Testament demonstrated the final integration of its line of thought.

This line of thought touched upon a major topic in the history of religion in Europe: priesthood. We know of many cultures that developed complex and powerful priesthoods, in concurrence or direct support of political, often regal power. Egypt, Sumer, Indian Brahmans and the Aztecs exemplify such a type of priesthood. The priesthoods of Greco-Roman cities and sanctuaries hardly shared in these characteristics. Each priest or group of priests cared for a specific cult or task, which was important but not subjected to any superior priest. They cared for the continuity of a cult or for the application of correct formulae, but they were not indispensable 'mediators' between men and gods. Occasionally, their personal conduct became a matter of interest, but such occasions were rare, and the attention was concentrated on very few offices, the Roman Vestal Virgins and the Flamen Dialis being one of them. Such moves occurred several times without lasting effects.[64] Like contemporary functionaries of Jewish synagogues, episcopoi and presbyters in groups oriented towards Christ were not indispensable mediators for god and his 'name' or 'son'. Engaging with a temporary development of the supreme pontificate, 'Hebrews' developed an image of a much more important priestly role. In modern Christianity, the mediating role of priests is still an unsolved matter of debate between

THEOLOGICAL HERITAGES

various churches. Even if the priestly and prophetic role of every believer is part also of Roman Catholic theology, the practical role, the emphasis and many corollaries differ widely between Protestant understandings of priesthood and the image and self-image of other 'clergies'. Ancient priesthoods form the part of an entangled history of religious thinking on the role of 'specialists' down into the modern age.

CHAPTER V

COLONIZING TIME

The Roman calendar in its technical as well as graphical form probably leads the list of the most unchanged and pervasive survivals from classical antiquity into the modern age. Today, it is of nearly universal use (even if not everywhere as the official version). Apart from the minor changes of the Gregorian reform, all other attempts at reform have been short lived. In the same manner as the Roman calendar organized the temporal framework of Rome and the Roman Empire, it provided the temporal organization of all the emerging European states – virtually unchanged. If we wonder why February has only 28 days, we would have to inquire into ancient chronography before the fourth century BC. And yet, we are not dealing with a story of easy proliferation and unquestioned universality. Universality was far from being taken for granted, in antiquity as in the early modern and modern periods. Until the early twentieth century, Europe was calendrically divided into Orthodox and Latin Christianity. Until the first half of the nineteenth century the Latin part was divided into countries, regions or even cities using the old Julian or the new – since 1582 – Gregorian calendar. Paying attention to the local character of ancient calendars, one soon becomes aware of the possibilities and problems of universalizing and localizing the Roman calendar. Shifting the focus from the atemporal chronological framework to changeable local texts furthermore shows the utilization of the calendar for construing images of history that are highly individual. Within a comparative approach these analyses of some less well-known features of the Roman calendar could serve to stimulate analysis of the early modern age. But the impulse does not stop there. The calendar is only the vanguard of a process, which could be termed 'colonizing time'. Down into the depths of the short days of winter and the darkest hours of the night, time is 'colonized' by measuring, organization and utilization. The ubiquity of watches has effectively supplemented the advance of the calendar. At the same time, the long history and the persistence of an ancient calendar signals cultural and, in particular, religious resources of resistance against rationalization and exchangeability. Religion presents itself as a quite successful strategy to make things different, to make times different.

Calendars in ancient Italy

Fifty copies or rather fragments of individual Roman calendars, called *fasti* in Latin, have been found up to now.[1] Roughly half of all items have been found in, or could be attributed to, the city of Rome. Most of the remaining ones belong to Latium, Etruria and Campania. The northernmost, the so-called 'Fasti Guidizzolenses', have been found in the surroundings of Brixia; the southernmost item, the 'Fasti Tauromenitani', belongs to Tauromenium, an Augustan colony in Sicily. The latter, actually, is the only copy found outside Italy itself.

In order to trace the significance of the distribution we have to have a closer look at the form and content of the *fasti*. Usually, the Roman calendar offers a synopsis of the whole year, representing 12 months in 12 parallel columns. Whereas the intercalary month of the republican calendar has been added as a thirteenth column in older calendars (see figure on following page), the single intercalary day of Caesar is no longer represented in the calendar. Even a close observer would not detect any rules or even necessities for intercalation (in fact, the legal annihilation of any intercalatory period is a hallmark of the Julian calendar).

The graphic organization of each month can be easily sketched. Usually, there are four columns to every month.

1) At the left margin, there is a column of letters running from *A* to *H*, repeating itself. These are the *litterae nundinales*, which indicate the cycle of the Roman week of eight days. As a year of 365

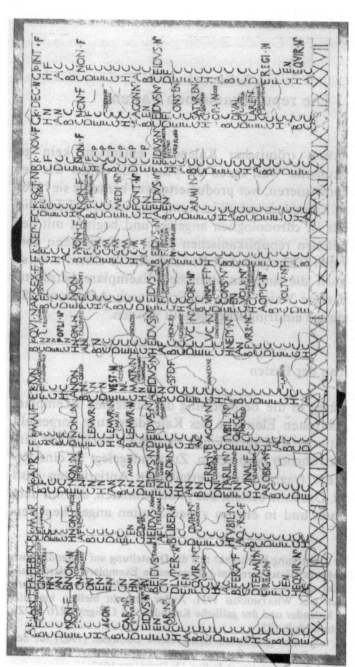

Fasti, Antiates maiores (with my own supplements; Rüpke, *Kalender und Öffentlichkeit*. Berlin: Walter de Gruyter, 1995).

days is made up of 45 *nundinae* and five additional days, the letter indicating the market days (*nundinae*) of the current year would change at the end of the year. In some copies, a parallel column for a planetary week of seven days was added as early as the Augustan age: hence a smooth transition to the latter form of the week was possible in the fourth century AD.[2] Down into the early modern period of printing, the same system was employed in order to make the use of the same calendar possible for several years.

2) The second column is made up of numbers indicating the time span that elapses before the next structuring day of the month, i.e. kalends, nones and ides; hence numbers are listed in a decreasing pattern: 2 January is 'the fourth day before the nones of January' (the latter being indicated for 5 January), 31 January is 'the day before the kalends of February'. Such a column, which renders usage of the calendar very easy, is found only occasionally and is lacking in the pre-Julian Fast: Antiates maiores, printed on the opposite page. Without it, people would simply have to count the days in the column. Today's system of counting all days of the month from the beginning became popular only in the early modern period.

3) The third column, in which nearly every day is marked somehow, indicates the legal – indirectly the religious – status of the day. An *F* indicates *fasi* – specific types of legal action are possible; *C* stands for *comitia*, which might be held on such a day; *N* indicates *nefas* and restriction of legal activities. *NP* – *nefas piaculum* – adds a religious sanction for a number of *nefas* – days that are *nefas* due to larger cultic activities, normally related to *feriae*, days consecrated to certain deities.[3] Usually the religious reasons are referred to in the form of an abbreviation in large letters that are similar to the *K*, *NON*, and *EID* of the kalends, nones and ides. For the month of July, for instance, *Popli*(*fugia*) and twice *Lucar*(*ia*) could be indicated.

4) Finally, a fourth category (to call it a column would be to exaggerate) adds in smaller letters some information about *dies*

natales, the founding days of temples. 'On this day a temple had been dedicated to Mars in the Campus' would be a standard rendering for an abbreviated *Marti in Campo* or the like. These dates are distributed very unevenly. In order to gain an audience, the dedication days of new temples concentrated on the ides and similar dates of reduced everyday activities. In some months, April for instance, as well as July, September and December, a series of *ludi* (games) are indicated, a category of ritual and popular entertainment that proliferated from the late republican period onwards, honouring gods as well as victories of emperors.

No one would expect a pocket calendar printed in Britain to represent the USA's Independence Day in bold letters. With this in mind, a comparative analysis of different printed calendars is possible and might even be revealing in terms of the nations' history and religious or political orientation. The *fasti*, however, were quite uniform. Despite the primarily local character of ancient societies, the list of festivals reproduced on the *fasti* from Urbinum Metaurense in northern Umbria is identical to the list of *fasti* from Venusia and would be identical to the list of *fasti* from Tarentum, if the latter were preserved for more than three days.

Judging by the limitations of reproducing the cultic variety of the capital in sometimes obscure Italian *municipia*, one cannot interpret the *fasti* as a document of the religious hegemony of Rome over Italy: the dates of the festivals reproduced everywhere are local Roman dates. The *fasti* are not even used to add local Italian festivals or cultic events. There is only one case of local additions:[4] Verrius Flaccus, the author of the Fasti Praenestini and an Augustan scholar, adds two local events to the list of Roman activities. Yet, this is done in a calendar of which the composition is already exceptional: it is the only calendar that integrates the reproduction of the Roman *fasti* and a running commentary on these *fasti*, the commentary being added by the extensive use of the space usually left for miscellaneous notes in the 'fourth column'. What, then, do we still learn from the *fasti* about Italian dating systems and religion?

Calendrical systems in ancient Italy

Different dating systems existed outside of Rome down to the time of the late Republic. The *liber linteus*, an Etruscan sacrificial calendar from the second or even first century BC, provides us with several dates of a calendar that numbered the days of the month from 1 to 30, perhaps still a lunisolar calendar,[5] while the Roman calendar – possibly an ancient offspring of the Eturian system – had been a solar one for nearly two centuries. A lunisolar calendar has months in accord with the lunar phases, and tries to be in step with the solar year by intercalating a whole month, whereas a purely solar calendar might use 'months' as conventional parts of the year, but is only interested in representing the length of the solar year. An Etruscan date from such a lunisolar calendar could still be used by 67 BC.[6] Exotic features from other Latin or middle-Italian calendars are reported by antiquarians. An inscription of the year 58 BC adds the dating *mense Flusare* to a Roman date of a specific day.[7] Thus it is difficult to decide whether the differences might have been reduced to different names of the months within an identical system of reckoning (a phenomenon widespread in the eastern Mediterranean). The same holds true for the information given by Suetonius in his biography of Augustus: that some Italian *civitates* made the day of Augustus' first visit to them the beginning of the year.[8]

Due to better sources, such a process can be reconstructed for the province of Asia. Here, in 9 BC a calendar reform replaced the former lunisolar calendar by a Julian calendar with traditional Macedonian names for the months and a New Year's Day on the birthday of Augustus (23 September). Details show the careful acculturation: months of 31 days, required by the Julian calendar, had not been used for conventional lunar months before; therefore the numbering was adapted to '29', '30a' and '30b'.[9] The decree was published by the proconsular governor, but would have been built upon the consensus of local elites. Nevertheless, many eastern cities and areas, even within the province of Asia Minor, continued to employ their old lunisolar systems. If a synchronism was needed, *hemerologia* (synopses) were at hand.[10]

It is the Italian *colonia civium Romanorum* of Taormina that illustrates the limits of adaptation best. The *fasti* found in 1962 are of the normal Romano-Italian type. What has looked so strange since its first publication has been the wording of the headline.[11] Within the fragmentary text, periods are defined that extend from 4 April to 31 May and from 1–30 July, hence periods of two times 29 and of 30 days. Very probably, these periods correspond to conventional lunar months used in the local Greek calendar, the dates of which were used in inscriptions before the fifth century AD. Two names of Roman goddesses, coordinated with Roman dates, would then be Latin paraphrases of the Roman names of the months for the local inhabitants: Vesta and Fors Fortuna seemed to have characterized the equivalent Greek months at Tauromenium – they are not translations of the otherwise known Greek names of the months.[12] Judging by the presumed length of the whole text above the calendar and the lists of magistrates, it is probable that equations for all the months of the year had been given – naturally for a specific year, perhaps the founding year of the colony or of an important institution.

The importance of the findings must be spelled out. Sicily was the oldest province of Rome, only a couple of kilometres away from the Italian mainland. Tauromenium was an Augustan colony of Roman citizens. And yet, here, the Roman calendar was not an instrument of practical use. The inhabitants and the local elite felt close to Rome and engraved the only non-Italian copy of the *fasti*, but they were in need of a mechanism of translation, a translation of the Roman calendrical system into Greek practice, even if Roman goddesses and Latin language formed the frame of reference. Clearly, even a Roman colony in Sicily was not as Roman as the easternmost elements of the Roman army, who – at Dura Europos – employed a Roman calendar, as demonstrated by the Roman dates of their *feriale*, their list of festivals preserved on papyrus.[13]

Judging from dated inscriptions, the technical system of the Roman calendar was adapted in Italy and in many parts of especially the Western Empire during the second and third centuries AD. One of the most notorious elements of the long process of adaptation is the Christian struggle for the correct date of the Easter festival. For a long period, again especially in the western parts of the Roman Empire, a date fixed in the Julian calendar, e.g. 25 March, or a Sunday after such a date, had been preferred.[14] Obviously local calendars not only remained in use for regulating everyday life of old and newly initiated Christians (the same is true for the Jews as far as epigraphical evidence can tell), but religious rhythms were translated into and adapted to the local calendar as well. One should not forget that a seven-day week was widely known due to astrological practices; it can be found in Roman *fasti* as early as the Augustan Fasti Sabini.[15]

When, at the large meeting of Christian bishops at Nicaea in 325, a date regulated by lunar phases finally prevailed – that is, a date regulated according to the local Palestinian calendar of the historical events – the victory was far from complete: fixed boundaries in terms of Julian dates for the changing date of the festival were an important element of the final compromise. In the twentieth century, an age of fruitless debate on calendar reform, it was not the *Roman* church that was opposed to fixing the date of Easter.[16]

Meanwhile, from the perspective of a bishop on the Council of Nicaea, the moveable date of Easter was a sort of last resort for the user of lunisolar calendars. For the cults of martyrs and other saints, liturgical calendars of fixed Julian dates without any reference to the lunar, Easter or weekly cycles had already been established, later called *sanctoralia*. They did not supersede the weekly rhythm of Sundays and working days for a local church, but formed the basis for cultic organization on the local level everywhere, with a few common dates even on the supra-local level.

It should be noted that it was precisely the primarily technical character of the Roman calendar that enabled its use for different ends, a sort of ideological emptiness and pragmatic handling that made it suitable even for different *religious* ends.

The diffusion of Roman festivals

Unfortunately, the distribution of *fasti* all over Italy tells us nothing about the adaptation of the cults indicated by these *fasti*. One has to turn to other sources to get more information on this topic. *Ferialia* would be an appropriate genre: this term is derived from an expression applied to a list of local festivals in an inscription from fourth-century Campania.[17] It has been suitably applied to other texts, the main feature of which is a comparable list. The most comprehensive example is the already-mentioned *feriale*, the list of festivals and commemorative dates given cultic expression at the Mesopotamian garrison of Dura Europos in the second quarter of the third century AD. The content of the list suggests a derivation from an Augustan order, obliging the whole military apparatus to perform certain cultic acts. Thus, the role of the imperial army in romanizing non-Latin groups is given a religious base.[18]

Outside of the *organization totale* of the military, the known lists are much shorter. From the earlier empire a larger list is known for Cumae, the 'Feriale Cumanum', naming about a dozen imperial dates.[19] Date, occasion, and sacrifice or rituals are specified. It is not possible to reconstruct the social framework of the cult – a *collegium* engaged in imperial cult is just a good guess. There is, however, a speculative character to the list: an exercise in polytheism, an attempt at defining the most appropriate deities for any given imperial festivals, thereby drawing – perhaps – more on antiquarian literature than on actual cult.

Imagination is much more restricted in the case of traditional popular Roman festivals practised in rural Italy. The so-called Fasti Guidizzolenses from northern Italy are not really *fasti*.[20] Their main feature is not the calendrical pattern, which is reduced to simple dates without further information. More interesting is the list of – seemingly – local festivals added to the same stone. Seven items for the second half of the year mostly name traditional Roman festivals and their respective dates: the Apollinaria (13 July), Neptunalia (23 July), Diana (Ides of August), Volkanalia (23 August), and finally for December the Septimontium (11 December), Saturnalia (17 December) and a festival for the Gallic deity Epona on the very next day. The temporal pattern of the festivals, the selection, is not necessarily extracted from the large list of Roman dates, but it definitely *is* a derivation from the calendar of the capital – even if it is hard to imagine a festival as firmly related to the topography of Rome as the Septimontium (the feast of the seven hills) being performed in northern Italy or Carthage where, according to Tertullianus, school holidays were given on the same occasion.[21]

As in the case of the Saturnalia and the New Year festivals on 1 January, which were observed throughout the Mediterranean world, the quality of general merry-making would be a central factor for the proliferation and diffusion of Roman dates. The staff of provincial governors, merchants and soldiers might spread an attractive custom in an anarchic process of examples, of copying and rejecting elements of Italian practices. Even if every specific Roman custom had been exchanged, the Roman character of the occasion as such would have remained as a permanent trace, just as African martyrs were celebrated in Rome as martyrs from Africa.[22]

It should be noted that even the detailed regulations of the Julian law of the *colonia* of Urso, the so-called *lex Ursonensis*,[23] do not include calendrical regulations. Here, it is the task of the first colonial council to define the number and seasonal position of the festivals (chapter 64 of the colonial charter, *Lex coloniae Ursonensis*). The only element of central definition and transfer of identity of the centre is formulated in chapters 70 and 71: there should be games or plays for the Capitoline triad and Venus, the goddess of the founder, Caesar.

The only strictly calendrical regulations stem from a *lex municipii* of Flavian times. It is among the norms concerning juridical procedure that the *lex Irnitana*[24] refers to non-locally defined dates: the dates concerned are strictly confined to imperial festivals. The standard expression is 'days which should be reckoned to the festive day or among the holidays on account of the veneration of the imperial family'. These days were set apart from those days on which games were held according to the decrees of local councils, but even they might be given their precise position in the local calendar by a local decision. No mechanism of central regulation is indicated, but the sanction is strict: even if all parties consent to deal with their legal problem on such a day, the results would not be valid (chapter 92 of the colonial charter, *Lex coloniae Ursonensis*). Social consensus, the need to demonstrate loyalty, and the potentially positive sanction of taking recourse to central, imperial authority by the defeated party would be the most effective guarantees of the universal observation of central calendrical decisions in a still thinly bureaucratized imperial state.[25]

Unfortunately, these conditions do not favour the creation of significant sources. Even for Rome we have no clear image of the temporal patterns of religious activities for the different social strata. We know about the basic rhythms as such. According to antiquarian sources, the recurrent cycle of 'market days' (*nundinae*) produced a sort of Sunday every eight days: a school holiday, time for body care, though not a day free of work.[26] In the same manner as for the first day following kalends, nones or ides, it was regarded as harmful to start important enterprises on the day after these *nundinae*.[27] Nevertheless, prior to the nineteenth century, we should not imagine anything like the (still) clear-cut weekly rhythm of some contemporary Western societies. Even the concentration of economic activities on only one in eight days is rather improbable for a metropolis like Rome. Apart from the seven-day week of the Jews – and less strictly organized the Christians – no ancient cult has organized itself on a truly weekly basis.

Another rhythm was defined by the monthly kalends and ides. By the time of Cato the Elder, these days were already expected to be honoured by small domestic sacrifices.[28] They were used for banqueting in honour of birthdays and similar occasions: this being the reason why so many famous Roman poets seem to be born on kalends or ides.[29]

On the yearly level, the differences must have been much greater. Only very few festivals, for instance the Saturnalia or New Year's Day (the kalends of January), would have pervaded all strata of society and included all areas of Rome's urban topography. The number of yearly festivals and the complexity of their cycles are an indicator of the complexity of society and the division of (religious) labour. The list of festivals given in the urban *fasti* is neither a representation nor a suitable indicator of a collective Roman identity.

In light of this urban complexity, it is difficult to assess the frequency of reproduction and the precise mechanisms of transfer of urban cultic dates into Italian or provincial communities. As the analysis of dated inscriptions from all over the empire shows, imperial festivals were the most effective export items, although a number of traditional Roman festivals might have merely served as calendrical points of reference for the publication of private dedications – on the aggregate level of private positioning of religious acts, traces of the pattern of kalends and ides can be detected as well.[30]

We do not know anything about the *nundinae*: no equations with Julian dates are known for the empire. Market days and respective rhythms of different length are known for Italy and beyond – but they are hardly direct imports from Rome. On the other hand, the favourable role of the Roman calendar for recurrent, uninterrupted cycles should not be overlooked. No other calendar – with the exception of minor groups like those at Qumran – was able to indicate civil dates in their respective rhythms for years in advance. Together with the already existent recurrent rhythm of the *nundinae*, this might have been a major and specific Roman factor in accommodating the Judaeo-Christian seven-day week. Whereas the planetary week was an important popular interpretative scheme, as we will see in the next chapter, the named factors must have been decisive on an administrative level.

Why were useless *fasti* produced and displayed?

I have come back to my point of departure, the *fasti*. Why did these representations linger, if the juridical and cultic contents of the urban calendar could be locally accommodated only to a certain, quite limited extent? The key to the answer is given by the distribution of the marble calendars – not in space, but in time. The oldest Roman *fasti* must have been painted around 170 BC; they can be reconstructed on the basis of a late republican painted calendar from Antium. The earliest marble copy, however, was located in the sanctuary of the Arval Brethren, newly endowed by Caesar, *divi filius*, the Augustus to be. This calendar was put up in the years after the victory at Actium (31 BC) in the area of the goddess Dea Dia, just outside Rome. There are several urban copies also dating to the time of Augustus, and just a few copies certainly datable to that period from Latium, Etruria and Campania. Yet already in Tiberian times, we find copies all over Italy – only for them to stop spreading just a couple of years later.

The parallel to the spread of imperial ideology and cult is obvious. With astonishing velocity the calendar of festivals was filling with imperial dates, births, accessions to the throne, marriages, victories and discoveries of assassination plots. Unlike the traditional festivals in the calendars, these new dates were not reduced to simple names like *Augustalia*. Not names but short explanations were added to the juridical character of these days in the *fasti*. 'This day is a holiday, for on this day Caesar has captured Alexandria' is such a phrase. Within a few years, such entries gave a specific profile to any written calendar, filling wide areas of what had previously been just a lightly inscribed surface.

The calendars were not a representation of the complex imperial cult of Rome that might be visited by tourists or delegations. Instead, the calendars were an independent medium to represent imperial celebrations, not festivals; they were not an auxiliary institution of urban cult as the primary mode of representation, but a complementary institution within the whole spectrum of imperial propaganda.

Yet propaganda is a problematic concept. Of course, official policy must have offered the formulas that could easily be integrated into the *fasti*. But a sort of central 'Her Majesty's Calendrical Office' to produce official copies of the latest version of the calendar is lacking. *Fasti* were set up by individuals, often by colleges, some perhaps by municipal authorities. This is a specific form of appropriation. It is a display of loyalty on the part of local elites – including Rome – and in Italy a kind of self-romanization, too. As far as we can tell from the fragmentary transmission of the marble copies, headlines naming the dedicant or dedicants were common. Self-representation was no less an element of the bundle of motifs that led to the production and display of *fasti*. The addition of a list of Roman consuls or a thin chronicle added to the interest and didactic value of a calendar;

the addition of a list of local magistrates or a list of the administrative functionaries of the dedicating college enhanced local or group identities.

Without any doubt there must have existed thousands of *fasti* in the form of books or book-rolls in antiquity, from Cicero's use of them down to the luxurious copy called the Chronograph or Chronicle of 354.[31] The practical superiority of the Julian calendar finally convinced most of the Mediterranean world. Yet – with a few and peculiar exceptions – marble copies stopped being produced after the time of Claudius or even Caligula. With a view to a generally booming epigraphic culture we can only surmise the reason: with *fasti*, the ratio between the whole of the text and the free parts of the text that could be used for the dedicant's own name, biography and achievements was rather disappointing. Other forms of liturgical activities and their epigraphical recording would have seemed more rewarding – and might nevertheless be done *pro salute Caesaris*. Thus, within a few decades, marble calendars went out of fashion.[32] Ancients could be as quick and economically rational as moderns.

Yet within those decades, marble calendars were very fashionable indeed. So far, I have spoken about epigraphy, but now I must address literature as well. Religion and cults have been of interest to Roman writers from early on. That includes festivals named in the *fasti*, but the *fasti* themselves were not the point of departure. As shown by extracts in Varro's book 'On the Latin language', he wrote a systematic treatise 'On the year', explaining all temporal categories. Treatises 'On the calendar', however, became popular in Augustan times.

Verrius Flaccus wrote 'On the calendar', extracts of which have survived in the inscriptional commentary of the 'Fasti Praenestini'. Ovid too wrote a commentary on the calendar, his famous *Libri fastorum*.[33] Others followed within a brief space of time, mostly during the first century of the Christian era. They are only known by incoherent quotations by Suetonius, Cornelius Labeo and Macrobius – authors who again wrote systematic treatises 'On the (Roman) year', not running commentaries on a specific form of the public representation of time. The sequence of the titles and interests reflected the coming into fashion of the marble calendars, and their downfall too.

The impulse to go beyond the boundaries of the 'calendar' genre is already visible in the writings of Ovid. In the original preface to the *Libri fastorum*, now at the beginning of the second book, Ovid announces a commentary on the *fasti* only. Praise of the emperor will be the most important topic – a topic in accordance with the contemporary production and diffusion of *fasti*, the necessary background to every adequate reading of his text. However, the object of the commentary is modified soon afterwards. At the end of the long passage on the first day of the year Ovid introduces the constellations of the stars, their rise and decline, as his second object. That is no improvement; it is no completion of the *fasti*, but the addition, the yoking together, of two totally different objects: the *fasti* on the one hand, and *parapegmata* – notes on the first and last visibility of the stars and some prognostics depending on them – on the other. Read as a commentary, the reader of the *Libri fastorum* has to switch to a new entry in the *fasti*, the text commented upon by Ovid's poetic commentary, every few lines. 'Who forbids?' Ovid asks on starting this practice[34] – and no person with humour would do so. The dates of the Julian calendar are not only a pattern of imperial history, but a cosmic, trans-Caesarian pattern. At least on the level of the temporal framework, Rome and the cosmos have become a unity.

Fighting for details?

It is necessary to summarize the findings so far. First, festival calendars are local calendars. Any serious central interest in unification of these local procedures was restricted to imperial cult and the army. Second, the rational calendrical systems of the Romans facilitated the integration of diverse rhythms. Calendrical dates themselves – kalends, ides – became decisive points of reference for the planning of activities; they did not form mere chiffres for underlying subtle divinatory systems. Third, on the religious level, the synopsis of precisely dated and hence coordinated cultic acts could be read as an offer of choice to other local cultures, the sheer number reducing the obliging character of the single date. This pattern was repeated by the Christian and later Catholic calendars of saints, combining a universal summation with the selection and additions of local cult. Disregarding all other areas and mechanisms of centralization, such a differentiation of form and content may be a distinctively Roman strategy of giving a common framework to an empire.

Turning to modernity, I would argue that despite the presence of the Julian calendar in significant parts of Europe all calendars were regional or even local calendars.[35] This is shown *ex negativo* by the far from successful calendar reforms of the sixteenth century, dealt with in the next paragraph. It could be illustrated by the attempts of the modern territorially defined states to locally monopolize the production of calendars and to censor every locally circulated calendar.[36] However, I shall focus on a rather private enterprise: the reinvention of historical calendars in sixteenth-century Protestant Germany – an action directly inspired by Roman antiquity. Unfortunately, as should not be forgotten, to focus on these processes is to lose sight of all the other calendars used in Europe, especially the Islamic lunar calendar, the foremost rival.

The age-old traditionality of the Julian calendar with its automatic intercalation and common graphic representation could not still every technical criticism, as became obvious in the thirteenth century, when the calendrical differences to the solar year added up to about a week's time. By the time of the Council of Nicaea, the spring equinox had been on 21 March; all regulations on determining the date of Easter depended on that date. Now, however, the astronomical fix point had in fact moved slowly to about 11 March of the Julian calendar. Hence, the necessity to improve the calendar was felt more and more. After many abortive attempts (the Council of Constance being one of the opportunities), the liturgical reforms of the Council of Trent and the authority granted to the Pope to formulate the details of the reforms and to implement them opened a way for a calendar reform. After years of debate, checks and diplomatic lobbying, Pope Gregory XIII introduced the reformed calendar and in 1582 brought dates in line by going directly from 4 to 15 October.[37]

It is difficult to deem the reform a success. For over a century Roman Catholic Europe used the dates of the new calendar, whereas the Protestant states of middle and northern Europe kept to the old one. If on 8 February a German Catholic wrote a letter to a Protestant in a neighbouring miniature state, his correspondent could still answer the letter – given the efficiency of early modern postal services – on 31 January. Two days later – that is, on 14 February – the answer would reach the Catholic initiator. What seems funny to us today was the normal state of affairs in those days, especially within confessionally mixed and heavily divided regions like Germany or the Helvetian confederation.

Obviously, it had been a mistake not to consult Protestant governments.[38] That is not to say that the consulting process with Catholic monarchs or universities had been intensive; it is even questionable that reservations had adequately been taken into account. Obviously, the leading and explicit role of the papacy turned the acceptance of an astronomical decision into a question of religious observance. The question of the calendar moved cities like Augsburg to the brink of civil war.[39] Last but not least, it cannot be denied that, judged by astronomical accuracy, better solutions may have been envisaged.[40]

The result is known. The Protestant states of Germany and Denmark accepted the Gregorian calendar in 1700, the Netherlands in 1710, Great Britain in 1752, and the last canton of Switzerland – the country of Bâle – only in 1844. Within the area of Orthodox Christianity Russia changed its time meters in 1918; a concurrent reform of the Greek Orthodox Church, at least resulting in a parallel intercalation for the next 800 years, took place in 1924.

What may be read as the route to success of the reform can also be read as ultimate failure. The acceptance and refusal of the Gregorian reform is to be seen within the framework of the formation of modern states on a biconfessional continent. The Gregorian reform was not the only calendar reform instigated by the Council of Trent. For the history of European religion, Trent and its empowering of the papacy to regulate liturgical and – obviously by implication only – calendrical matters[41] marks the attempt to abolish the existence and functioning of local or regional liturgical calendars by replacing them with a universal one. Again, the bishops granted authority to the Pope to execute their initiative. The *Breviarium Romanum* of 1568 and the *Missale Romanum* of 1570 promulgated a so-called *calendarium universale* or *calendarium ecclesiae universae* that was intended to replace and delegitimize every local Catholic (and by implication, of course, Protestant – the differentiation is far from clear cut) calendar. Despite the preceding growth of the importance of the Roman liturgy in some parts of Europe, such a calendar was a massive novelty, destroying age-old practices. The attempt failed, even if the Apostolic tried to force the intended rules until the Second Vatican Council in the 1960s.[42] Local rulers or bishops and monastic orders tried to keep their profiles of festivals and saints, if necessary by including them in the universally legitimizing Roman calendar.

From this point of view and in this context, there is another aspect to the Gregorian reform. It not only claimed to change local calendars, but also attempted to delocalize or universalize them at the same time. That might be acceptable as a new element of the calendar for the new, confessionally defined union of Catholic rulers – these being the same people, however, who fought for their independence on the liturgical level at the same time. The abolition of local calendars was not acceptable for the emerging Protestant states. When, from 1700 onwards, they accepted the reform calendar, it had lost its universalizing implications and was reduced to a technical element of firmly established Protestant local calendars.

The calendar as a tool to construct history

The bitter fighting about calendars is only understandable if one takes into account additional aspects of these texts – that is, the utilization of the calendar as a formal point of reference not just of strictly calendrical information. I had earlier hypothesized on the beginning of the popularity of the graphic representations of the Roman system of annual time-reckoning as an attempt to find a visual form for the synopsis of Roman military history: these events were embodied in the vowing and building of temples and the annual celebrations in honour of their dedications.[43] Integrating a few minor modifications, this form became canonical for the calendars of Roman antiquity. Further information was added only by combination, by putting lists of magistrates below painted calendars or by adding lists of martyrs or bishops to the codex pages of book calendars. From antiquity, only Ovid's versified commentary on the Roman calendar, the *Libri fastorum* as described above, was a sort of exception, as the running commentary allowed for the integration of long descriptions or aetiologies for single dates. However, it has to be stressed that Ovid's book did not serve as a calendar. Ovid skipped dates and concentrated on days of interest.

A permanently growing interest in astrology and the growing importance of printing techniques in the fifteenth century brought graphical representations of calendars to the fore. For the educated public, Ovid became a central figure in this context. Apart from dozens of manuscripts (around 170 known in total), an adaptation of his work was composed: in 1516 Iohannes Baptista Mantuanus (Giovanni Battista Spagnoli) wrote 12 *libri fastorum*, bringing Ovid up to date and supplementing the second half of the year, never versified by Ovid.[44]

Ovid's texts were known to Paul Eber, a friend of Martin Luther and a professor of grammar and protestant theology at Wittenberg. Known to him, too, were the Roman *Fasti triumphales* that had been found in 1548, a list of dates of republican triumphs. As early as 1550, Eber published a *Calendarium historicum* of no less than 482 pages, a calendar featuring historical events and (more and more) narratives to each of the 365 days of the year.[45] Dates from antiquity feature as prominently as dates of early modern history and the history of the Reformation. But the number of dates from both periods shifts. From edition to edition, and especially since the translation of the *Calendarium historicum* into German in 1582 – the year of the Gregorian reform – antiquity moves ever further into the background.[46]

Yet it is not the degree of classicism that is important. What is important is the form and its growing popularity. From antiquity onwards,[47] and throughout the Middle Ages, calendars include historical annotations, which finally came in the form of a calendrical systematization of historical dates and narratives, namely the lives and passions of the saints. Despite the lack of liturgical necessities, the most popular and widespread martyrologies are derived from the textual tradition of the monk Usuard of Saint-Germain-des-Près (written after 858), who produced a martyrology giving entries for every single day.[48] Quite a number of medieval liturgical books adapted to local custom display calendars that are but summaries of this martyrology.[49] Turning again to antiquity, Eber reinvented the form, but thoroughly changed the contents. His lead was taken up. In 1570 Caspar Goltwurm, who had already composed a profane historical calendar, published his ecclesiastical calendar, a 'Kirchenkalender', arranging narratives of the lives of the saints in due order for each day. Of course, this is drawing on the aforementioned tradition, but it is a reaction to and adaptation of Eber's Protestant calendar. For the history of German literature, these historical calendars and their manifold versions for different audiences are to be seen as the starting point of the 'calendar stories' and the popular calendars of the seventeenth to twentieth centuries.[50]

Conclusion

The calendrical genre summarily presented in the last section demonstrates the capacity of the calendar to be modified to non-discursive statements of individual or collective identity.[51] Taking up associations of contemporary liturgical practice and classical literature, calendars could be modified far beyond and much quicker than local festival practices or official systems of time-reckoning. The emerging territorial states of early modern Europe needed a common rational calendrical system, just as much as the Romans a millennium before. At the same time, an interest in temporal frameworks grew, accelerated by the emerging boundaries of modern European political systems.

In recognizing the success of the Roman Julian calendar in the long term and the resistance of the Gregorian calendar to the far-reaching calendar reforms of the French revolution and Stalin's attempt to replace the week of seven days, including a Sunday as a holiday, by a continuous working week of five days, we cannot forget its delayed reception in the Roman Empire, furthered only by the power of Roman armies and the importance of Roman administration. Even an instrument widely stripped from its earlier religious associations was seen as a competitor and aggressor against local identities. As a consequence, the story told for the early modern calendar was again a local story. The concentration on German sources resulted in a chronological focus on the sixteenth, rather than fourteenth or fifteenth centuries; it resulted in a focus on the age of confessionalization rather than the Italian Renaissance. But the story did not end here. The Gregorian calendar was introduced into Japan after the reforms of the 1860s. In many countries, even if not the first calendar to be used, it is the second, whether in Egypt, Israel or in many Asian countries. It was a tool of modernization, despite many internal incoherencies and historical survivals. In its technical quality in tracing the solar and stellar year it could wonderfully accommodate astrological interests. To these I shall turn in the next chapter.

CHAPTER VI

DEALING WITH THE FUTURE: DIVINATION BY CALENDARS

To be forced to make decisions in the face of uncertainty is one of the major challenges in everyday life and more so when decisions of far-reaching consequences are concerned. The assumption that the gods might help in such a situation is an important part of religion and its instrumental use in the lives of individuals and communities of believers. You might pray to the gods or the one god for guidance and continuous help. When you have already reached a point of crisis, be it social or medical, military or emotional, you might put more weight behind your prayer by accompanying it with sacrifices or donations, or you might promise such a donation in case of a positive outcome. Votives, as presented in the Introduction, are a powerful tool to give substance to a communication with an addressee who is not symbolically present and visible. Ancient as well as modern religion is fundamentally communication with and about the divine (or even less tangible: transcendent).[1] Internet religion is as much a new way of socializing with others as a new medium for communication with the divine.[2]

Many strategies to deal with uncertainty, however, are not overly religious on first sight. In following up on the ancient history of the widespread Gregorian – for many readers 'our' – calendar, this chapter will take a look into ancient practices that are imbued with very different logics and beliefs and might switch their religious appearance as much as similar practices do today, often stemming directly from ancient calendrical and astrological practices. It is the use of time that will be under scrutiny, and we should take a closer look at concepts and practices, which are as unsystematically attested as even more recent daily practices and 'popular beliefs'.

The equal quality of units of time is an advantage for free planning, be it military or economic or private. There is no guidance as to the use of time. Sometimes, such guidance is longed for, be it traditional or rational. For Roman religion, a layer of secondary qualifications was laid upon the surface of the *fasti* calendar, covering purposes that were not catered for by the days for assemblies or lawsuits. The term *dies religiosi* is the generic term for all dates with a negative connotation in the Roman taxonomy of time.[3] The term connects these dates with *religio*, 'religious scruples', which quite generally warns against all kinds of activity and especially against starting any enterprise of import on these dates. There are no positive sanctions for these dates. However, a 'bad end' is presented as a natural consequence if the warnings are not heeded.[4] The opposite is formulated in positive clauses. We find terms such as *dies proeliares*, days on which a battle may be fought, or *dies comitiales*,[5] days on which the popular assembly may be called together. The latter term found its way directly into the official vocabulary and into the Roman calendar in the form of the *fasti*. The significance of the terms 'pure days' (*dies puri*) and 'solemn days' (*sollemnes*) is still uncertain.[6]

In terms of numbers, the largest group within the 'days of religious scruples' is that of the 'days following' (*dies postriduani*) – that is, those days directly following the monthly orienting days of the kalends, nones and ides. Together they were called 'black days' (*dies atri*).[7] One could note in a calendar a day of a particularly bad event as a *dies vitiosus*, which then might be added to the category of 'black days'. This is an empirical date, but it is not confirmed by repeated experience, as is claimed for the 'days following'.

It is important to note the differences between *dies religiosi* and *dies atri*. The usual *dies religiosi* were days on which cult was performed, which then marked the particular quality of the whole day. The best examples are those days on which a subterranean pit called *mundus* was open (*mundus patet*). Whatever may be behind the rite, people mostly saw it as a direct and potentially dangerous link that was established to the underworld, similar to the festivals of the Lemuria in May.[8]

There were other more specific *religiones*. There were not to be any weddings on *feriae* due to an agrarian saying about ploughing, which equated the first breaking-up of the soil with the defloration of the bride;[9] the opening of the *aedes Vestae* from 7–15 June made these days *religiosi*;[10] the weapons dance of the Salii in March led to a special code of conduct for the Flaminica Dialis and made weddings at this time inadvisable.[11]

The relevant norms vary greatly in character. There are rigid cult directives for a public priestess such as the Flaminica, as well as vaguer words of guidance where it is hard to tell whether they have normative power or are just counterfactual thinking. We know from other sources that the days on which the *mundus* pit was open were subject to restriction on many activities.

Another group of 'unlucky days' draws on different origins. In a sacred context, these days are rather inconspicuous; their negative character became apparent only over the course of time, mostly in the context of military defeat. The *fasti* note only one such instance: the defeat of the Romans on the Allia by the Gauls on 18 July.[12]

That this is more than the conservation of a historical event is shown by further unlucky events on the same date. The well-known annihilation of 306 Fabians on the Cremera, dated by Ovid to 13 February,[13] was in part dated to the same day as the Gallic catastrophe.[14] This peculiar Roman point of view was continuously confirmed by repetition. In yet another case, this time for 11 June, in Ovid's commentary on the calendar he notes two defeats on the same day.[15] A tendency towards accumulation and intensification can also be found when it comes to military success, as in the notes on 1 and 2 August, obviously bringing together more and more festive occasions.[16]

In the continuation of structurally analogous processes, the in itself accidental conjunction of an event with a repeatedly proven infelicitous element became an *omen*, which, in this case, hinged not so much on dates, but more on contingent detail of political decision-making processes: in 310 BC, the beginning of poll-taking on a *lex curiata de imperio* by the Faucian *curia* was deemed a bad omen since it was this very same *curia* which had also led the ballot in the year of the Gallic conquest of Rome and the defeat at the Caudian passes. This tradition was underscored by Livy with the account of Licinius Macer, citing the catastrophe on the Cremera to this *curia*'s discredit.[17]

The psychological mechanism of this strategy seems obvious: in order to come to terms with extraordinary negative events, the contingency of the disaster is interpreted in intangible, inevitable terms. This is evident in nearly all contemporary sources, as when Nero's great fire of Rome in AD 64 is dated to 19 July, a date that is cited as coinciding with the Gallic capture and burning of Rome.[18] It served also, however, the Roman psycho-hygiene of historical consciousness. Military catastrophes were handled by ascribing a certain quality to the *dies religiosus*.

The play with historical dates gave a certain air of empiricism and rational control of action to the qualification of certain dates in the eyes of the ancients, though it is quickly undermined. The documents on the ritual dealing with prodigies, which were written down in the *commentarii* of the supreme pontiffs, note only very few 'defeats'. With the exception of the *dies Alliensis*, the dates are not noted in the calendars; only very few traditions concerning dates are actually tangible.[19] The Roman aristocracy kept no ritual or other institutional form of documentation of defeat.[20] It is an extensive group of days, the *dies postriduani*, which makes the disproportion of historical fact and calendrical consequence so obvious: within the whole calendrical year only one single fixed date, the Battle of the Allia, is actually noted in the calendar, a date which – not one, but three days after the ides – fits so uncomfortably that it had to be conceptualized as being intimately linked to a sacrifice two days prior to the event.[21]

The evidence on defeats is not altogether surprising, given more recent calendrical practices. 'Anniversaries' have become a major feature of contemporary practices of commemoration. Groups, and in particular nations, construe their identity by establishing recurring dates characterized by festive commemorative practices or even general merry-making. The proclamation of a new constitution and constitutional form (Republic, e.g. Turkey), free elections ('Freedom day', South Africa), or a revolutionary event (storming the Bastille in France), or, in a post-colonial world, very often 'independence days' (e.g. United States of America) form such calendrical identity markers. The medial duplicity of the actual celebration and the calendrical representation far beyond actual practice was certainly an ancient invention. Such days usually imply victories rather than defeats. Only infrequently did victorious groups commemorate defeats or martyrs' days as the basis of a minority identity. All such days, however, do not allow generalization for the purposes of everyday action. If they provoke further action, it is the definition of alternative days of memory by oppositional groups.

Reading the calendar

In contrast to the alleged inductive exploitation of *dies postriduani* as days on which nothing new must be attempted,[22] the common definition as days following the kalends, nones and ides lets us assume that these days gained religious prominence only *via* the technical system of the calendar. This is not marked in the *fasti*, in which they are marked as *F(as)*. The sacred status, which was appointed by the pontiffs and which was accompanied by detailed cultic regulation,[23] speaks to a systematic, not inductive, rationale for the *ater* quality, which is seen in connection to the orienting days, but which is not explained.

There is much room for argument concerning the actual rationale. The large number of days concerned, the connection to the central orienting days (which were especially important in the Roman calendar before the reform of the late fourth century BC, though still recognized later on), the extent of the limitation, and the later narrative connection to the greatest catastrophe in Roman history indicate a massive political interest in the negative connotation of these days.[24] In looking at the interdict on weddings held on kalends, nones and ides, an interdict actually based upon *dies postriduani* might point us in the right direction: the primary aim would then not be the restriction of action on the following days, but the restriction of action on the orienting days that served as holidays and assembly dates. The considerable preparations needed for ventures such as travelling, for example, which would severely limit availability and interest in socio-political activities, could in this way be kept away from orienting days.[25]

The assertiveness of these regulations is presented in the calendar.[26] There is no known *dies natalis* for any temple nor any triumph noted for a *dies postriduanus*. Dates noted in the calendars, even from the Republic, concur with the given prohibitions: horse parades on 14 September and in November do not postulate a sacrifice. The *vitulatio*, a rather obscure form of victory ritual and explicitly termed a sacrifice, took place on 6 July, the day before the nones. All other comparable entries belong to the imperial age. Now, the positioning of new *feriae* for victories, imperial birthdays and other celebrations[27] was oriented towards the accuracy of memorial days, and could easily coincide with *dies atri*, thus disregarding older sacral regulations.[28]

However uncertain such an explanation may remain, the attempt to explain *dies postriduani* by way of the preceding orienting days is supported by a parallel development. The days immediately after those days which marked the middle *nundinal* week days also came to be noted as *dies inominales*.[29] We are dealing with those days which within the *nundinal* week held the second position in terms of preferences for holidays, a process of growth which was presumably a result of the growing societal and urban complexity. Imperial antiquarians could not identify any official reasoning for this classification, but Gellius spoke about the avoidance of kalends, nones and ides as current practice.[30]

For a long time now, *ater* has been explained with a view to *Quinquatrus* and other italic forms[31] like the suffix *–atrus* as 'day(s) after the ides': these were termed 'black', since they belonged to that part of the month in which the moon waned, became darker; the first days of this period were then supposed to have been termed *dies ater*.³² This hypothesis did not remove all problems. Should not the last day (or the last night) of this period be better termed *dies ater*? It is not at all far-fetched to describe the time of the waning moon phase as 'dark'; on the contrary, once accepted into a culture,³³ it is difficult to understand how it could be so completely forgotten as to allow for the conferment of the following days to the first half of the month – especially in a culture such as that of Rome, which deemed a string of activities advisable or inadvisable in connection with the waning or waxing of the moon.³⁴

With the social and ritual explanation of *dies atri* being connected to the functions of the 'orienting days', which no longer follow the lunar phases of construction, a new perspective is given to the term itself and its origin. Instead of employing an unexplained suffix in order to further mystify the adjective, the obvious answer must suffice: the employment of adjectives of colour like black or white in order to mark out lucky or unlucky circumstances was widespread in antiquity.³⁵ It was quite common to mark your own calendar with black and white pins.³⁶

There is no doubt that any Roman would have understood *dies ater* as simply an 'unlucky day'.³⁷ The later *dies aegyptiaci* were so called since 'Egyptian' was synonymous with 'black'. Even in the fifth century, as cited by Polemius Silvius, this origin of the *dies atri* was known. In employing a euphemism, *dies communes*, 'normal days',³⁸ the interpretation of *ater* is once again stressed. The entire complex is a paradigm for the social role of religion that can only come to full fruition within the context of cultural studies: socio-political interests (the orienting days), imbued with a strong religious component, were encoded in precise religious language (*dies atri*). This was no mere 'priestly fraud'. The new religious dates had to be integrated and systematized within the ritual system. As part of this system, it remained independent of the modification of the original social function due to the rearrangement of the calendar during the decemviral reform; it gained new momentum in a differentiated, far from uniform, popular religiosity in analogous developments: apart from the following days to the middle *nundinal* days, the days following the *nundinae* were soon also branded with similar associations and restrictions. Since this information refers to the emperor Augustus it is not possible to ascribe it to any kind of 'lower-class superstition'.[39]

Chronomancy: choosing the lucky day

The extension of the concept of *dies atri* and all other classes of day that needed special behavioural regulations points to the increased need for action control, an aid to the decision-making process along a timeline. This is relatively easy to explain. In almost any complex situation asking for more than routine actions, the question of 'what to do?' is followed by the question of 'when to do it?' In the high density of simultaneous social actions, there has to be at least some kind of coordination between the most important potential actions and processes: the most opportune moment, the *kairos*, had to be chosen. This kind of timing not only coordinates sequences of action in their progression, but also in their speed. It demands an immensely high, potentially never satisfactorily met level of information.

With a view to any uncertainties concerning the action, especially if no plausible alternative is given, the point of time at which a certain action is performed is often the only available factor that the agent has at his or her disposal. It seems therefore only logical if, in the general uncertainty in which the action is to take place, the action is focused with regard to time. As an answer to this kind of focused action, the Roman religion provided a number of practices that allowed for rational, systematized rules.[40] In so far as we define 'instrumental religion' as a functional medium for the reduction of contingency, it includes appropriate techniques. Divinatory practices and practitioners can stand in marked contrast to the dominating organized religion of any culture, as can still be seen when regarding astrology in modern-day Europe, a technique which stands with no connection to the structures and teachings of the Christian churches, neither with respect to organization, nor world view.[41] Insurance companies and banks that reduce the risk of payment obligations for the economy can be viewed as specific modern and non-religious forms of contingency reduction.[42] For the individual, these kinds of questions regularly appear in existential situations, which always connect to divinatory practices; their lists are hardly different from any modern-day demand for divination: the focus is on love, social relations and economical, especially speculative, success.[43]

Of central importance at Rome were the auspices, a technique that includes the interpretation of spontaneous signs, but which was predominantly used as a means to gather information in a specific situation. The paucity of the range of auspicy that had developed over time, and the neglect of certain kinds of auspicy depicted in Cicero's *De divinatione*, is easily interpreted as a development towards more manageable and more informative practices of divination. Divination is not on a downhill path in general; auspicy is rather supplanted by haruspicy and astrology.[44] The question the diviner wishes to have answered is 'Can I do this action *today*?' A negative reply does not refer to the question per se; it only refers to the day: not a strict 'No!', but 'another day', *alio die*. In reference to an astrological term, this can be termed as 'catarchontomancy' – divining good dates for the start of new activities.

Although the augural discipline recognized private auspices (for instance, for weddings),[45] in most cases even the simplest divinatory practices are much too complex for everyday use (the exception being central political actions). In addition, the required *auspicatio*, as well as any other kind of divinatory practice (such as extispicy in the course of sacrifice) can only be performed on a set date. A degree of certainty gained by employing divination is bought at the price of added uncertainty during the whole process.[46]

The proposed thoughts do not lead to an evolutionary history of divination in Rome or elsewhere. They merely circumscribe the area in which calendrical divination must be understood. In comparison to the above-mentioned practices of individual exploration of any course and time of action, the general qualification of days as advantageous or disadvantageous – in all possible modifications and specifications – is an extremely low-cost, quick and easy method for the reduction of uncertainty, which touches on the entire range of actions and enables planning and coordination, due to its obvious publicity. It is hardly surprising, then, that a corresponding composition and use of the calendar can be found in many societies:[47] the known (i.e. socially plausible) quality of any day reduces uncertainty; the future, or rather ongoing history, is no longer entirely open to any possibility. Calendrical astrology is the most common form of lay astrology in history.[48] The definition of the divinatory quality of a given day was most often seen, as it was in Rome, in relation to the month, in many cases governed by moon phases. Especially in Asian cultures, in which the Gregorian calendar as an economical calendar is superimposed upon local moon calendars, there is a conscious recourse to lunation.

Numerous associations connected to moon phases as well as complex rituals make it easy to assume that the moon as a subject, or at least as a plausible guarantor, played a large role in regard to days noted as unlucky. This kind of thinking is, however, misleading. Even in efficient moon calendars, the definition of certain daily numbers, recognising any natural fluctuations, is of little natural, astronomical plausibility. It follows that the quality of certain days should be left well alone, especially in cases of notable interruptions in the natural length of a month by the insertion or repetition of days, as was done in Greece, or more precisely in Athens. Another way of employing the calendar is shown by the Roman usage in which the month itself no longer bears any relation to the moon phases – which goes to show that in a secure tradition the calendar posed a sufficiently plausible frame of reference, though highly artificial, which – as is shown in this context – does not need any recourse to actual astronomical phenomena. The written form of unlucky days belongs to the earliest 'calendrical' documents in the world of the eastern Mediterranean. In Babylonia, these texts are to be seen within the context of a rich literature on *omina*; they consequently list practitioners arranged chronologically and by expertise.[49] In the Greek world, two Mycenean documents give information about the quality of days, chronologically arranged; the given formula *o-u-(ki)-te-mi* is consistent with classical *ou thémis* ('unlawful') within the context of the 'unlucky days' (*hemerai apophrades*).[50] I do not know of any comparable documents for Rome; the rules for the placement of *dies atri* were very simple, though; a well-organized written calendar was given, and therefore the need for a comparable instrument was not really there. Simplicity and clarity in regard to good and bad days has numerous advantages, though also many drawbacks. A lack of complexity due to an over-sophisticated degree of generalization no longer has any successive selection: all days, both good and bad, are equally good and bad, so this gives only minimal aid in the decision-making process. Even modern-day magazine astrology, which succeeds in believably dividing all humanity into 12 cohorts depending on birth, is more complex due to the weekly changes in their prognoses. It is the operability of the prediction in connection with a simple yet comprehensive overall structure that makes this kind of astrology (and others in its wake) so appealing to the masses.

The most common method of marking out complexity within a calendar that is designed to order and arrange was the combination of two deferring elements or even calendars (alternatively every day of the year is treated as different, as in Mesopotamia and Egypt[51]). The combination of week and month creates from the simple elements of 'Friday' and 'thirteenth day of the month' an ominous 'Friday the thirteenth'. The combination of a seven- or fourteen-day 'week' and another eight-day planetary week gives guidance to action for the Shan people in northwest Thailand.[52] Ten *t'ien-kan*-days in connection with 12 *ti-chih*-days create a 60-day divinatory cycle in China.[53]

Very long, triple or multiple cycles allow for extraordinary complexity,[54] which in its hyper-differentiation does not provide useful guides for everyday life, but does gain a predicative, historio-theological advantage: for Rome, the connection is attested by the birth horoscope – systematically speaking a constellation of a number of significant astronomical cycles in extended circuits – of the city of Rome itself, of Romulus and of Augustus.[55] In all this, one factor must not be forgotten which is just as important as practical orientation: the human willingness to play, which, despite all systematized world views or plausible reasons and beyond any actual need for action and any elementary fear of the unknown, counts and marks these cycles.[56]

Collision of *nundinae*

The interplay of different cycles and their respective 'black days' can also be shown for Rome. They are first met in the late Roman Republic. Here, we find a collision between the ongoing cycle of the *nundinae* and the orienting days. Without any definite proof, it is safe to assume that the character of the *nundinae* will have dominated the 'hosting day', following the logic of the system; in the case of a collision with *feriae*, the *feriae*-character will have been retained, but it will not have hindered the holding of markets.[57] In extraordinary cases, it was possible to avoid a collision by moving the market day, as Cassius Dio, the Greek historian and Roman senator of the Severan era, notes for the year AD 44, and which he claims was a long-held practice.[58] The criteria for moving market days were determined by the unhindered holding of public festivals; they are based, then, on practical not religious considerations.

This is contrasted with another type of collision that led to a completely different kind of adjustment: if a *nundinal* day coincided with the first day of the year or with the nones, it was considered extremely unlucky. Macrobius relates this belief, which can also be found in Cassius Dio, as having existed long before his day.[59] The underlying concept is clear: the single day, which in the republican era was inserted occasionally, or theoretically every fourth year between the Terminalia (23 February) and the intercalatory month, presented a variable with which it was possible to avoid the collision of *nundinae* with 1 January and with the nones. The details mentioned by Macrobius conform with what we have seen so far; this includes the single intercalary day, the timing of the intercalation – which the author himself no longer understood, as can be seen by his addition of *vel mensis intercalaris* – and the social meaning of the nones. To this must be added the negative value of certain dates, and the interpretation of the intercalation, which was viewed as a remedy to the collision.

Looking at the evaluation of the collision, we do not find anything of significance in an intercultural comparison, as shown by the combination of cycles mentioned above. Traditions note cases of the unlucky collision of *nundinae* and the first day of the year only for the years 78 BC and – in Macrobius' example – AD 52.[60] There are no indications that this belief is much older. The *nundinae* had given a continuous and socially accentuated structure to the week – as can be seen with regard to the holidays – ever since the decemviral reform, but there was no differentiated characterization of these eight days. Any associations concentrate entirely on the continued system of the orienting days that were rigorously upheld even after the reform: here we find on the second and (between the nones and the ides) sixth day of the 'week' the *dies atri* and *dies inominales*.

If the transfer did not take place at the very beginning – and as mentioned previously there is no indication that it did – it is most likely that a new impulse for making the analogy was needed. This is probably to be found in the convergence with the astrological planetary week, which left its first traces in Rome at the end of the first century AD.[61] Such an origin – or better, inspiration – of the association is borne out by that type of catarchontomancy, literally: divining by a starting day, for which the day of the week of the first day of the year – *nundinae* or not – characterizes the entire following year.[62]

The Roman reason for such an evaluation of *nundinae* and nones can be found in an almost contemporary source – that is, Augustus' avoidance of their respective following days, which in both cases refers to the negative particle heard in the terms.[63] This explains why the combination of the two days was so very negative: Macrobius' historical thesis may be important for its historio-cultural contents in view of the continuous practice of a funerary cult for the kings; as political motivation for the first century (and earlier) it is, however, useless.

The historical development becomes clearer when taking into account the remedy: the intercalation of one day. The first – and, it must be noted, only – noted case belongs to the year 41 BC.[64] That the practice, as Dio claims, was in fact older is contradicted by the given examples of collisions in the preceding period, or at least is cast into significant doubt.[65] The absurdity of the assumption is easily shown: in the republican calendar, all *nundinal* letters are used for the nones between March and December, except for the *G*. If the collision between *nundinae* and nones was to be avoided, February – the only possible opportunity – has to be intercalated in such a way as to make the valid *nundinal* letter for the nones a *G*. Come the new year, however, this became a *D*, thus making the intercalation of three days, or, by using a *mensis Interkalaris*, even seven days, necessary to avoid a renewed collision. Such a system was simply not practicable.

With the fixed intercalary scheme provided by the Julian calendar, intercalation motivated by the reasons given above became nigh on impossible. The only certain case we know of is said to have fallen in the years directly following the reform. A contradiction? More likely a hint at the character of 'anti-collisionary intercalation', which was nothing more than a misunderstood interpretation of the new Julian intercalation.

Granting this, it is fitting to accept the factual content of Dio's note on intercalation in the year 41 BC. Since intercalation for some decades – due to the complicated interpretation of Caesar's intercalary directions[66] – took place every third year, the first one, which still fell in Caesar's own day, must have taken place in 44 BC. Since this initial intercalation, a primary intercalation of one day in the second year after the reform, could naturally not yet constitute a rhythm, the job had to be transferred to the second intercalation taking place in either 41 or 40 BC, depending on the reckoning of the intercalary directions. It was only with the first intercalation after the death of the great reformer and dictator that his reform of the calendar can be judged accepted and established. The analysis of the reform has shown that the intercalary directions were not distributed pamphlet-wise among the people, but rather that the practice of oral announcement was upheld, even though it must have been clear to anyone that the reformed system negated the need for further decision, and that the ritual became quite superfluous under these circumstances. Regarding these conditions it becomes instantly obvious as to why for parts of the population, maybe even the largest part, the need for interpretation of the intercalation of 41 BC was wanting: why intercalation now? Why only one day even after the end of the Caesarian reform?

The interpretative tool used must have been the one that we find in Dio and Macrobius. It grants that, without intercalation, the *nundinae* would in fact have fallen on 1 January 40 BC, thus granting an at least rudimentary divinatory quality to the market days in the form that Augustus gave them. It is possible that the collision of *nundinae* and 1 January was given meaning only then and in the course of the Lepidian revolt: the coincidence does not offer certainty of the occurrence of this *nundinal* concept in the year 78.

The result: neither for the time before nor for the time after 41 can we reckon on 'anti-collisionary intercalation'. Even in 41 BC only a few people believed that intercalation served to avoid *nundinae* for the first day of the coming year; this intention must not be assumed for the agents of the intercalation, the pontiffs. They were faced with a set of different problems when they decided on the intercalation.

The planetary week

A *nundinal* superstition is a marginal phenomenon, not just with respect to its mixture of astrological concepts and Roman calendar practice. In the course of the imperial age, it is not the reference to *nundinal* days that plays the major part in calendrical divination, but the Greek form of the planetary week. Known in Rome since the Augustan era, it gains quick popularity in the early imperial age, and widespread belief during the second century even in the western provinces of Gaul.[67]

As a divinatory instrument for action directives, the highly differentiated qualities of the different days characterize the planetary weekly rhythm.[68] As a system of only seven days, the astronomical and theological realities being a given, and being traditional, it is easy to handle, and provides in its seven-day rhythm – which constantly adjusts to the economically, socially and politically present eight-day rhythm of the *nundinae* – a high degree of fascination that keeps up the interest. The use of the seven planetary gods provides a divinatory instrument with iconographic elements that can easily be adjusted to fit new forms. Be it in the written form of names, or graphically in the form of portrait busts, the seven-part structure is quickly adapted to many different contexts. From the simple graffito[69] to clay models – a case in point being the one found in Treves, which allowed mass production of three-dimensional copies of weekday 'calendars' – to intricate inscriptions, stones to the weekday divinities, and large architectural elements like the Septizodium in third-century imperial Rome,[70] everything was possible.

Demands for a higher complexity and playfulness could be met by combination with other chronological elements. For a stricter astrological use, the combination with *Lunaria* proved useful, the graphic depiction of moon phases,[71] which can be traced just as much as the weekdays by moving little pins.[72] The pin calendars in the Roman thermae of Trajan and in south-west German Rottweil, both dating to the second century AD, demonstrate the heightened complexity in combination with the zodiac.[73]

The multiple possibilities for variation show a playful use of the astrological instrument, which is only in exceptional cases like the 'Chronograph of 354' combined with Roman *fasti*.[74] Even in the case of both systems being used in combination, as in the case of grave inscriptions, the two respective instruments remain separate.

The division may appear strange at first sight; they fulfil, however, important functions. Divinatory practices tend to a certain overdetermination; a conducive effect for the alleviation of action-preventing fears in terms of choosing the moment is in part counteracted by the determination of the moment, which no longer regards a social context of action or factual circumstance. The Roman practice in a military context shows that this kind of calendar-driven, overdeterminate divination is dealt with by simply ignoring it.[75]

Today, the planetary week and the zodiacus are probably the single most important divinatory tools. Classifying everybody into seven or twelve groups, being related to the simplest calendrical knowledge, the ancient technique allows for everyday orientation as well as everyday mockery. The latter, however, is not a product of a more rationalist age. Derision reintroduces the reduction of complexity achieved by the divinatory method as well as the uncertainty that has probably existed since the day that divination came into being.

Conclusion

This chapter has highlighted two features of ancient religion which are only loosely connected to modern notions of religion – that is, divinatory practices and different uses of the calendar. Of course, many religions provide a list of holidays or even a liturgical year, and such phenomena have been addressed in the previous chapter. Divinatory practices based on instruments of daily use and offering 'cheap' orientation are hardly associated with religion and religious affiliation. Sparing the number 13 in seat numbers of aircrafts (widespread) or in floor numbers (less widespread) is not seen as consonant or dissonant with 'ordinary' religious beliefs held by clients or entrepreneurs. Thus, 'religion' itself is a concept that today serves strategic aims. It opens up a space for individual, social, even public and financial action, especially secured by the human right of religious freedom. Hence, classification as 'religious' is consequential. Early modern astrological tractates did stress in their introductions or dedications their compatibility or even foundation in biblical beliefs in 'Christian' nations. Today's astrology in many Western as well as Asian cultures is conceptually clearly differentiated from 'ordinary' religious or ritual practice. But specialists might know better and give much more complexity to these systems of orientation than is offered by astrology in newspaper columns.

CHAPTER VII

THE PRESENCE OF DEATH IN LIVED RELIGION

Lived religion

Is my juxtaposition of death and life more than a linguistic pun without any clear objective? I hope it is. The concept of 'lived religion' has been developed for the description and analysis of contemporary religion by Meredith McGuire in a book published in 2008.[1] It is my attempt to employ this concept within the field of ancient religion. In its application to contemporary social analysis, the concept of lived religion does not address thriving religious communities or the latest theological fashions. Instead, it starts from a methodological individualism, focusing on the individual's 'usage' of religion. But there is more to it. 'Lived religion' does not ask how individuals replicate a set of religious practices and beliefs preconfigured by an institutionalized official religion within their biography – or, conversely, opt out of adhering to tradition. Instead, 'lived religion' focuses on the actual everyday experience, on practices, expressions and interactions that could be related to 'religion'. Such 'religion' is understood as a spectrum of experiences, actions, and beliefs and communications hinging on human communication with superhuman or even transcendent agent(s) – for the ancient Mediterranean usually conceptualized as 'gods'. Ritualization and elaborate forms of representation are called upon for successful communication with these addressees.

Dealing with one of the most pervading areas of 'religion', this chapter reflects on practical necessities as well as on culturally stabilized forms of rituals and concepts. These are of utmost importance. It is important to keep in mind that individual practices are not entirely subjective. The existence of religious norms, exemplary official practices, control mechanisms and enforcement should be taken into account (even more than has been admitted by McGuire). It is precisely such institutions and norms that tend to predominate in the surviving evidence from antiquity. To deal with this situation, the term 'appropriation', as developed by Michel de Certeau, is very helpful.[2] The specific forms of religion-as-lived are barely comprehensible in the absence of specific modes of individual appropriation (to the point of radical asceticism and martyrdom), cultural techniques such as the reading and interpretation of mythical or philosophical texts, rituals, pilgrimages and prayer, and the various media of the representation of deities in and out of sanctuaries.[3] The notion of agency implicit in the notion of appropriation – far more so than with 'reception' – is not free of problems. In view of the normative tagging of teachings, traditions, narratives, etc. in the field of religion, the description of *how* ideas are taken up and the specification of processes of reception are of particular importance. The lived-religion approach offers a frame for a description of the formative influence of professional providers, of philosophical thinking and intellectual reflections in literary or reconstructed oral form, of social networks and socialization, of lavish performances in public spaces (or performances run by associations) with recourse to individual conduct in rituals and religious context. This valuation and methodological primacy of the individual is more than a radicalization of approaches to differentiate the practices of ever more narrowly defined groups and communities.[4]

However, the analysis does not merely describe the contrast between norms and practices or the influence of one on the other. Ideally, even the intersubjective dimension of religious communication can be accessed through the records of the individuals by enquiring into their communication, their juxtaposition, their sharing of experiences and meaning, their specific usage and selection of culturally available concepts and vocabulary, as Nancy T. Ammerman has put it.[5] Thus, meanings constructed by situations rather than coherent individual world views should and will be identified. Logical coherence is secondary to the effectiveness of religious practices for the purposes desired and called 'practical coherence' by McGuire.

In my attempt to apply the perspective of lived religion to death in the centre of the Roman world (and again, for practical reasons, I concentrate on the late republican period and the early Empire[6]) I will concentrate (after dealing with the practical problems of death as a starting point) on burial and grief rituals, divinization, thinking about the afterlife, and tombs and grave monuments.

Practical problems[7]

The death of a person leads to a number of problems,[8] which may even serve as parameters for intercultural comparison.[9] The most urgent problem is, first, that of disposal of the rapidly decomposing body, which quickly turns into a health risk for the living. The second problem is the effect on the family and, third, changing social positions as a result of the death. In some cases this includes a change of social standing for the family or group affected. Without being able to cover all aspects, I will focus on the loss of social capital. A fourth point is that on the death of a person, the interaction with this person necessarily changes – I will explain this further shortly. Finally, my fifth point is that all these aspects are just as important for the person or persons concerned: more precisely, the anticipation of all these points by the living.

My first point, the removal of the body, is largely dealt with in juridical regulations. The Law of the Twelve Tables is said to have restricted burials to areas outside the city (Cicero, *De Legibus* 2.58). Judging by the archaeological evidence, this must have been polemically directed against earlier and – judging by the literary evidence – probably ongoing practice.[10] The municipal law of the colony Urso in Hispania Baetica, founded by Caesar in 44 BC, regulates the building of an *ustrinum*,[11] a crematorium (*Lex Ursonensis* ch. 74). The particular smell of such institutions might have signalled to the traveller – unintentionally – that he or she was approaching the city.[12]

The most comprehensive regulations are given in a fragmentary text found in Puteoli on the Gulf of Naples, most likely dating to the Augustan age. This text is a municipal reference frame for the temporary lease of an undertaker's monopoly. Most notable are regulations intended to ensure the speediest way of getting a corpse out of the house and out of the city area; a minimal number of able-bodied workers are employed and clear priorities are given:[13] members of council, children and adolescents as well as suicides are given precedence.[14] The enterprise is denoted by a term that turns the name of a Roman cult district of identical function into a generic term: *Lucus Libitinae*, the grove of the goddess Libitina.[15]

While the removal of the body from Puteoli is undertaken for a fee depending on the distance of the ride, the final deposit – and I consciously use factual, impious language in order to separate the aspects analytically – is met with a wide range of possible costs. The quickest and cheapest way to deposit a body was to dump it in a pit that was repeatedly filled with chalk; a method that was also employed by Rome's richer families in case of epidemics. The holocaust of a body, the complete destruction by fire, demands high temperatures, therefore technical complexity and an abundance of fuel: in other words, it costs a lot of money. Cheaper than inhumation of the body is a burial by urn, which demands less space. However, we are not able to specify these costs further or set them in relation to the costs of inscriptions or the costs for the funeral cortege. The favour that burning seems to have found with the Roman republican upper class might have been due to the fact that the two distinct phases of cremation and inhumation of the incinerated body offered two separate occasions for public events.

My second and third points – the effect on the family and changing social positions – require less explanation. On the death of a *pater familias* – we are again in Rome and under the sovereignty of the Roman law – his sons become fully emancipated citizens, and the dependence of his wife, now a widow, is in the normal practice of *manus*-marriage terminated, at the very least drastically altered. The loss of a child may end hopes of family continuity (and that also means hopes of an own grave cult) or set in motion considerations for adoption or manumission of slaves (with according requirements). In the Puteolan text, children were given preference in treatment; their funeral was classified as *funus acerbum*, 'unripe funeral'. The range of possible social consequences on the deaths of acting consuls or even an Augustus, or the deaths of rich matrons or wage-earning labourers need not be detailed here. For the social strata that is, in its grave monuments, the most accessible to us, the problem may be postulated that the immediate or larger family, the *gens*, was threatened by a loss of social capital, the stability of networks and the reciprocity of mutual support in their expectation security – as I read 'social capital' in this context. Here, funerary rituals allowed not only to remember, but in speeches, monuments, and inscriptions to reconfigure, the *persona* of the deceased.[16]

My fourth point brings us to the endangerment of interaction with the deceased due to the loss of immediate, interactive presence. I phrase this maybe in a somewhat more complicated way than I could have, since multiple forms of interaction and communication are not actually based on immediate face-to-face interaction. Social presence may well be expressed by the agency of legal representatives or by life-sized statues in the market squares of communities or provinces whose patron or administrator one once was, a fact that Seneca points to in his *Consolations*.[17] There is an alternative to representation, namely physical preservation. For Rome, Harald Mielsch has argued that the popularity of sarcophagi – probably usually combined with techniques of embalmment – took its start from a special interest in children's sarcophagi.[18] They offered an intimate familial form of presence of the deceased. Portrait features integrated into mythological figures (sometimes even outright portraits) would strengthen this aspect; the usual lack of inscriptions underlines the intended intimate setting.[19] This is in a way a revival of Etruscan sarcophagi showing married couples, which fall out of use slightly earlier.[20] It is significant that accusations of witchcraft as causing premature death – a rare accusation in Greco-Roman antiquity – focused on women and children.[21] The whole development of sarcophagi, gaining in frequency from around AD 120 onwards, must be seen in the context of developments of motifs and interests that were already present in first-century ash urns as with the growing popularity of inhumation, gaining momentum from around 150 onwards.[22]

Such a statuary presence continued past the point of death without any (visible) modification. Many times, there will have been doubts, and letters written to already deceased persons, which, if not answered, did not offer definite conclusions. But a founding hero or a patron saint could not, of course, substitute for a living and giving patron who was ready to represent the group's interests (although semantics and labour division may change in the course of the centuries). When the statue, the representing sign, no longer refers to a breathing person as referent, the very sign changes in content and the practices addressed to this sign change likewise. One might even raise the question: is there anybody referred to at all? For those belonging to the immediate circle, the question may become much direr in dream visions, auditions or other forms of supernatural communication. In this context, a field opens up of forms – and problems – of continuing presence to which we will return later on. At least in an abstract form the question of validity of a testament is also to be answered, which marks the control of the deceased over his goods before any living users. Roman law did not leave this control unrestricted,[23] but it did support the will of a person that is no longer alive (much more than does the institution of the legal portion under the German title of inheritance laws). The institution of the will, the awkward institution of the *testamentum*, assuring the ongoing will of somebody already dead, was very consequential here and found a corresponding place in philosophical, Epicurean thinking.[24]

I come to my fifth point. In the view of the mortal being, dying in the future, the problems of appropriate social presence in view of familial absence are just as prevailing. Anyone approaching the city saw engraved upon the markers to their left and right along the streets statements concerning the afterlife, be it the denial of any post-mortal existence, neutral statements – 'here lies' or 'here rests' – or the utterance of a vague hope.

Traditions and norms: burial and grief rituals

The culmination point of many of the problems outlined above is the immediate temporal environment of dying. Considering the sources, the areas most accessible to us are the routinized and ritualized, i.e. the culturally stabilized forms. A division between the phenomena denoted in these terms is not always easy, though necessary: the *Lex Libitinae Puteolana* regulates the routine of removal of bodies as much for those cases in which an elaborate ritual followed – as was the case for council members – as in the case of suicides who are denied any kind of burial.[25] Employing the performance term we have learned to see that such a ritual gives space to individual interpretation, emotional engagement and individual articulation much more than it hinders it, while at the same time giving a code to the ritual, supplying forms and standards. It is telling that we have examples of emotional overzeal, the abandonment of ritual standards, exclusively for public grieving rituals, e.g. the burning of Caesar's body in the forum of the excessive grief for the heir apparent, Germanicus.[26] A similar amount of individual variation must be considered for rituals on a smaller scale. At the same time, professional mourners and gestures of self-mutilation remain primarily cultural forms, as do acts of destruction such as the killing of prisoners of war in gladiatorial games to honour the deceased, acts that ethnologist Karl Meuli interprets as *Trauerwut*, 'violent grief'.[27] A ritual anomy of grief precedes the technical acquisition of a new status in the decision of ritual arrangement.

The description of an (elite) burial ritual is found in the late republican writer and antiquarian Varro's *de vita populi Romani*, a book which is only extant in fragments.[28] According to Varro, whose 'Antiquities of things divine' has been of importance in Chapter II, the entire time from the point of death to the actual burial is marked by the wearing of mourning garb; for women this seems to have been a hooded cloak called *ricinium* (later: *mafurtium*).[29] Since the early Roman law of the 'Twelve Tables' prohibited the use of more than three *ricinia* and a small purple tunica,[30] this probably refers to garments that were given to the deceased: the wearing of multiple tunicas was, especially for women, not common.[31] For the burial proper, black or dark cloaks were worn and hair dress left at home. This phase was accompanied by public lamentations in the form of praise for the deceased by paid singers or the family servants, and continued in the funeral cortege. Varro puts the last, already post-mortal phase of human existence in the power of the *dea Nenia*, a divinity bearing the name of the *naenia*, the mourning song.[32] In Varro's reconstruction of an ideal burial ritual, the song lasts until the cremation is over; the chorister marks the end of the ritual with the words 'you may leave'.[33] According to Cicero, the Twelve Tables limited the number of flute players at burials to ten.

To be added to the preceding cortege is the funerary oration, the *laudatio funebris* on the forum for persons of high social standing. This form of public oration for deceased magistrates developed at the end of the fourth century,[34] and was in singular cases also known for women beginning at the latest in the first century BC (with a view to Caesar's funerary oration for his aunt Julia, widow of Marius). It will at least in these cases have modified the role of the *praefica*.

The ritual described so far is, with its focus on public praise on the way to the crematorium, clearly one accompanying the burial of adults. Children – sources term them 'sons' – were buried by the immediate family (in the ancient sense without a doubt including the family's slaves) without a larger public being invited.[35] Ancient sources speculate as to the reason, and point to the status of both family and office of the father. It is easier, however, to see in this practice the simplest form that can also be seen in the *Lex Puteolana*: the need to dispose of the body quickly, which is only when there is need or interest in securing social capital beyond death in the form of lavish public funerary corteges, the *exsequiae*.

The burial ritual has not yet come to its end with the cremation. Burial itself is still necessary. Sources differ in this respect; literary sources date to a time in which cremation had only just become established as the norm practised by the elite – that is, the late Republic and early Empire – and to late antiquity, in which cremation dominates literary description, but was no longer the common practice. We find numerous variations not only geographically – in different provinces – and chronologically, but even in any one necropolis.[36]

Concerning inhumation – a potentially less complex form of burial, lacking in some of the possibilities of conspicuous consumption offered by the double ritual of burning and burying ashes – the body is deposited without any further alteration. Ideally, the sacrifice of a pig is performed at the grave (*porca praesentanea*), the meat remaining uneaten.[37] The remains are instead added to the grave or buried close by. Cicero interprets the practice in terms of the ritual and legal constitution of the grave site, which may visually be marked by pottery.[38] Interpreting the sacrifice as a cleansing ritual for the family is problematic, however, since it remains within the burial phase. It is much more likely that the sacrifice was directed at Ceres and related to the opening of the ground; abstaining from a meal in connection with the sacrifice marks the distance to the dead.[39] We do not know how much such intellectual thinking and ritual regulation were appropriated by people differing in familial traditions, social status and means.

It is telling that the regulations which have come down to us mostly concern cremation ritual, formulating norms and luxury restrictions, beginning with the Twelve Tables as cited by Cicero and including Cicero's own commentary on the laws. Apparently, the attraction of cremation rituals must be seen in the greater possibilities for a ritual public display and theatricality, for which the Homeric epic provided heroic antecedents. Elaborate processions and cremations are interconnected right up to the consecration rituals of the emperors, including expensive biers that were – or so I believe – demonstratively destroyed rather than removed after inhumation.

There were numerous other possibilities for public display in terms of cremation, including the use of special kinds of wood for the pyre – the *Lex Puteolana* seems to have dealt with this topic in its first column[40] – scented perfumes, oversized wreaths for the deceased, and incense burners or altars. When Varro considers the use of cypress wood for the pyre, he is very aware of smells and unpleasant odours for the audience. Other objects may also have been added to the fire. It is unclear whether the pig was sacrificed at the same time: remains of pigs' bones were found in the debris – as were remains of other animals.[41]

Concerning the fire described, two variations are given. One was the use of a crematorium (*ustrinum*), a fixed structure. The alternative was an individual pyre, the use of which dominates ancient literature, a good choice if an *ustrinum* was not available and for more elaborate cremations.[42] The individual pyre sites of the emperors were conserved in somewhat monumentalized forms.

Concerning the burning, a distinction had to be made between human ashes and the ashes of the burning more generally. The division was laborious: larger bones were typically collected (*ossa legere*) and purified with wine, as was a part of the less differentiated human ashes. It is telling that Propertius, in his personal poetry speaking for the early Augustan age, connects the touching and collection of bones with an especial intensity, intimacy and individuality (e.g. Propertius 4.7) – just as telling is that it was exactly this practice that was prohibited by the Twelve Tables and in Cicero's *Laws* (Cicero, *De legibus* 2.60), thus apparently going against common practice, if Propertius is any indicator to go by.

The cremation and collection of the bones is, normally, though not necessarily, followed by deposition within an urn and the final placement or burial. It must be stressed that the ashes thus collected were often only a small part of the actual human ashes, which could weigh around four pounds for an adult, sometimes only three or four ounces for some regions or periods.[43] During the burial proper, the remains may be complemented by other remains of the cremation – often carefully and selectively chosen, leaving pottery shards behind[44] – which were then deposited next to or above the human ashes. This brings us to the burial site, where renewed or final sacrifices were performed and new depositions made, which makes us right in asserting that there was a double interment in the case of incineration.[45] In cases in which the urn was kept at home during the time it took to complete the memorial or to set up a communal grave site, this can in fact be termed a secondary burial.

It remains unclear whether, in the recovery of the urn, the pontifical demand for at least partial covering with earth was fulfilled. Since we have no sources telling us so, it is fruitless to speculate whether someone may have argued that this demand was already fulfilled by burying the incineration ashes, which already included human ashes. Such depositions can be found, by necessity, in the vicinity of crematoria and graves.

Eight days after the cremation or burial and at the end of the *feriae denicales* the ritual sequence comes to an end in the *cena novemdialis*, which seems to coincide with a meal of *silicernium* at the grave site.[46] Again it was possible to create publicity by the choice of location or the accompanying programme of *munera* – literally 'duties', actually gladiatorial games; Caesar, for example, used the death of his father to stage magnificent gladiatorial combat.[47]

The lack of any discussion of the beginning of the *feriae* shows that a rather rapid succession of death, cremation and burial is assumed. Such a sequence is assumed also in the *Lex Puteolana* in which the only fragmentary first column seems to regulate, apart from the lease of the *ustrinum*, the lease of an altar (*ara*) and Chalcidium, probably a roofed structure under which part of the ceremony would be held. The late antique Virgil commentator Servius reports that houses in which death had recently occurred were marked by a spray of cypress. This would likely have accompanied the entire period in which members of the family were excused, even excluded, from public functions as *funestus* or *funesta*, and abstained – as far as economically possible – from work.[48] The sweeping of the house, purification by the heir, called a 'sweeper', and a sacrifice to the *Lar familiaris* will also have belonged to the end of this period and the return to normalcy, at which time hair and beard could be shorn again.

The sequence of sacrifices to the family *lar* or *penates*, the meal including the holocaust of the *porca praesentana* and the concluding sacrifice and meal at the grave, mark out the transition of the deceased from the living to the divinized ancestors.[49] This concurs with a possible ritual logic concerning the choice of communication and addressees of the sacrifices, and finds a parallel in the legal sector, since for the entire period of the burial, the deceased was still recognized as signatory for all renderers of services.⁵⁰ The process involves gestures of intimacy and division, and, most of all, gestures of ostentation towards the public when the deceased was an adult. The choice of cremation or burial is to be seen in this context, and lies not in any notion of the status of the deceased. If the theory that the attraction of incineration was greater due to its higher degree of visibility, then the decline of said practice has to be seen in terms of changes in publicity and public visibility in the late imperial age, correlating to the changes in the inscriptional culture of the time.⁵¹ The elaborate pictorial programme of the sarcophagi dating mostly to the second century AD points to a different, more intimate public than do the pyre and grave monuments of the late Republic and early imperial age.⁵²

Divinization

I have already hinted at the interpretation of the sacrificial sequence as a reconstruction of divinization, and would like now to come back to the topic. The grave site is a place of special significance; in conducting a ritually correct assignation of the dead, it becomes a *locus religiosus*. The status of a cenotaph must have been open to dispute, as it is the subject of an imperial rescript in the time of Marcus Aurelius in which the lack of religious quality is noted. It was, therefore, just like an unused grave, still for sale. Without any binding force on society, the *locus religiosus* constitutes a cult site that must be kept free of all other obligations.⁵³ This concurs with addressing the dead in the ancestor cult. In this context, one does not speak of *maiores*, the elders, as happens in the public and political sphere, but of *di parentes* (divine parents) or, in a standardized euphemistic adjective that no longer works in classical times, of *di manes*, 'good gods'. Beginning in the late Republic, both dedicatory inscriptions and grave inscriptions mark the ownership, or rather the transfer of ownership, of the grave to the *di manes* of the deceased, or place both parties side by side without grammatical connection, in two datives as *Dis manibus Gaii* or *Dis manibus, Gaio* … The plural indicates de-individualization on a conceptual level, which has no further bearing on the subsequent individualization of the social persona of the deceased that usually follows in the inscription text.

There is no doubt that what we find here is genuine cult – real graves often contain tubes that allow for the direct transfer of part of the sacrifice to the addressee. Legally, the cult is not restricted; the grave site does not lose its religious value no matter how long the interval.[54] The status of the addressed deities can, however, only be determined in the negative sense. They are, first of all, neither ghosts nor spirits, nor *lemures* that were dreaded and guarded against at the festival of the *Lemuria* by providing them with cheap foodstuff.[55] Neither are they divinities like the ones that were worshipped in temples, the genesis of which was enacted in the consecration ritual of the emperors, in which the soul was carried to the heavens by an eagle, thus in the cremation being severed from the body: a case of philosophical systematization in actual, ritual practice.

But it was not only the emperors who were thus transferred into the divine sphere. Divinization into the plural form of *di manes* was a prospect for every Roman, but this form of address was obligatory only for the family, as Cicero notes at the end of the laws on religious practices in his 'On laws': *suos leto datos divos habento*[56] – the deceased family members were to be treated as divine beings, from which follows, as Plato already states, that grief ought to be restricted to a minimum. Rejecting the conjecture *suos* and reading *nos* as given by the manuscripts, this legal text also reads like a consolation. But this kind of consolation points to the cultic memory of those left behind, not to a personal, post-mortal future. Death is the end of mortality, but the subsequent immortality is no longer one's own. But how could it be conceptualized?

Life after death

In looking at formulaic inscriptions and even extravagant grave monuments, it is difficult to get any sense of the prevailing notions concerning the beyond. The choice of a pyramid as a grave monument by the late republican or early Augustan Gaius Cestius Epulo, who was both tribune of the plebs and member of the priestly college of the Epulones, cannot be explained by reading the inscription. Neither is the choice of burial of Marcus Terentius Varro explained by looking at any of his extensive writings: he had his grave fitted out according to neo-Pythagorean rules.[57] Extensive speculation as to what follows death can be found in the *Consolations* of Seneca, for instance to his mother Helvia, or other similar passages in larger literary productions. This holds true as much for Cicero's 'Dream of Scipio' in his treatise *On the Republic* as for Aeneas' descent into the underworld in book 6 of Virgil's *Aeneid*. The concepts found in these cases hark back to Greek philosophy and mythological traditions and develop them systematically; employing philosophical language, the *animus* that is released from the body at the time of death becomes a medium of post-mortal evolution. These writings often had significant impact, and the consequences of the texts cannot be understated. However, it must be noted that these writings were still texts that were born out of a distinct situation, as in the case of 'consolations' (as written for instance by Seneca or Cicero) or writings of similar literary function, which (a) are not to be left out of any kind of history of the beyond, and (b) demonstrated synchronically in their various times notions of the beyond, which (c) had very little or no effect on subsequent actions. In saying this, I do not want to claim the opposite: Varro's example speaks as much of individual options as do Dionysian *thiasoi* and the findings of Orphic gold tablets, passes to the underworld, in Rome.[58]

Grave monuments

For obvious reasons, concerning the decorations of grave sites we have mostly archaeological data. My central thesis runs as follows: with a view to the aforementioned problems concerning death, the composition of grave sites concentrated on the problem of social presence. This normally means ensuring a continued presence in the collective memory within society. While the preservation of the memory of a single person within a cultural memory is determined by practices that the individual can hardly control – I am thinking of historiography, musical hymns, canonization, monuments – ancient dead were mostly interested in the preservation of the name, as well as their achievements and, in some cases, their likenesses along much-frequented streets leading to the cities. Visibility might be combined with the luxury offered to the deceased and the intimacy for the survivors provided by a garden, which could exceed the usually 100 to 400 square feet up to five iugera, around 70,000 Roman square feet, or 12,500 square meters.[59]

The aristocrat Petronius captured this intention in his depiction of the symposium and self-portrayal of Trimalchio – a depiction that is certainly not limited to the circles of rich freedmen.[60] Features that can be generalized are: monumentality (200 x 200 feet), initially to make the passer-by pause and read (in this case a sundial); individualization in depicting professional success and a happy family life, but also wariness of the all-too-frequent misuse or reuse of sites, leading to the institutionalized protection of the grave site and its cult (for example, by employing a guardian); and special mention within the testament.

The grave of the baker Marcus Vergilius Eurysaces could serve as an example, even if not every detail of the reconstruction is beyond doubt. The monument was put up in the second half of the first century BC along one of the major trunk roads in an area of numerous elaborate graves, the monument itself most likely being the largest of these. Legal and stylistic indicators echo the decade of 30 to 20 BC.[61] In an unusual and therefore instantly noticeable use and arrangement of machines for the mixing of dough,[62] which echo the placement of columns in other architecture, it gains in monumentality. A frieze made out of small, barely discernible pictures depicts Eurysaces' large enterprise. The formulation of the inscription might point to the baker's special status as entrepreneuer – *redemptor*.[63] Eurysaces himself is depicted, together with his wife Atistia, on the far side of the monument, facing away from the city, in life-sized statues. It should be noted that such statuary and imagery connected with tombs might have been a very important factor in overcoming the traditional Jewish reservation against images in the traditions of Christian art.[64]

The inscriptions not only depict an unusually tight connection between monument and memory, but also point to the burial of the wife in a bread basket. The grave monument itself – and this is the central point – does not have any noticeable space for the deposit of Eurysaces' remains, though it is possible that an urn in the form of a basket found separately was part of the monument.[65]

The fierce competition for individualized representation found both in the late Republic and the early Empire can be stated as much for grave monuments as for the coins of the first century BC.[66] What is lacking are notions of a post-mortal existence in this particular form of the successful perpetuation of the depicted person; for the favoured philosophy of the upper strata of Roman society, Epicureanism, this spells out the total decomposition of the body and the end of any kind of existence after death in the wake of its atomization. Concerning the statue pair and the inscription of Atistia, I would like to stress two points, though.

First, concerning statues: a practice begun in Rome in the late fourth century BC, these were a highly attractive form for the multiplication and perpetuation of one's own social presence, both before and after death. I cannot here give a detailed historical anthropology of the far from linear development of human statuary in the ancient Mediterranean and adjoining regions (I am thinking of early Iron Age Celtic and Italian statuary and the Etruscan warriors of Capestrano from the middle of the first millennium BC), though that is desperately needed. For Rome itself, it is important to point to the struggle for the erection of statues in the public sphere – that is, in central spaces of the city.[67] This struggle is to be seen in connection with the question of collective recognition of individual feats – in publicly granting a statue or the space in which to erect it – as well as the intrusion of statuary forms of depiction on grave monuments. This was achieved by depicting, for example, fixed bases on low- or half-relief grave images. This choice of depiction speaks clearly to the continuity of notions of social presence;[68] even the appearance of Africanus in the Somnium Scipionis is defined by this imagery.[69]

Second, the *panarium*, the bread basket as the form of the urn. In Petersen's analysis of the monument he conclusively shows how telling the monument is in regard to the role that one's profession played for the deceased: it is not only an instrument of social recognition, but provides a comprehensive set of signs and symbols.[70] This conclusion can also be generalized: the author of the *The Shepherd of Hermas*, a Christian text written in the second century AD, himself a producer of and trader in salt, presents his visions within a world of white salt mountains.[71] No alternative worlds of the unknown beyond are expostulated and explored: it is rather the economic world and social status of the author and his supposed audience that becomes an image of the natural and social order as much in life as in death.

Conclusion

As observable in the Roman period, death found a specific place in lived religion. Public norms aimed for the quick removal of the body from the city and immediate disposal outside of it. A quick restructuring of the family within a brief mourning period in accordance with the will and testament of the deceased, especially as concerns the slaves (i.e. their possible manumission), was a subsequent aim shared by many. In the upper echelons of society, a quick and massive mobilization of the social capital of the deceased in the funerary cortege and laudatory speech by the main heir was valued. This was aimed at an unspecified reciprocity, since the social positioning of the children must already have occurred during the lifetime of the deceased. A quick change in the status of the deceased was one of the consequences. The failure to answer to the calling of one's name (*conclamatio*) is taken as proof of death; there is no longer the possibility of shared meals, though the deceased is still recognized as legal partner for all services connected to the funeral. This is followed by the transfer to the plural of the divinized ancestors worshipped at a cult site outside the city; cult within the house is only demanded by neglected ghosts and spirits.

These perspectives had consequences for the living to anticipate. What remains for the mortal in this respect is to ensure a social presence via grave monuments as sometimes highly individual projects. There were plenty of ways to project such a monument. The public addressed depended on social status and changed over time. It was not always an urban one. Beginning in the second century AD, this is recognized in that people chose a more intimate form of burial: the sarcophagus and the cubiculum in the catacombs. Death can be withdrawal from society, radicalized by the Christians in making god the spectator of post-mortal existence, and denying society power even over the body. Those in pursuit of the afterlife as a veritable god had to turn to their fellow citizens: it was widely accepted that divinization could only be realized through the community. And only in this way was death the beginning of an immortality that was not granted to many. And for those, it did not last for long, even if the restricted periods of the individual occupation of tombs in the cemeteries of contemporary European cities were probably surpassed. In this respect, ancient individuality went beyond the modern notion.

This observation is all the more important as the interest and belief in an ongoing personal existence was not very intensive in Greco-Roman cultures. This widespread reluctance to imagine a personal afterlife was shared by many Jews, in particular in the period before the destruction of the Temple. Egyptian pyramids and the magnificent tomb interiors of central Etruria well into the Roman period demonstrate that this reluctance was not without alternatives. Ancient Christianity, however, became probably the most important vector of transporting ideas of post-mortal existence into the modern world. Churches from the early modern period, as well as cemeteries from the nineteenth and twentieth centuries, present in their cenotaphs and tomb decorations motifs of a belief in the continuity of personal identity and family relationships beyond death, which are far more radical than what most people raised in Greco-Roman practices would have admitted. Not by becoming a god oneself, but by God's benevolence and love, stimulated (if not to say, ensured) by the prayer of others and oneself and one's own moral conduct, such a post-mortal status could be nearly assured. In many European countries one feature of the complex developments referred to as secularization has been that consensus in these matters has given place to a variety of beliefs and indications of beliefs (and non-belief) in public cemeteries, which might parallel the ancient state, but which has been modified by an additional loss of hope in a continuing social presence within the context of mass societies.

CHAPTER VIII

CONCLUSION

Based on a sketch of a particularly important variety of 'ancient religion', this book has offered a few deeper looks into the fabric and contradictions of ancient religious practices, institutions and ideas. By looking into details, I have tried not to stress big differences between ancient and modern religion, but to use the complexities of ancient religion in order to offer starting points for readers' reflections on their own religious environment, so different in, for example, Manchester and rural Louisiana, Singapore and Canberra, Lancaster and South Dakota – so different in lived traditions.

Different trends and forms of individualization – and the contrasting development of de-individualization in the form of 'religionization' – was considered in the first chapter. The establishment of 'religions' happened in the formation of groups enforcing uniformity by standards of belief and ritual practice, and maybe even the development of an internal jurisprudence (as in late ancient Christianity and, less easy to place, the tiny but growing strand of Rabbinic Judaism). In both respects – widespread individual options and the drawing of borderlines – Greco-Roman antiquity had been seminal. With regard to the privatization of religion as the formation of fundamentalist movements and the severe punishment of heretics, the opposition of individualization and de-individualization is of primary importance today.

Religious change and the traditional character of religion have been reviewed through the lenses of ancient historiography of religion. Again, the open admittance of change and accommodation, as much as the claim of a return to a religion's original forms and intentions, has proved to be a major topic and challenge to the self-image of today's religions, as well as the political and scientific ways of dealing with these very religions. Eternal truth is, as many traditions critically reflect, condemned to appear in temporal phenomena. Traditionalism as the open acceptance of dynamics could accommodate new alliances or end older ones.

The third chapter dealt with another inherent dilemma of religion: entertaining belief in powerful transcendent beings or realities. Stressing the invisible character of these powers makes it difficult to communicate with them and bring them to bear on daily life. Identifying the divine with a set of man-made symbols lays them open to manipulation and critique. Waves of iconoclasm and of powerful artistic representation have shifted the balances down into today's theological and intellectual debates.

The same holds true for one of the problems addressed in the fourth chapter: contrasting splendid public ritual and the imagination of divine perfection in the case of the supreme priest. Ritual, and criticism of ritual, fight for intellectual and – or! – aesthetic attractiveness of religion and religious thinking. Reform movements remove rituals and feel the necessity to compensate, either in imaginary terms or by a change of media, for instance bringing music into the place of visual arts.

What is mere culture and what is really religious? The fifth chapter thematized this perennial question with regard to the calendar, but the question is repeated in many instances in contemporary discussion or even juridical strife. The question is asked in respect to, for example, Christmas trees, as well as the headscarf, Sunday practices and questions of piety with regard to corpses. It is a question without an answer, but the discussion itself is an important part of religious discourse.

The sixth chapter makes a slight shift. Popular culture, exemplified by astrology then and now, and public religion – honoured, controlled, and robbed of much of its daily impact – has been treated in its most consequential and most widespread form in connection to the calendar – still a major phenomenon in Western societies, and far more so in Asian societies. Getting rid of the marker of 'religion' opens new fields of application

CONCLUSION

across religious boundaries, but at the same time it endangers its respectful position in society and the complex apparatus of reflections and institutions associated with this marker.

Finally, cosmological and social status have been contrasted with regard to burial practices and afterlife beliefs. For many, here is religion in its very essence; for others, it is far less so. Lived religion is as much individual religion as a socially embedded phenomenon, and gods might be used to stress either side of the balance. This certainly holds true for ancient and modern religion.

SOME SUGGESTIONS FOR FURTHER READING

The notes refer to research literature concerning the specific topics dealt with in the chapters. As introductory reading I recommend J.N. Bremmer, *Greek Religion* (Oxford, 1994) and J.A. North, *Roman Religion* (Oxford, 2000) as very short overviews of Greek and Roman religion respectively. For a more detailed overview see R. Parker, *Athenian Religion: A History* (Oxford, 1996), *On Greek Religion* (Ithaca, 2011), J. Rüpke, *Religion of the Romans* (Oxford, 2007) and J. Rüpke, *A Companion to Roman Religion* (Malden, Mass., 2007) (with introductory chapters on the ancient religions of Judaism and Christianity, fully acknowledging their historical contexts). Etruscan religion, hardly dealt with in this book, is a less well-known but important religious tradition in the western Mediterranean: J.-R. Jannot, *Religion in Ancient Etruria* (Madison, Wis., 2005). For the east Mediterranean region, Egyptian religion remains a vital tradition down into late antiquity: F.O. Dunand, C. Zivie-Coche, *Gods and Men in Egypt: 3000 BCE to 395 CE* (Ithaca, 2004).

Research on modern religion(s) is too manifold to allow any serious recommendation. Facts about the history of religion might be gathered in the *Encyclopedia of Religion* (New York, 2005 ff) or *Religion in Past and Present* (Leiden, 2008 ff.). A very good selection of aspects of and approaches to contemporary religion is given in the three large volumes edited by Hent de Vries: *Political Theologies: Public Religions in a Post-Secular World* (New York, 2006), *The Future of the Religious Past* (New York, 2008), *Religion: Beyond a Concept* (New York, 2008). The rise of the modern discipline of the study of religion, respectively history of religion, is described in H.G. Kippenberg, *Discovering Religious History in the Modern Age* (Princeton, 2002).

Large-scale historical accounts tend to either employ problematic evolutionistic generalizations or the paradigm of 'world religions', neatly separating instead of embedding cultural practices and beliefs. The methodological state of the art is summarized in S. Engler, M. Stausberg (ed.), *The Routledge Handbook of Research. Methods in the Study of Religion* (London, 2011).

NOTES

Introduction

1 See the discussion in Hodges, Richard and David Whitehouse, *Mohammed, Charlemagne & the Origins of Europe: Archaeology and the Pirenne Thesis* (London, 1983).
2 See Bowersock, G.W., *Hellenism in Late Antiquity* (Cambridge, 1990).
3 Eisenstadt, S.N. (ed.), *The Origins and Diversity of Axial Age Civilizations* (Albany, 1986); Arnason, Johann P. and Björn Wittrock (eds), *Eurasian Transformations, Tenth to Thirteenth Centuries: Crystallization, Divergences, Renaissances* (Leiden, 2004).
4 Marchand, Suzanne L., *Down from Olympus: Archaeology and Philhellenism in Germany, 1750–1970* (Princeton, 1996); Morley, Neville, *Antiquity and Modernity* (Oxford, 2008).
5 Kippenberg, Hans G., 'Religious history displaced by modernity', *Numen* 47 (2000), pp. 221–43; Dawson, Lorne L., 'Privatisation, globalisation, and religious innovation: Giddens' theory of modernity and the refutation of secularisation theory', in J.A. Beckford and J. Walliss (eds), *Theorising Religion: Classical and Contemporary Debates* (Aldershot, 2006), pp. 105–19.
6 For example, Parker, Robert, *On Greek Religion* (Ithaka, 2011); Rüpke, Jörg, *Religion of the Romans*, ed. and trans. by Richard Gordon (Cambridge, 2007).
7 Cf. Beard, Mary, John North and Simon Price, *Religions of Rome. 2 vols.* (Cambridge, 1998).
8 For a history of the term 'religion' see Smith, Jonathan Z., 'Religion, religions, religious', in C.M. Taylor (ed.), *Critical Terms for Religious Studies* (Chicago, 1998), pp. 269–84.
9 The subsequent text follows closely my chapter 'Roman religion', in Flower, Harriet I. (ed.), *The Cambridge Companion to the Roman Republic* (Cambridge, 2004), pp. 179–95.
10 Linderski, Jerzy, 'The augural law', *Aufstieg und Niedergang der Römischen Welt* II.16.3, pp. 2146–312.
11 See Cicero, *De diuinatione* 1.28; Livy 4.2.5; Festus p. 316.18–20 Lindsay; Ausonius *Opuscula* 16.12.12 Prete.

12 Barton, Tamsyn, *Ancient Astrology* (London, 1994), pp. 32–7; Stuckrad, Kocku von, 'Jewish and Christian astrology in late antiquity: a new approach' *Numen* 48 (2001), pp. 1–40.
13 Wiseman, Timothy P., 'Lucretius, Catiline, and the survival of prophecy', in T.P. Wiseman, *Historiography and Imagination: Eight Essays on Roman Culture* (Exeter, 1992), pp. 49–67; 133–9.
14 Rüpke, Jörg, 'Divination et décisions politiques dans la République romaine', *Cahiers Glotz* 16 (2005), pp. 217–33.
15 Rosenberger, Veit, *Gezähmte Götter: Das Prodigienwesen der römischen Republik* (Stuttgart, 1998).
16 See Ziolkowski, Adam, *The Temples of Mid-Republican Rome and Their Historical and Topographical Context*. Saggi di Storia antica 4 (Rome, 1992).
17 Bernstein, Frank, 'Complex rituals: games and processions in Republican Rome', in Rüpke, Jörg (ed.), *A Companion to Roman Religion* (Oxford, 2007), pp. 222–34.
18 Rüpke, Jörg, *Domi Militiae: Die Religiöse Konstruktion des Krieges in Rom* (Stuttgart, 1990), pp. 217–34; Östenberg, Ida, *Staging the World: Spoils, Captives, and Representations in the Roman Triumphal Procession* (Oxford, 2009).
19 See Rüpke, Jörg, *Religiöse Erinnerungskulturen: Formen der Geschichtsschreibung im antiken Rom* (Darmstadt, 2012), chapter 'Fasti: Quellen oder Produkte römischer Geschichtsschreibung?'.
20 For the *pax deorum*, see e.g. Livy 31.8–9.
21 Livy 41.17.3; Cicero *Philippica* 14.22; Naiden, Fred S., *Ancient Supplication* (Oxford , 2006).
22 Rüpke, Jörg, *Domi Militiae*, p. 216.
23 Rüpke, Jörg, *Religions of the Romans*, trans. Richard Gordon (Oxford, 2007), pp. 155–7. See Forsén, Björn, *Griechische Gliederweihungen: Eine Untersuchung zu ihrer Typologie und ihrer religions – und sozialgeschichtlichen Bedeutung*. Papers and monographs of the Finnish Institute at Athens 4 (Helsinki, 1996) and Schörner, Günther, *Votive im römischen Griechenland: Untersuchungen zur späthellenistischen und kaiserzeitlichen Kunst – und Religionsgeschichte*, Altertumswissenschaftliches Kolloquium 7 (Stuttgart, 2003) for Greece.
24 See Luckmann, Thomas, *The Invisible Religion: The Problem of Religion in Modern Society* (New York, 1967).
25 For the critique of these concepts see Eidinow, Esther, 'Networks and Narratives: A Model for Ancient Greek Religion', Kernos 24 (2011), 9–38; Kindt, Julia, *Rethinkig Greek Religion* (Cambridge, 2012)
26 Livy 10.47.6–7; Ovid, *Metamorphoses* 15.622–744.
27 See Bakker, Jan T., *Living and Working with the Gods: Studies of Evidence for Private Religion and its Material Environment in the City of Ostia (100–500 AD)*. Dutch monographs on ancient history and archaeology 12 (Amsterdam, 1994). Bassani, Maddalena, *Sacraria: ambienti e piccoli edifici per il culto domestico in area vesuviana*. Antenor Quaderni 9 (Roma, 2008).
28 Pailler, Jean-Marie, *Bacchanalia: la répression de 186 av. J.-C. à Rome et en*

NOTES

italie: vestiges, images, tradition. Bibliothèque des écoles françaises d'Athène et de Rome 270 (Rome, 1988).
29 Guthrie, W.K., *Orpheus and Greek Religion: A Study of the Orphic Movement* (New York, 1966) (2nd ed. 1997); Edmonds, Radcliffe G. (ed.), *The "Orphic" Gold Tablets and Greek Religion: Further Along the Path* (Cambridge, 2011).
30 Livy 2.27.5: *collegium mercatorum*; 5.50.4: *collegium Capitolinorum.*
31 See Wiseman, Timothy P., 'Liber myth, drama and ideology in republican Rome', in C. Bruun (ed.), *The Roman Middle Republic: Politics, Religion, and Histography c. 400–133 B. C.* Acta Instituti Finlandiae 23 (Rome, 2000), pp. 265–99.
32 See Scheer, Tanja S., *Mythische Vorväter: zur Bedeutung griechischer Heroenmythen im Selbstverständnis kleinasiatischer Städte.* Münchener Arbeiten zur Alten Geschichte 7 (München, 1993); Erskine, Andrew, *Troy between Greece and Rome: Local Tradition and Imperial Rome* (Oxford, 2001).
33 Rüpke, Jörg, *Religion in Republican Rome: Rationalization and Ritual Change* (Philadelphia, 2012).
34 Rüpke, Jörg, 'Charismatics or professionals? Analyzing religious specialists', *Numen* 43 (1996), pp. 241–62.
35 Rüpke, Jörg, *Fasti Sacerdotum: A Prosopography of Pagan, Jewish, and Christian Religious Officials in the City of Rome, 300 BC to AD 499* (Oxford, 2008).
36 *Lex Acilia* of 191 BC, see Rüpke, Jörg, *The Roman Calendar from Numa to Constantine: Time, History, and the Fasti,* trans. by David M. Richardson (Boston, 2011), pp. 84 f.
37 This hypothetical historical reconstruction and deconstruction of the supposedly 'Numaic calendar' is fully discussed ibid.
38 Aberson, Michel, *Temples votifs et butin de guerre dans la Rome republicaine* (Rome, 1994); Orlin, Eric M., *Temples, Religion and Politics in the Roman Republic* (Leiden, 1996).
39 Cancik, Hubert, 'Rome as sacred landscape: Varro and the end of republican religion in Rome', *Visible Religion* 4/5 (1985/6), pp. 250–65.
40 Rüpke, Jörg, *Fasti sacerdotum: Die Mitglieder der Priesterschaften und das sakrale Funktionspersonal römischer, griechischer, orientalischer und jüdischchristlicher Kulte in der Stadt Rom von 300 v. Chr. bis 499 n. Chr,* Potsdamer altertumswissenschaftliche Beiträge 12/1–3 (Stuttgart, 2005), pp.1419–40.
41 Gustaffson, Gabriella, *Evocatio Deorum: Historical and Mythical Interpretations of Ritualised Conquests in the Expansion of Ancient Rome* (Uppsala, 2000); Ferri, Giorgio, *Tutela urbis : il significato e la concezione della divinità tutelare cittadina nella religione romana.* Potsdamer altertumswissenschaftliche Beiträge 32 (Stuttgart, 2010).
42 MacBain, Bruce, *Prodigy and Expiation: A Study in Religion and Politics in Republican Rome.* Collection Latomus 177 (Brussels, 1982), corrected by Rosenberger, Veit, 'Prodigien aus Italien: Geographische Verteilung und religiöse Kommunikation', *Cahiers Glotz* 16 (2005), pp. 235–57.

Chapter I

1 This chapter has been reworked from my 'Hellenistic and Roman Empires and Euro-Mediterranean Religion', *Journal of Religion in Europe* 3 (2010), pp. 197–214.
2 Jaspers, Karl, *Vom Ursprung und Ziel der Geschichte*. New ed. (München, 1988).
3 Eisenstadt, Shmuel N., 'Die Achsenzeit in der Weltgeschichte', in H. Joas and K. Wiegandt (eds.), *Die kulturellen Werte Europas* (Frankfurt a. M., 2005), pp. 40–68, here p. 41.
4 Merlin, Donald, *A Mind So Rare: The Evolution of Human Consciousness* (New York, 2001).
5 Eisenstadt, Shmuel N. (ed.), *Kulturen der Achsenzeit: Ihre Ursprünge und ihre Vielfalt* (Frankfurt a. M., 1987); Árnason, Jóhann P., Shmuel N. Eisenstadt and Björn Wittrock (eds), *Axial Civilizations and World History* (Leiden, 2005).
6 Árnason, Eisenstadt and Wittrock: *Axial Civilizations*.
7 Eisenstadt, Shmuel N. 'Allgemeine Einleitung: Die Bedingungen für die Entstehung und Institutionalisierung der Kulturen der Achsenzeit', in id., *Kulturen der Achsenzeit: Ihre Ursprünge und ihre Vielfalt* (Frankfurt a. M., 1987), pp. 10–40.
8 Árnason, Eisenstadt and Wittrock: *Axial Civilizations*.
9 Wittrock, Björn, 'Cultural crystallizations and world history: the Age of ecumenical renaissances', in J.P. Árnason and id. (eds), *Eurasian Transformations, Tenth to Thirteenth Centuries: Crystallizations, Divergences, Renaissances* (Leiden, 2004), pp. 41–73, at pp. 47–56.
10 Ibid., 46.
11 Woolf, Greg, *Becoming Roman: The Origins of Provincial Civilization in Gaul* (Cambridge, 1998).
12 Firmicus Maternus, *De errore profanarum religionum* 7.
13 Animals: Cicero, *De natura deorum* 3.39 and again in 3.48; *Belus*, i.e. Baal in 3.42; Egyptian variants: 3.54–59; *religio*: 2.8.
14 Cicero, *Pro Flacco* 69: *Sua cuique civitati religio, Laeli, est, nostra nobis*.
15 See Rüpke, Jörg, 'Religious pluralism', in A. Barchiesi and W. Scheidel (eds), *The Oxford Handbook of Roman Studies* (Oxford, 2010), pp. 749–52.
16 For example, North, John, 'The development of religious pluralism', in J. Lieu, id. and T. Rajak (eds), *The Jews Among Pagans and Christians: In the Roman Empire* (London, 1994), pp. 174–93.
17 Minucius, *Octavius* 6.1; similar the Egyptian intellectual Athenaeus, *Deipnosophistes* 1.20c–d.
18 *Asclepius* 24; see Clifford Ando, *The Matter of the Gods: Religion and the Roman Empire* (Berkeley, 2008), p. 155, n. 20.
19 Minucius, *Octavius* 20.6.
20 For example, Acts 4.17; Josephus, *Bellum Judaicum* 2.8.1.
21 Lactantius, *De mortibus persecutorum* 34.
22 See Ando: *Gods*.

NOTES

23 See Veyne, Paul, *L'Empire Gréco-Romain* (Paris, 2005), pp. 454–5.
24 Brief account: Smith, Jonathan Z., 'Religion, religions, religious', in M.C. Taylor (ed.), *Critical Terms For Religious Studies* (Chicago, 1998), pp. 269–84.
25 Cf. Musschenga, Albert W., 'The many faces of individualism', in A. van Harskamp and id. (eds), *The Many Faces of Individualism*. Morality and the meaning of life 12 (Leuven, 2001), pp. 3–24. The distinction is made 'between *individualisation* as an objective process of social change, *individuation* as development of personal identity, *values of individuality* which express views on personal identity that emerge in the process of individualisation and are used to legitimise that process, and *individualist doctrines* in which (some of) these values are linked up to certain conceptions of man and of society', here p. 5.
26 Expressive as well as utilitarian individualism would be involved – as defined by Bellah, Robert N., *Habits of the Heart: Individualism and Commitment in American Life* (Berkeley, 2008).
27 Hahn, Alois, 'Zur Soziologie der Beichte und anderer Formen institutionalisierter Bekenntnisse: Selbstthematisierung und Zivilisationsprozeß', *Kölner Zeitschrift für Soziologie und Sozialpsychologie* 34 (1982), pp. 407–34. id., 'Differenzierung, Zivilisationsprozeß, Religion: Aspekte einer Theorie der Moderne: René König, dem Begründer der Sonderhefte, zum 80. Geburtstag gewidmet', *Kölner Zeitschrift für Soziologie und Sozialpsychologie. Sonderheft* 27 (1986), pp. 214–31, at pp. 225–8.
28 See Halman, Loek, 'Individualism in contemporary Europe', in A. van Harskamp and A.W. Musschenga (eds), *The Many Faces of Individualism*. Morality and the meaning of life 12 (Leuven, 2001), 25–46, at p. 29, on the role of the modern welfare state.
29 See North: 'The development of religious pluralism'.
30 See Bendlin, Andreas, 'Peripheral centres – central peripheries: religious communication in the Roman Empire', in Cancik and Rüpke (eds), *Römische Reichsreligion und Provinzialreligion* (Tübingen, 1997), pp. 35–68.
31 Thus Rüpke, Jörg, 'Apokalyptische Salzberge: Zum sozialen Ort und zur literarischen Strategie des "Hirten des Hermas"', *Archiv für Religionsgeschichte* 1 (1999), pp. 148–60.
32 Taylor, Charles, *Sources of the Self: The Making of the Modern Identity* (Cambridge, 1989). I am grateful to Matthias Huff for the qualification.
33 Bowes, Kim, *Private Worship, Public Values, and Religious Change in Late Antiquity* (Cambridge, 2008).
34 See McGuire, Meredith B., *Ritual Healing in Suburban America* (New Brunswick, 1988), pp. 240–57.
35 Harris, William V. and Holmes, Brooke (eds), *Aelius Aristides Between Greece, Rome, and the Gods* (Leiden, 2008); Petsalis-Diomidis, Alexia, 'Sacred writing, sacred reading: the function of Aelius Aristides' self-presentation as author in the Sacred Tales', in B.C. McGing and J. Mossman (eds), *The limits of Ancient Biography* (Swansea, 2006), pp. 193–211; id., *Truly Beyond Wonders. Aelius Aristides and the Cult of Asklepios* (Oxford, 2009).

36 Bendlin, Andreas 'Vom Nutzen und Nachteil der Mantik: Orakel im Medium von Handlung und Literatur in der Zeit der Zweiten Sophistik', in D. Elm von der Osten, J. Rüpke and K. Waldner (eds), *Texte als Medium und Reflexion von Religion im römischen Reich* (Stuttgart, 2006), 159–207. Belayche, Nicole and Jörg Rüpke, 'Divination et révélation dans les mondes grec et romain: presentation', *Revue d'Histoire des Religions* 224 (2007), pp. 139–47.

37 Stuckrad, Kocku von, *Das Ringen um die Astrologie: Jüdische und christliche Beiträge zum antiken Zeitverständnis* (Berlin, 2000).

38 Janowitz, Naomi, *Icons of Power: Ritual Practices in Late Antiquity* (University Park, 2002). Athanassiadi, Polymnia, 'Dreams, theurgy and freelance divination: the testimony of Iamblichus', *Journal of Roman Studies* 83 (1993), pp. 115–30.

39 Gordon, Richard, 'Aelian's peony: the location of magic in Graeco-Roman tradition', *Comparative Criticism* 9 (1987), pp. 59–95; id., 'Imagining Greek and Roman magic' in V. Flint (ed.), *Witchcraft and Magic in Europe 2: Ancient Greece and Rome* (London, 1999), 159–275; id., 'Magic as a topos in Augustan poetry: discourse, reality and distance', *Archiv für Religionsgeschichte* 11 (2009), pp. 209–28.

40 Schilling, Heinz (ed.), *Konfessioneller Fundamentalismus : Religion als politischer Faktor im europäischen Mächtesystem um 1600 [Kolloquium zum Thema "Konfessionsfundamentalismus in Europa um 1600. Was waren seine Ursachen, was die Bedingungen seiner Überwindung?" vom 5. bis 8. Juni 2005]* (München, 2007); Schilling, Heinz, Thóth, István György and Muchembled, Robert, *Religion and cultural exchange in Europe, 1400–1700* (Cambridge, 2006); Lieburg, Fred van (ed.), *Confessionalism and Pietism: Religious Reform in Early Modern Europe [Proceedings of ohe First Conference of the Dutch, Nordic and American Network Programme on "Cultural History of Pietism and Revivalism", held in November 2004 in Dordrecht, . . . organised by the Huizinga Institute for Cultural History . . .]* (Mainz, 2006); Greyerz, Kaspar von *et al* (ed.), *Interkonfessionalität – Transkonfessionalität – binnenkonfessionelle Pluralität: Neue Forschungen zur Konfessionalisierungsthese* (Gütersloh, 2003).

41 Mulsow, Martin, *Moderne aus dem Untergrund: Radikale Frühaufklärung in Deutschland; 1680–1720* (Hamburg, 2002), —, *Die unanständige Gelehrtenrepublik : Wissen, Libertinage und Kommunikation in der Frühen Neuzeit* (Stuttgart [u.a.], 2007), Mulsow, Martin and Popkin, Richard Henry (ed.), *Secret Conversions to Judaism in Early Modern Europe* (Leiden, 2004).

42 See e.g. Noll, Mark A., *The Rise of Evangelicalism: The Age of Edwards, Whitefield and the Wesleys,* A history of evangelicalism: People, movements and ideas in the English-speaking world 1 (Downers Grove, Ill., 2005); Hölscher, Lucian, *Geschichte der protestantischen Frömmigkeit in Deutschland* (München, 2005).

NOTES

Chapter II

1 See the radical position of Vinzent, Markus, *Christ's Resurrection in Early Christianity and the Making of the New Testament* (Farnham, 2011).
2 See Reynolds, Gabriel Said (ed.), *The Qur'ān in its Historical Context [1]* (London, 2008); Neuwirth, Angelika, *Der Koran als Text der Spätantike: Ein europäischer Zugang* (Berlin, 2010).
3 For the following I extensively rely on research more fully presented in Rüpke, Jörg, 'Construing "religion" by doing historiography: historicisation of religion in the Roman Republic', *History of Religion* 2013, forthcoming.
4 For a critical review see Grethlein, Jonas, *The Greeks and Their Past: Poetry, Oratory and History in the Fifth Century BCE* (Cambridge, 2010); see also Lianeri, Alexandra (ed.), *The Western Time of Ancient History: Historiographical Encounters with the Greek and Roman Pasts* (Cambridge, 2011).
5 Rüsen, Jörn, 'Some theoretical approaches to intercultural comparative historiography', *History and Theory* 35/4 (1996), pp. 5–22, here p. 8.
6 Halbwachs, Maurice, *On Collective Memory* (Chicago, 1992; originally 1925); Nora, Pierre and Ageron, Charles-Robert, *Les lieux de mémoire 1: La République* (Paris, 1984); Ricoeur, Paul, *Time and Narrative* (Chicago, 1984–85).
7 Rüpke: *Römische Erinnerungs Kulturen*, pp. 139–52.
8 For the latter, Rüpke, Jörg and Ulrike Rüpke, *Antike Götter und Mythen* (München, 2010).
9 See Klein, Kerwin Lee, 'On the emergence of memory in historical discourse', *Representations* 69 (2000), pp. 127–50 – on the terminological strategies and social contexts of the use of 'memory' rather than 'history'. I am grateful to Karl Galinsky for the reference.
10 Rüpke, Jörg, *Fasti Sacerdotum*, no. 2818.
11 Davies, Jason P., *Rome's Religious History: Livy, Tacitus and Ammianus on their Gods* (Cambridge, 2004).
12 See Cancik, Hubert, *Religionsgeschichten: Römer, Juden und Christen im römischen Reich. Gesammelte Aufsätze 2* (Tübingen, 2008), p. 4, for the focus on the institutional history of religion.
13 Livy 37.50; 38.1–11.
14 Livy 39.5.14 ff.
15 Rüpke, Jörg, *The Roman Calendar from Numa to Constantine: Time, History and the Fasti* (Malden, MA., 2011), pp. 88–90 and the critical evaluation of the dating by Feeney, Denis, *Caesar's Calendar: Ancient Time and the Beginnings of History*. Sather classical lectures 65 (Berkeley, 2007), here p. 143, in n. 24.
16 Rüpke: *The Roman Calendar*, pp. 93–5.
17 Ibid., p. 95; Rüpke: *Religion in Republican Rome*, pp. 152–71, (also for the following).
18 Rüpke, Jörg, 'Representation or presence? Picturing the divine in ancient Rome', *Archiv für Religionsgeschichte* 12 (2010), pp. 183–96.
19 I base my argument on the assumption that their indications about Varro's work and some sequences of quotations are reliable. This is the basis of the

edition on which I gratefully rely: Cardauns, Burkhart, *M. Terentius Varro, Antiquitates rerum divinarum. 1: Die Fragmente. 2: Kommentar.* Akademie der Wissenschaften und der Literatur, Mainz, Abhandlungen der Geistes – und sozialwissenschaftlichen Klasse 1 (Wiesbaden, 1976).
20 Varro, *De lingua latina* 5.74.
21 Pliny, *Naturalis Historia* 18.285–6; Varro, *De re rustica* 1.1.6.
22 Censorinus, *De die natali* 17.8.
23 Augustine *De ciuitate* dei, 6.4, p. 251.13–16.
24 See fr. 6–9; on which see Rüpke, Jörg, 'Varro's tria genera theologiae: religious thinking in the late republic', *Ordia prima* 4 (2005), pp. 107–29.
25 Augustine *De ciuitate* dei, 7.17, p. 295.22 introducing Varro, *Antiquitates rerum diuinarum* fr. 228.
26 Caeser, *De bello Gallico* 6.17.1.
27 See Rüpke: 'Religious pluralism', p. 750.
28 See Rüpke: *Römische Erinnerungs Kulturen*, pp. 165–73.
29 See e.g. Brownlee, John S., *Political Thought in Japanese Historical Writing: From Kojiki (712) to Tokushi Yoron (1712)* (Waterloo, 1991); Bowring, Richard John, *The Religious Traditions of Japan, 500–1600* (Cambridge, 2008).

Chapter III

1 See Schmidt, Francis, 'Polytheisms: Degeneration or Progress?' *History and Anthropology* 3 (1987), pp. 9–60. This chapter is based on my article 'Representation or presence? Picturing the divine in ancient Rome', *Archiv für Religionsgeschichte* 12 (2010), pp. 183–96.
2 Cicero, *De domo sua* 51: *te meam domum consecrasse, te monumentum fecisse in meis aedibus, te signum dedicasse.*
3 Varro, *Antiquitates rerum diuinarum fr.* 18 and 38 Cardauns; Servius Auctus, *In Aeneidem* 1.505; Cardauns, comm. ad loc. 1976, 147.
4 Izzet, Vedia, 'Tuscan order: the development of Etruscan sanctuary architecture', in E. Bispham and C.J. Smith (eds), *Religion in Archaic and Republican Rome and Italy: Evidence and Experience* (Edinburgh, 2000), pp. 34–53.
5 See Ornan, Tallay, *The Triumph of the Symbol: Pictorial Representation of Deities in Mesopotamia and the Biblical Image Ban* (Fribourg, 2005), p. 171.
6 See Mylonopoulos, Joannis (ed.), *Divine Images and Human Imaginations in Ancient Greece and Rome*, Religions in the Graeco-Roman World 170 (Leiden, 2010) for the range of possibilities and reactions.
7 Varro, *Ant. rer. div. fr.* 38 Cardauns.
8 Thus e.g. Clarke, John R., *Looking at Lovemaking: Constructions of Sexuality in Roman Art, 100 B.C. – A.D. 250* (Berkeley, 1998), pp. 174–7; Balch, David L., *Roman Domestic Art and Early House Churches* (Tübingen, 2008), p. 118 f.
9 Kastenmeier, Pia, 'Priap zum Gruße: Der Hauseingang der Casa dei Vettii in

NOTES

Pompeji', *Mitteilungen des Deutschen Archäologischen Instituts, Römische Abteilung* 108 (2001), pp. 301–11, here pp. 307–11.
10 Clarke, John R., *Art in the Lives of Ordinary Romans: Visual Representation and Non-Elite Viewers in Italy, 100 B.C.–A.D. 315* (Berkeley, 2003), p. 86.
11 Cf. Clarke: *Art in the Lives of Ordinary Romans*, p. 89. Cf. Cic. *ND* 1.83.
12 Cic. *De Natura Deorum* 1.81; Epicureans: 1.76–84.
13 Clark, Anna J., *Divine Qualities: Cult and Community in Republican Rome* (Oxford 2007), p. 184.
14 See ibid., 128–31. The average height of a honourific statue including basis was about three metres (Fejfer, Jane, *Roman Portraits in Context* (Berlin, 2008), p. 18).
15 See e.g. for geography: Crang, Mike, 'Picturing practices: research through the tourist gaze', *Progress in Human Geography* 21 (1997), pp. 359–73.
16 Cic. *De Natura Deorum* 1.84.
17 Stewart, Peter C.N., *Statues in Roman Society: Representation and Response* (Oxford, 2003), p. 31. See also Fejfer: *Roman Portraits*, pp. 20–25, for the archaeological evidence of the first century BC.
18 Seneca, *De superstition fr.* 36 Haase = *fr.* 69 Vottero (Augustine, *De ciuitate dei* 6.10), trsl. partly from Beard, Mary, John North, et al., *Religions of Rome 2: A Sourcebook* (Cambridge 1998), p. 234.
19 Martin, Dale B., *Inventing Superstition: from the Hippocratics to the Christians* (Cambridge, 2004), p. 96.
20 Mitchell, W. J. Thomas, *What do Pictures Want? The Lives and Loves of Images* (Chicago, Ill., 2005).
21 Cic. *Dom.* 108–112. Trans. on the basis of *The Orations of Marcus Tullius Cicero*, trans. C.D. Yonge (London, 1891).
22 Steuernagel, Dirk, 'Wozu brauchen Griechen Tempel? Fragen und Perspektiven', in H. Cancik and J. Rüpke (eds), *Die Religion des Imperium Romanum. Koine und Konfrontation* (Tübingen, 2009), pp. 115–38, here pp. 124–6.
23 Hesberg, Henner von, 'Die Statuengruppe im Tempel der Dioskuren von Cori: Bemerkungen zum Aufstellungskontext von Kultbildern in spätrepublikanischer Zeit', *Mitteilungen des Deutschen Archäologischen Instituts, Römische Abteilung* 113 (2007), pp. 443–61. According to Pliny (*NH* 36.185) mosaics were installed in the Capitoline temple of Jupiter in 149 BC.
24 Ibid., p. 458 f. and 456.
25 Gellius, *Noctes Atticae* 6.1.6; Livy 26.19.5. See Rüpke, Jörg, *Religion of the Romans*, ed. and trans. by Richard Gordon (Cambridge, 2007), p. 20.
26 See Lubtchansky, Natacha and Pouzadoux, Claude, 'Montrer l'invisible: Introduction', in S. Estienne (ed.), *Image et Religion dans l'Antiquité Gréco-Romaine: actes du colloque de Rome, 11 – 13 décembre 2003* (Naples, 2008), pp. 15–8.
27 See Ando, Clifford, 'Signs, idols, and the incarnation in Augustinian metaphysics', *Representations* 73 (2001), pp. 24–53 for Augustine's thinking and struggling with older tradition and Wallraff, Martin, 'Viele Metaphern – viele Götter? Beobachtungen zum Monotheismus in der Spätantike', in J. Frey, J.

Rohls and R. Zimmermann (eds), *Metaphorik und Christologie* (Berlin, 2003), pp. 151–66.
28 See e.g. Cassius Dio 43.45 on statues of Caesar and Pliny the Younger, *Panegyricus* 52,3 (Pliny the Elder, *Naturalis Historia* 34,15 f. attests the oldest statue made of gold for the republic).
29 Ouwerkerk, Coenraad A.J. van, '"Effigies Dei" and the religious imagination: a psychological perspective', in D. van der Plas (ed.), *Effigies Dei: essays on the history of religions* (Leiden, 1987), pp. 156–70, see here p. 161. This is a stronger notion than the 'aura of facticity' provided, according to Clifford Geertz, 'Religion as a cultural system', in M. Banton (ed.), *Anthropological Approaches to the Study of Religion* (London, 1966), pp. 1–46, here p. 1, by specifically religious ritual.
30 Gordon, Richard L., 'The real and the imaginary: production and religion in the Graeco-Roman world', *Art History* 2 (1979), pp. 5–34. Cf. Steiner, Deborah Tarn, *Images in Mind: Statues in Archaic and Classical Greek Literature and Thought* (Princeton, 2001), p. 79: container, vessel, residence.
31 Cf. Hubbeling, Hubertus G., *On Symbolic Representation of Religion: Groninger Contributions to Theories of Symbols* (Berlin, 1986).
32 Stewart: *Statues in Roman Society*, pp. 208–14. Lamps: ibid., p. 207.
33 Hesberg, Henner von, 'Dona cano divum: Eine Relief aus Köln mit der Wiedergabe eines Jägers vor einem Heiligtum der Diana', in J. Gebauer (ed.), *Bildergeschichte: Festschrift Klaus Stähler* (Möhnesee, 2004), pp. 208–20, see here pp. 214–15; cf. Stewart: *Statues in Roman Society*, 215–21.
34 Cf. for this factor, which has not been analysed here, Versnel, Hendrik S., 'What did ancient man see when he saw a god? Some reflections on greco-roman epiphany', in D. van der Plas (ed.), *Effigies Dei: Essays on the History of Religions* (Leiden, 1987), pp. 42–55.
35 See Donohue, Alice A., *Xoana and the Origins of Greek Sculpture* (Atlanta, 1988). Scheer, Tanja S., *Die Gottheit und ihr Bild: Untersuchungen zur Funktion griechischer Kultbilder in Religion und Politik* (München, 2000).
36 See Heyberger, Bernard and Naef, Silvia (ed.), *La multiplication des images en pays d'islam: de l'estampe à la télévision (17. – 21. siécle); actes du colloque Images: Fonctions et Langages. L'Incursion de l'Image Moderne dans l'Orient Musulman et sa Périphérie, Istanbul, Université du Bosphore (Boğaziçi Üniversitesi), 25 – 27 mars 1999* (Würzburg, 2003); Naef, Silvia, *À la recherche d'une modernité arabe: L'évolution des arts plastiques en Egypte, au Liban et en Irak* (Genéve, 1996). There is no explicit denial of images in the Qur'anic text; the usual scriptural basis is the mentioning of pagan sacrificial slabs (5:90).

Chapter IV

1 Stroumsa, Guy G., *The End of Sacrifice: Religious Transformations in Late Antiquity* (Chicago, 2009). This chapter follows closely Rüpke, Jörg, 'Starting

NOTES

sacrifice in the beyond: Flavian innovations in the concept of priesthood and their repercussions in the treatise "To the Hebrews"', *Revue d'histoire des religions* 229 (2012), pp. 4–30.
2 Cf. Stroumsa, Guy G., *Barbarian Philosophy: The Religious Revolution of Early Christianity* (Tübingen, 1999), pp. 40–1.
3 See below. Koester, Craig R., 'Hebrews: a new translation with introduction and commentary', in *The Anchor Bible*, vol. 36 (New York, 2001), p. 50 opts for a date between 60 and 90; Attridge, Harold W., *The Epistle to the Hebrews: A Commentary* (Philadelphia, 1989), p. 9, pp. 60–100.
4 See Scholer, John M., *Proleptic Priests: Priesthood in the Epistle to the Hebrews*. Journal for the Study of the New Testament Supplement Series 49 (Sheffield, 1991), p. 83.
5 Lincoln, Andrew, *Hebrews: A Guide* (London/New York, 2006), p. 45; rather optimistic: Mason, Eric Farrel '*You are a Priest Forever': Second Temple Jewish Messianism and the Priestly Christology of the Epistle to the Hebrews* (Leiden, 2008), p. 203.
6 Loader, William R.G., *Sohn und Hohepriester: Eine traditionsgeschichtliche Untersuchung zur Christologie des Hebräerbriefes*. Wissenschaftliche Monographien zum Alten und Neuen Testament 53 (Neukirchen-Vluyn, 1981), p. 100.
7 Sceptical: Koester: 'Hebrews', pp. 59–60. Hurst, Lincoln Douglas, *The Epistle to the Hebrews: Its Background and Thought* (Cambridge, 1990), p. 133, stresses, apart from the Septuagint (in particular Ps 8) and the Old Testament traditions of Acta 7, the Pauline theology and contemporary Jewish apocalyptic (4 Ezra, 1 Enoch), but the priestly figure 'remains a riddle'.
8 See Aitken, Ellen Bradshaw, 'Portraying the temple in stone and text: the Arch of Titus and the Epistle to the Hebrews', in G. Gelardini (ed.), *Hebrews: Contemporary Methods – New Insights*. Biblical Interpretations Series 75 (Leiden, 2005), pp. 133–6, for an early Domitian date by supposing that Hebrews directly reacted to the imagery of Titus as displayed in the Arch of Titus.
9 Attridge: *The Epistle to the Hebrews*, p. 7.
10 Ibid., p. 10.
11 Molthagen, Joachim, 'Die Lage der Christen im römischen Reich nach dem 1. Petrusbrief: Zum Problem einer domitianischen Verfolgung', *Historia* 44 (1995), pp. 422–58.
12 See Urner, Christiana, *Kaiser Domitian im Urteil antiker literarischer Quellen und moderner Forschung* (Augsburg, 1993), p. 49 f.
13 For the latter and his underrated reception see Urner: *Kaiser Domitian*, p. 319.
14 Leberl, Jens, *Domitian und die Dichter: Poesie als Medium der Herrschaftsdarstellung*. Hypomnemata 154 (Göttingen, 2004), p. 343.
15 Ibid., p. 344 f.; Nauta, Ruurd R., *Poetry for Patrons: Literary Communication in the Age of Domitian*. Mnemosyne suppl. 206 (Leiden, 2002), pp. 327–35, likewise underlines the fact that poetic honouring of the emperor need not imply personal imperial patronage.

16 See Clauss, Manfred, *Kaiser und Gott: Herrscherkult im römischen Reich* (Stuttgart, 1999), pp. 112–32.
17 Gordon, Richard, 'The veil of power: emperors, sacrificers and benefactors', in M. Beard and J. North (eds), *Pagan Priests: Religion and Power in the Ancient World* (London, 1990), pp. 201–31.
18 Rüpke, Jörg, *Fasti Sacerdotum,* no. 1017; *Corpus Inscriptionum Latinarum (CIL)* 6.31294 = *Inscriptiones Latinae Selectae (ILS)* 258; *CIL* 6.40453.
19 Rüpke, *Fasti Sacerdotum,* no. 1470; *CIL* 9.4955 = *ILS* 267 and *CIL* 3.12218; *Notizie delle scavi (NS)* 1899.64 attests membership among the *XVviri* already for AD 72.
20 See Stepper, Ruth, *Augustus et sacerdos: Untersuchungen zum römischen Kaiser als Priester.* Potsdamer altertumswissenschaftliche Beiträge 9 (Stuttgart, 2003), pp. 35–9 and 45; Haeperen, Françoise van, *Le collège pontifical (3ème s. a. C.-4ème s. p. C.): contribution à l'étude de la religion publique romaine* (Bruxelles, 2002), p. 153 f.
21 Haeperen: *Le collège pontifical,* pp. 94–6.
22 Rüpke: *Fasti Sacerdotum,* 2008, pp. 57–66.
23 And after his release from imperial service: Abramenko, Andrik, 'Zeitkritik bei Sueton: Zur Datierung der Vitae Caesarum', *Hermes* 122 (1994), pp. 80–94.
24 Suetonius, *Titus* 9.1; trsl. J.C. Rolfe, Loeb Library.
25 Livy 27.8.4–10; Valerius Maximus 6.9.3; Rüpke, *Fasti Sacerdotum,* no. 3393.
26 Cf. Paulus ex Festo p. 293,8–9 L; Varro, *De re rustica* 2.1.20 and Pliny, *Naturalis historia* 8.206 with Ovid, *Amores* 3.8.23 *purus . . . sacerdos* in a metaphorical way.
27 For details see Parker, Robert, *Miasma: Pollution and Purification in Early Greek Religion* (Oxford, 1983).
28 Ovid *Fasti* 4.731–4; 6.225–234 of Augustan times.
29 Thus Stepper: *Augustus et sacerdos,* p. 147.
30 *Coins of the Roman Empire in the British Museum (CREBM)* 2,300 ff. 7a ff. = *Roman Imperial Coinage (RIC)* 2, Domitian 11–23.
31 Suetonius, *Domitianus* 8.3–4; corroborated by Dio 67.3.3 f.
32 As argued by Stéphane Gsell, see Jones, Brian W., *The Emperor Domitian* (London, 1992), p. 218.
33 Hardie, Philip, *Statius and the Silvae. Poets, Patrons and Epideixis in the Graeco-Roman World* (Liverpool, 1983), p. 203 n. 68; Jones: *The Emperor Domitian,* p. 101 on Statius, *Silvae* 1.1.36.
34 *CIL* 6.826 = 6.30837a-c = *ILS* 4914 = Année epigraphique (*AE*) 2001.182.
35 Suet. *Domit.* 4.4.
36 *CREBM* 2, no. 419–438; rightly stressed by Harry O. Maier.
37 Suet. *Domit.* 5, see Jones: *The Emperor Domitian,* pp. 102–6 for details and further evidence.
38 See Fredrick, David, 'Architecture and surveillance in Flavian Rome', in A.J. Boyle and J.W. Dominik (eds), *Flavian Rome: Culture, Image, Text* (Leiden, 2003), pp. 205–9 on the characteristics of Domitian's architecture.

NOTES

39 Suet. *Domit.* 1.2 and 9.1.
40 Fishwick, Duncan, *The Imperial Cult in the Latin West: Studies in the Ruler Cult of the Western Provinces of the Roman Empire.* III: 1. EPRO 145 (Leiden, 2002), p. 95, see also 96 f. See Kantiréa, Maria, *Les dieux et les dieux Augustes: Le culte impérial en Grèce sous les Julio-claudiens et les Flaviens. Etudes épigraphiques et archéologiques.* Meletemata 50 (Athens, 2007), p. 84 for a new routine of dedications in Greece.
41 Clauss: *Kaiser und Gott*, p. 120 f.; for the location see the suggestion of Candilio, Daniela, 'Indagini archeologiche nell'aula ottagona delle Terme di Diocleziano', *Numizmatika i Sfragistika* vol. 1/2 (1990/91), pp. 165–83.
42 Stat. *Silv.* 5.1.38 and 74.
43 Suet. *Domit.* 13.2: *dominus et deus*; see Stat. *Silv.* 1.1.62: *forma dei praesens.*
44 Throne: Plin. *Paneg.* 52.1; statue: Stat. *Silv.* 5.1.189–191. Stat. *Silv.* 1.1.74: *salve, magnorum proles genitorque deorum.*
45 See Coleman, Kathleen M., 'The emperor Domitian and literature', *Aufstieg und Niedergang der römischen Welt* II.32.5 (1986), pp. 3087–115; Cancik, Hubert, 'Größe und Kolossalität als religiöse und aesthetische Kategorien: Versuch einer Begriffsbestimmung am Beispiel von Statius, Silve I 1: Ecus maximus Domitiani imperatoris', *Visible Religion* 7 (1990), pp. 51–68.
46 For references to Trajan's divine status see Levene, David S., 'God and man in the classical latin panegyric', *Proceedings of the Cambridge Philological Society* 43 (1997), pp. 66–103, esp. 78–82.
47 An important strategy in this as in earlier panegyrics, see ibid., p. 78. Quotation: Plin. *Paneg.* 64.2.
48 Levene: 'God and man', p. 81.
49 Cf. Nauta: *Poetry for patrons*, pp. 412–4 for *topoi* dealing with honorific speeches and poetry.
50 Koester: 'Hebrews', p. 59.
51 For example, Hughes, Philip Edgcumbe, *A Commentary on the Epistle to the Hebrews* (Michigan, 1977), p. 169; Gräßer, Erich, 'An die Hebräer', in Gnilka, J. et al. (ed.), *Evangelisch-katholischer Kommentar zum Neuen Testament*, Bd. XVII/ 2 (Zürich/Braunschweig/Neukirchen, 1990), p. 245.
52 Koester: 'Hebrews', p. 187; see Martin, Alain, *La titulature épigraphique de Domitien.* Beiträge zur klassischen Philologie 181 (Frankfurt a. M., 1987).
53 Rissi, Matthias, *Die Theologie des Hebräerbriefs: Ihre Verankerung in der Situation des Verfassers und seiner Leser* (Tübingen, 1987), p. 52.
54 Koester: 'Hebrews', p. 297, 359, 448, 381.
55 Bruce, Frederick Fyvie (ed.), *The Epistle to the Hebrews.* Rev. ed. (Michigan, 1990), p. 170.
56 As used in 1 Colossans 1.18 or Romans 8.29.
57 Cf. the list of qualities collected by Hagner, Donald A., *Encountering the Book of Hebrews: An Exposition* (Grand Rapids, 2002), p. 104, and Gray, Patrick, 'Brotherly love and the high priest Christology of Hebrews', *Journal of Biblical Literature* 122 (2003), pp. 335–51.
58 Gelardini: 'Hebrews, an ancient synagogue homily for tisha be-Av', p. 123.

59 Ellingworth, Paul, *The Epistle to the Hebrews: A Commentary on the Greek Text* (Michigan, 1993), p. 78; cf. DeSilva, David A., *Perseverance in Gratitude: A Socio-Rhetorical Commentary on the Epistle 'to the Hebrews'* (Grand Rapids, 2000), p. 58 f.
60 Ellingworth: *The Epistle to the Hebrews*, p. 79; see also DeSilva, David A., 'Exchanging favor for wrath: apostasy in Hebrews and patron-client relationships', *Journal of Biblical Literature* 115 (1996), pp. 91–116.
61 See Käsemann, Ernst, *Das wandernde Gottesvolk. Eine Untersuchung zum Hebräerbrief* (Göttingen, 1957), p. 72.
62 Gray, Patrick, *The Epistle to the Hebrews and Greco-Roman Critiques of Superstition* (Leiden, 2004), p. 221; sim. Vanhoye, Albert, *Structure and Message on the Epistle to the Hebrews*. Studia biblica 12 (Rom, 1989), p. 16; Isaacs, Marie E., 'Priesthood and the Epistle to the Hebrews', *Heythrop Journal* 38 (1997), pp. 51–62, esp. p. 56.
63 Rüpke, Jörg, 'Early Christianity in, and out of, context', *Journal of Roman Studies* 99 (2009), pp. 182–93, esp. pp. 191–2.
64 See Rüpke, Jörg, 'Performanzkultur: Zur Sichtbarkeit von Religion und religiösen Spezialisten im antiken Rom', in B. Beinhauer-Köhler, D. Pezzoli-Olgiati and J. Valentin (ed.), *Religiöse Blicke – Blicke auf das Religiöse: Visualität und Religion* (Zürich, 2010), pp. 149–163; —, *Von Jupiter und Christus: Religionsgeschichte in römischer Zeit* (Darmstadt, 2011).

Chapter V

1 An excellent edition (unfortunately skipping all chronological material of the texts) of all texts then known is offered by Degrassi, Attilio, *Inscriptiones Italiae* 13.2 (Roma, 1963). For more recent finds see Rüpke, Jörg, *Kalender und Öffentlichkeit: Die Geschichte der Repräsentation und religiösen Qualifikation von Zeit in Rom* (Berlin, 1995).
2 Astronomical information is given in the Fasti Venusini (*Inscriptiones Italiae* 13.2, p. 56–59). See Rüpke, Jörg, *The Roman Calendar from Numa to Constantine: Time, History, and the Fasti*. Trans. by David M. Richardson (Boston, 2011), pp. 162–3; Stuckrad, Kocku von, *Das Ringen um die Astrologie: Jüdische und christliche Beiträge zum antiken Zeitverständnis* (Berlin, 2000).
3 Rüpke: *Roman Calendar*, pp. 48–52.
4 The local character of the *dies vern(arum)* of the Fasti Antiates ministrorum is doubtful, see Rüpke: *Kalender und Öffentlichkeit*, p. 144 f.
5 Belfiore, Valentina, il Liber linteus di Zagabria: Testualità e contenuto. Biblioteca di Studi Etruschi 50 (Pisa, 2010). On the older Tabula Capuana see Woudhuizen, Fred, *The Etruscan Liturgical Calendar from Capua* (Amsterdam, 1996), and Cristofani, Mauro, *Tabula Capuana: Un calendario festivo di età arcaica* (Firenze, 1995).
6 *Inscriptiones Latinae liberae rei publicae* 589.
7 Ibid., 508.

NOTES

8 Suetonius, *Augustus* 59.
9 Laffi, Umberto, 'Le iscrizioni relative all'introduzione nel 9 a.c. del nuovo calendario della provincia d'Asia', *Studi Classici e Orientali* 16 (1967), pp. 5-98.
10 Rüpke, Jörg, 'Hemerologion', *Neuer Pauly* 5 (1998), pp. 342-3; Stern, Sacha, *Calendars in Antiquity: Empires, States, and Societies* (Oxford, 2012), 269.
11 See Rüpke: *Kalender und Öffentlichkeit*, pp. 133-6; Ruck, Brigitte, 'Die Fasten von Taormina', *Zeitschrift für Papyrologie und Epigraphik* 111 (1996), pp. 271-80.
12 *Inscriptiones Graecae (IG)* 14.429.
13 Fink, R. O., A. Hoey and W.F. Snyder, 'The Feriale Duranum', *Yale Classical Studies* 7 (1940), pp. 1-222.
14 Rüpke: *Roman Calendar*, pp. 157-160.
15 *Inscr. It.* 13.2, p. 52f.
16 Appendix to the *Constitutio de sacra liturgia* of the second Vatican council (*Conciliorum oecumenicorum decreta*, Bologna, 1973, p. 843).
17 *Inscr. It.* 13.2, p. 283 from AD 387.
18 Stoll, Oliver, *Zwischen Integration und Abgrenzung: Die Religion des Römischen Heeres im Nahen Osten. Studien zum Verhältnis von Armee und Zivilbevölkerung im römischen Syrien und den Nachbargebieten*. Mainzer Althistorische Studien 3 (St. Katharinen, 2001); Reeves, M. Barbara, *The Feriale Duranum, Roman Military Religion, and Dura-Europos: A Reassessment* (Buffalo, 2004).
19 *Inscr. It.* 13.2, p. 279.
20 *Inscr. It.* 13.2, p. 235.
21 Tertullian, *De idolatria* 10.3.
22 Cf. Saxer, Victor, *Morts, martyrs, reliques en Afrique chrétienne aux premiers siècles* (Paris, 1980).
23 *CIL* 1, p. 594 = *ILS* 6087.
24 Edition: González, Julián, 'The lex Irnitana: a new copy of the Flavian municipal law', *Journal of Roman Studies* 76 (1986), pp. 147-243; Crawford, Michael, *Roman Statues* (London, 1996), no. 24.
25 Rüpke, Jörg, 'Religion in lex Ursonensis', in Ando, Clifford and id. (eds), *Religion and Law in Classical and Christian Rome* (Stuttgart, 2006), pp. 34-46.
26 See Rüpke, Jörg, *Religion of the Romans* (Cambridge, 2007), pp. 197 f.
27 Suet. *Aug.* 92.2; see Rüpke: *Kalender und Öffentlichkeit*, pp. 563-87.
28 Cato, *De agricultura* 143.
29 See Gellius 2.24.14; Martial 4.66.3.
30 See Herz: *Untersuchungen zum Festkalender der römischen Kaiserzeit* (Diss. Main 1975), p. 50, for private dedications in Egypt made by persons of Roman origin.
31 Stern, Henri, *Le calendrier de 354: Étude sur son texte et ses illustrations* (Paris, 1953); Salzman, Michèle Renée, *On Roman time: The codex-calendar of 354 and the rhythms of urban life in Late Antiquity* (Berkeley, 1990).
32 Cf. Rüpke: *Roman Calendar*, pp.140-5.

33 The title given in Tristia 2.549 f. and elsewhere is just a synonym for *de fastis* within the genre of commentary: Rüpke, Jörg, 'Ovids Kalenderkommentar: Zur Gattung der Libri fastorum', *Antike und Abendland* 40 (1994), pp. 125–36.
34 Ovid, *Fasti* 1.295.
35 The basic facts are given in Grotefend, Hermann, *Taschenbuch der Zeitrechnung des deutschen Mittelalters und der Neuzeit*, 13th ed. (Hannover, 1991).
36 See e.g. Masel, Katharina, *Kalender und Volksaufklärung in Bayern: Zur Entwicklung des Kalenderwesens 1750 bis 1830* (St. Ottilien, 1997), p. 64 ff.
37 Coyne, George V. and Michael A. Hoskin (eds), *Gregorian Reform of the Calendar: Proceedings of the Vatican Conference to Commemorate its 400th Anniversary, 1582–1982* (Città del Vaticano, 1983).
38 Tractates abound in the seventeenth century. See for instance Ellrod, Jacob, *Calendarium Praeter Julianum & Gregorianum Tertium sive Intermedium, das ist: Mittel-Calender, in welchem einige, jedoch unvergreiffliche Mittel vorgeschlagen werdne, wie nach inhalt des juengst Anno 1654 zu Regensburg publicirten Reichs-Abschieds die beeden wieder einander lauffende Alt und Neue Calender, naeher zusammen gebracht, verbessert und hoffentlich gar vereinigt werden koennen, in 59 Fragen* (Hof, 1659), p. 17.
39 Cf. Kaufmann, Thomas, 'Römisches und evangelisches Jubeljahr 1600: Konfessionskulturelle Deutungsalternativen der Zeit im Jahrhundert der Reformation', in C. Bochinger and J. Frey (eds), *Millennium: Deutungen zum christlichen Mythos der Jahrtausendwende* (Gütersloh, 1999), pp. 73–136.
40 Cf. Osiander, Lucas, *Bedencken Ob der newe Päpstische Kalender ein Notturfft bey der Christenheit seie / unnd wie trewlich diser Papst Gregorius XIII. die Sachen darmit meine...* (Tübingen, 1583).
41 See the decrete of referral *Super indice librorum, catechismo, breviario et missali* of the final day of the council (*Conciliorum oecumenicorum decreta*, Bologna, 1973, p. 797), 4 December, 1563.
42 Ibid., pp. 50f.; *Constitutio De sacra liturgia* 111: *Ne festa sanctorum festis ipsa mysteria salutis recolentibus praevaleant, plura ex his particularis cuique ecclesiae vel nationi vel religiosae familiae relinquantur celebranda, iis tantum ad ecclesiam universam extensis, quae sanctos memorant momentum universale revera prae se ferentes* (*Conciliorum oecumenicorum decreta*, Bologna, 1973, p. 839).
43 Rüpke: *Roman Calendar*, pp. 95–105.
44 The lasting interest is demonstrated by improved editions during the second half of the sixteenth century: *Fastorum libri XII. A mendis permultis, quibus hactenus scatebant, repurgati* (Köln, 1561 (1562)); *Opera 2* (Antwerpen, 1576); see Trümpy, Hans, *Die Fasti des Baptista Mantuanus von 1516 als volkskundliche Quelle* (Nieuwkoop, 1979).
45 Kühne, Heinrich, *Das Calendarium Historicum des Paul Eber* (Wittenberg, 1971), pp. 54–65. The programme, as formulated on p. 20 ff. of the edition of 1551, names the 'birthdays of the most important men, pagan festivals, risings of the stars and events of private individuals'.
46 Eber, Paul, *Calendarium historicum, Das ist Ein allgemein Calender / in*

NOTES

welcem uff ein jeden tag durchs gantze Jar / eine namhaffte Geschicht oder Historien / aus heiliger Schrifft und sonsten / so sich voriger oder neulicher zeit hin und wider in der Welt zugetragen /kürtzlich vermeldet und gezeigt wird: Vor XXX Jaren in das latein zusammen getragen / von dem Ehrwirdigen Herrn Paulo Ebero der heiligen Schrifft D., Itzt aber von seinen Sönen / dem gemeinen Vaterland zum besten verdeutschet / und mit vielen newen Historien vermehret worden (Wittenberg, 1582). The text concentrates on the history of the recent centuries, antiquity is almost disregarded.

47 See Rüpke: *Kalender und Öffentlichkeit*, pp. 151–60 on the *Fasti* of Polemius Silvius of AD 448/9; and Dulabahn, Elizabeth Snowden, *Studies on the 'Laterculus' of Polemius Silvius* (Bryn Mawr, 1987).

48 Palazzo, Eric, *A History of Liturgical Books from the Beginning to the Thirtheenth Century* (Collegeville/Minnesota, 1998), p. 164.

49 Ibid., p. 23, following Jounel, Pierre, *Le culte des saints dans les basiliques du Latran et du Vatican au XIIe siècle* (Rome, 1977). The differentiation of the genres is analysed by Hennig, John, 'Kalendar und Martyrologium als Literaturformen', *Archiv für Liturgiewissenschaft* 7 (1961), pp. 1–44.

50 Sührig, Hartmut, *Die Entwicklung der niedersächsischen Kalender im 17. Jahrhundert* (Frankfurt a. M., 1979); Rohner, Ludwig, *Kalendergeschichte und Kalender* (Wiesbaden, 1978).

51 Cf. Zerubavel, Eviatar, 'The French republican calendar: a case study in the sociology of time', *American Sociological Review* 42 (1977), pp. 868–77.

Chapter VI

1 Rüpke, Jörg, 'Dedications accompanied by inscriptions in the Roman Empire: Functions, intentions, modes of communication', in J. Bodel and M. Kajava (eds), *Dediche sacre nel mono greco-romano: Diffusione, funzioni, tipologie/Religious Dedications in the Greco-Roman World: Distribution, Typology, Use*, Acta Instituti Romani Finlandiae 35 (Roma, 2009), pp. 31–41, Stavrianopoulou, Eftychia, *Ritual and communication in the Graeco-Roman world*, Kernos: Supplément 16 (Liège, 2006); for the modern age: Tyrell, Hartmann, Krech, Volkhard and Knoblauch, Hubert (ed.), *Religion als Kommunikation*, Religion in der Gesellschaft 4 (Würzburg, 1998); Malik, Jamal, Rüpke, Jörg and Wobbe, Theresa, *Religion und Medien. Vom Kultbild zum Internetritual*, Vorlesungen des Interdisziplinären Forums Religion der Universität Erfurt; Bd. 4 (Münster, 2007); Simon, Udou.a. (ed.), *Reflexivity, Media, and Visuality*, Ritual Dynamics and the Science of Ritual 4 (Wiesbaden, 2010).

2 Cf. Taylor, Mark C., *About Religion: Economies of Faith in Virtual Culture* (Chicago, 1999).

3 Gellius 4.9.5 f.; 5.17.1; Macrobius, *Saturnalia* 1.16.27. This chapter is based on my arguments in *Kalender und Öffentlichkeit: Die Geschichte der Repräsentation und religiösen Qualifikation von Zeit in Rom*.

Religionsgeschichtliche Versuche und Vorarbeiten 40 (Berlin, 1995), in particular pp. 563-592.
4 Fest. 348.22-30 L; Gell. 4.9.5-6.
5 Paul. Fest. 253.12-14 L; Macr. *Sat.* 1.16.15-18. On the disregard of such norms in certain military situations, see below and Goodman, M.D. and Holladay, A.J., 'Religious scruples in ancient warfare', *Classical Quarterly* 36 (1986), pp. 151-71. On the calendrical regulation of Greek military campaigns, see Pritchett, W. Kendrick, *The Greek State at War* (Berkeley, 1971), esp. pp. 116-26; 179, 185-6.
6 Cf. Macr. *Sat.* 1.16.24 and 28.
7 Macr. *Sat.* 1.16.21.
8 Cf. Varro in Macr. *Sat.* 1.16.18 and Fest. 144.14-146.2 L. See Degrassi, Attilio, *Inscriptiones Italiae* 13.2 (Roma, 1963), p. 361, and, with detailed references, Wissowa, Georg, *Religion und Kultus der Römer* (München, 1912, repr. 1971), p. 144, on the danger potential 235, for which see Ov. *fast.* 5.485-490.
9 Macr. *Sat.* 1.15.21.
10 Fest. 296.12-14 L.
11 Ov. *fast.* 3.393-8; first half of June: 6.225-234.
12 *Inscr. It.* 13.2.189 (F. Amit.); *Inscr. It.* 13.2.15 (F. Ant. mai.); see also Lucan. 7.409 and Ovid. *rem.* 219 f. Verrius Flaccus gives much detail in Gell. 5.17.2; Livy 6.1.1-2 and Macr. *Sat.* 1.16.21-24.
13 Ov. *fast.* 2.193-6; see Harries, Byron, 'Ovid and the Fabii: Fasti 2.193-474', *Classical Quarterly* 41 (1991), pp. 150-68.
14 *Inscr. It.* 13.2.208 (F. Ant. min.). Cf. Livy 6.1.11 f. and Plutarch, *Camillus* 19.1; Macr. *Sat.* 1.16.23.
15 Ov. *fast.* 6.563-8.
16 Horatius, *Carmina* 4.14.34-38; *Inscr. It.* 13.2.191 (F. Amit. 2. 8.); Plutarch, *Caesar* 56 (Liberalia).
17 Livy 9.38.15-16. The dates in question are 477, 387, 321, and - the event cited - 310 BC.
18 Tacitus, *Annales* 15.41.2.
19 For example, the defeat in the battle of Lake Trasimene, dated 22 June (Ov. *fast.* 6.763-8), and the battle of Cannae, dated 2 August (Gell. 5.17.5). See also Grafton, Anthony T. and Noel M. Swerdlow, 'Calendar dates and ominous days in ancient historiography', *Journal of the Warburg and Courtauld Institutes* 51 (1988), pp. 14-42.
20 Cf. Rosenstein, Nathan, *Imperatores victi: Military Defeat and Aristocratic Competition in the Middle and Late Republic* (Berkeley, 1990).
21 Cf. Livy 6.1.11 f. and Gell. 5.17.1 f. Any further unspecific cases prove that the ancient writers fully endorsed the theologumenon of empiric fact; their uncertainty shows that they cannot reconcile it with historical argument. Cf. Plutarch's critique in *Quaestiones Romanae* 25.
22 Varro *ling.* 6.29.
23 Macr. *Sat.* 1.16.24 f.; Gell. 4.6.10; cf. Bauman, Richard A., *Lawyers in Roman*

NOTES

Republican Politics: A Study of the Roman Jurists in their Political Setting, 316–82 BC (München, 1983), p. 77 on this passage.

24 On the strategy and function of these exemplary narratives, cf. Rüpke, Jörg, 'You shall not kill – hierarchies of norms in ancient Rome', *Numen* 39 (1992), pp. 58–79, see here p. 71 f.

25 Thus Plut. *q. R.* 25.

26 Also notable for the Fasti triumphales, which – in 459, 223, 175, 93, 34, 27, and 21 BC – note triumphs *a. d. quartum nonas* or *idus*, but never a triumph on the *dies ater*.

27 Cf. Lydus, *De mensibus* 4.65 for 2 April; ibid. 4.168, for 2 and 6 November. On the 6th the colossus is crowned (*Inscr. It.* 13.2.249, F. Fil.), on 16 October the slaves (*vernae*) celebrate in Antium (cf. p. 144).

28 Cf. the entries in the Fasti Viae dei Serpenti and Antiates ministrorum, which note funerary celebrations (*inferiae*) for Drusus for 14 September, the day after the ides (*Inscr. It.* 13.2.215; 209).

29 Plutarch *q. R.* 25 (*mor.* 269e) notes these kinds of conclusions by analogy as typical for *deisidaimonia*.

30 Gell. 5.17.3–5; likewise Macr. *Sat.* 1.16.26.

31 Varro, *ling.* 6.14; Fest. 304.33–306.8 L; cf. p. 228.

32 Wackernagel, Jacob, *Vorlesungen über Syntax mit besonderer Berücksichtigung von Griechisch, Lateinisch und Deutsch. Zweite Reihe* (Basel, 1924). Cautious consent in Ernout, Alfred and Meillet, Antoine, *Dictionnaire étymologique de la langue latine: Histoire des mots* (Paris, 1959), 1.53.

33 With regard to the large amount of material compiled by Wackernagel: *Vorlesungen über Syntax*.

34 Cf. the material compiled by Tavenner, Eugene, 'The Roman farmer and the moon', *Transactions and Proceedings of the American Philological Association* 49 (1918), pp. 67–82. The agrarian authors as primary sources are to be supplemented by Pliny's *Naturalis historia* and Virgil's *Georgicon libir*.

35 The material presented in Radke, Gerhard, *Die Bedeutung der weißen und der schwarzen Farbe in Kult und Brauch der Griechen und Römer* (Jena, 1936), esp. p. 65. More generally Berlin, Brent and Paul Kay, *Basic Color Terms: Their Universality and Evolution* (Berkeley, 1969).

36 Radke: *Die Bedeutung der weißen und der schwarzen Farbe*, p. 65. The well-known passage in Petron cited above (30.4); the phrase *lapillis melioribus* (Mart. 9.25.5; Cens. 2.1) is also to be seen in connection.

37 Cf. Afranius, *Comediae* 163: *Septembris heri kalendae, hocedie ater dies*. Virgil, *Aenis* 6.429; Propertius 2.11.4; Seneca, *Dialogi* 7.25.3..

38 Macr. *Sat.* 1.16.21. Information regarding the mentioned euphemism harks back to Suetonius: Suet. *frg.* p. 155.3 f. = Isidorus, *De natura rerum* 1.4.

39 Suet. *Aug.* 92.2.

40 In general, Johnston, Sarah Iles and Peter T. Struck (eds), *Mantikê: Studies in Ancient Divination*. Religions in the Graeco-Roman World 155 (Leiden, 2005); Rüpke, Jörg, 'Divination romaine et rationalité grecque dans la Rome du

deuxième siècle av.n.è.', in Stella Georgoudi, Renée Koch-Piettre, Francis Schmidt (eds), *Signes, rites et destin dans les sociétés de la Méditerranée ancienne*. Religions in the Graeco-Roman World 174, Leiden: Brill, 2012, 479–500; id. et al., 'Divination romaine I. Einleitung A. B. E. II. Öffentliche Divination in Rom A. B. D. E.', *Thesaurus cultus et rituum antiquorum 3*. Los Angeles: Paul Getty Museum, 2005, 79–104.

41 See for example Curry, Patrick, *Prophecy and Power: Astrology in Early Modern Period* (Princeton, 1984); Wayman, Alex, 'The human body as microcosm in India, Greek cosmology, and sixteenth-century Europe', *History of Religions* 22 (1982), pp. 172–190; Campion, Nicholas and ebrary Inc, *History of Western Astrology: Volume II: The Medieval and Modern Worlds* (London and New York, 2009).

42 Cf. Baecker, Dirk, *Womit handeln Banken? Eine Untersuchung zur Risikoverarbeitung in der Wirtschaft* (Frankfurt a. M., 1991), who does not, however, pay adequate attention to the time factor.

43 Compare topics mentioned on curse tablets compiled by Gager, John G. (ed.), *Curse Tablets and Binding Spells from the Ancient World* (New York, 1992); cf. also Iuv. 6.575.

44 Bouché-Leclercq, A., *Histoire de la divination dans l'antiquité 1: Introduction, divination hellénique* (Paris, 1879), —, *Histoire de la divination dans l'antiquité 2: Les sacerdoces divinatoires* (Paris, 1880), —, *Histoire de la divination dans l'antiquité 3: Oracles de Dieux* (Paris, 1880), —, *Histoire de la divination dans l'antiquité 4: Divination italique* (Paris, 1882) still remains the primary material collection. On the history of astrology in Rome comprehensively: Cramer, Fredrick H., *Astrology in Roman Law and Politics* (Philadelphia, 1954); Schmid, Alfred, *Augustus und die Macht der Sterne: Antike Astrologie und die Etablierung der Monarchie in Rom* (Köln, 2005).

45 Cic. *div.* 1.28.

46 Cf. Elias, Norbert, *Über die Zeit: Arbeiten zur Wissenssoziologie 2* (Frankfurt a. M., 1988), p. 18 as well as the mention of discontinuity of self coercion (*passim*).

47 Leitz, Christian, 'Die Nacht des Kindes in seinem Nest in Dendara', *Zeitschrift für ägyptologische Studien* 120 (1993), pp. 136–65 (Egypt); Labat, René, *Hémérologies et ménologies d'Assur* (Paris, 1939), pp. 13–28; Miles, Suzanna W., 'An analysis of modern middle American calendars: a study in conservation', in S. Tax (ed.), *Acculturation in the Americas* (New York, 1967), pp. 273–84, Graulich, Michel, 'The metaphor of the day in ancient Mexican myth and ritual', *Current Anthropology* 22 (1981), pp. 45–60; Whittaker, Gordon, *Calendar and Script in Protohistorical China and Mesoamerica: A Comparative Study of Day Names and their Signs* (Bonn, 1991).

48 Eriksson, Sven, *Wochentagsgötter, Mond und Tierkreis: Laienastrologie in der römischen Kaiserzeit* (Stockholm, 1956), p. 13 f.

49 Rochberg, Francesca, *The Heavenly Writing: Divination, Horoscopy, and Astronomy in Mesopotamian Culture* (Cambridge [u.a.], 2004), —, '"If P, then Q": Form and reasoning in Babylonian divination', in A. Annus (ed.), *Divination*

NOTES

and Interpretation of Signs in the Ancient World, Oriental institute seminars 6 (Chicago, 2010), pp. 19–27.

50 Ventris, Michael and John Chadwick, *Documents in Mycenaean Greek: Three Hundred Selected Tablets from Knossos, Pylos and Mycenae with Commentary and Vocabulary* (Cambridge, 1956), p. 311 (no. 207 = V280). See also no. 172 = KN02; Mikalson, Jon D., *The Sacred and Civil Calendar of the Athenian Year* (Princeton, 1975).

51 Langdon, Stephen, *Babylonian Menologies and the Semitic Calendars* (London, 1935), p. 156; Leitz, Nacht des Kindes.

52 Tannenbaum, Nicola, 'Shan calendrics and the nature of Shan religion', *Anthropos* 79 (1984), pp. 505–15.

53 Cf. Schipper, Kristofer and Wang, Hsiu-huei, 'Progressive and regressive time cycles in Taoist ritual', in J.T. Fraser, N. Lawrence and F.C. Haber (eds), *Time, Science, and Society in China and the West* (Amherst, MA., 1986), pp. 185–205, and more detailed Whittaker: *Calendar and Script*, pp. 5–146.

54 Cf. Strobel, August, 'Weltenjahr, große Konjunktion und Messiasstern', *Aufstieg und Niedergang der römischen Welt* II.20.2 (1987), pp. 988–1187 and Campion, Nicholas, *The Great Year: Astrology, Millenarianism and History in the Western Tradition* (London, 1994) for occidental cultures; or Whittaker *Calendar and Script*, pp. 147–9 for the combination of a 260-day year cycle in combination with the solar year of the Maya.

55 Ancient epigraphic and literary horoscopes in Neugebauer, Otto and Henry B. van Hoesen, *Greek Horoscopes* (Philadelphia, 1959); Jong, I. de and K.A. Worp, 'A Greek Horoscope From 373 A. D.', *ZPE 106* (1995), pp. 235–240; Schmidt, *Augustus*.

56 Cf. Huizinga, Johan, *Homo Ludens: Vom Ursprung der Kultur im Spiel* (Reinbek, 1956).

57 The Fasti Amiterni note 15 and 19 July, both *NP*-days (i.e. *feriae*) as *merk(atus)* (*Inscr. It.* 13.2.189).

58 Dio 60.24,7.

59 Macr. *Sat.* 1.13.16–19.

60 Dio 40.47.1.

61 See p. 456 ff.

62 Agnes Kirsopp Michels, *The Calendar of the Roman Republic*, (Princeton, 1967) p. 167.

63 See above and Suet. *Aug.* 92.2.

64 Dio 48.33.4. As a comparison with Macrobius shows, Cassius Dio's account that a day was left out in later times is most likely to have been a construct of the author (or an immediate source) with which he attempted to salvage the Julian year, rather than any actual practice in 41/40 BC.

65 Unger, Georg Friedrich, 'Nundinalfragen', *Jahrbücher für classische Philologie* 41 (1895), pp. 495–520.

66 See Rüpke, *Kalender*, p. 382 f.

67 Cf. P.M. Duval, Paul-Marie, 'Les dieux de la semaine', *Gallia* 11 (1953), pp.

282–93. The strength of the reception is proportional to the degree of Romanization. For Africa, cf. Tert. *nat.* 1.13; *idol.* 10.
68 See for example Juvenal, 6.569–576; Ammianus Marcellinus 28.4.24 (AD 369 ce). The moon as sign giver is clearly articulated here. The different daily qualities of the ancient planetary week are illustrated by the depiction of days in the Chronograph of 356 (images in Salzman, Michèle Renée, *On Roman Time: The Codex-Calendar of 354 and the Rhythms of Urban Life in Late Antiquity* (Berkeley, 1990), figs 8–12). On modern actual social differentiation of daily qualities (weekdays, weekends), see Zerubavel, Eviatar, *The Seven Day Circle: The History and Meaning of the Week* (Chicago, 1985), esp. pp. 107–29; Sorokin, Pitrim Alexandrowitsch, *Sociocultural Causality, Space, Time: A Study of Referential Principles of Sociology and Social Science* (New York, 1964), p. 190 f.; historically: Schreiber, Georg, *Die Wochentage im Erlebnis der Ostkirche und des christlichen Abendlandes* (Köln, 1959).
69 *Inscr. It.* 13.2.305: Index nundinarius Pompeianus. See also *CIL* 4.5202 = *NS* 1879.44 und *CIL* 4.6779 = *NS* 1901.330.
70 Cf. Maass, Ernst, *Die Tagesgötter in Rom und den Provinzen: aus der Kultur des Niederganges der antiken Welt* (Berlin, 1902), pp. 1–153.
71 The structure of simple lists of 30 moon days to be seen in two graffiti, the Index nundinarius Pompeianus (*Inscr. It.* 13.2.305) and the Index nundinarius from Dura Europos (Snyder, Walter F., 'Quinto nundinas Pompeis', *Journal of Roman Studies* 26 (1936), pp. 12–18, im. 2), the Parapegma Musei Neapolitani (*Inscr. It.* 13.2.307 = *CIL* 10.1605), and the only fragmentally extant inscription from Veleiae (*Inscr. It.* 13.2.313) are similar. More intricate designs are the Index nuninarius Latinus (*Inscr. It.* 13.2.301), and the Parapegma urbanum thermarum Traiani (*Inscr. It.* 13.2.309). On the combination of moon and planets see Eriksson, *Wochentagsgötter, Mond und Tierkreis*, p. 37; on the Lunaria see also Wistrand, Erik, *Lunariastudien* (Göteborg, 1942).
72 On the technique, cf. Eriksson: *Wochentagsgötter, Mond und Tierkreis*, pp. 22–7. The tradition of the parapegmata in Lehoux, Daryn, *Astronomy, Weather, and Calendars in the Ancient World: Parapegmata and Related Texts in Classical and Near-Eastern Societies* (Cambridge, 2007) following Rehm, Albert, *Parapegmastudien: mit einem Anhang Euktemon und das Buch De signis* (München, 1941).
73 Cf. Eriksson: *Wochentagsgötter, Mond und Tierkreis*, pp. 17–37.
74 An Egyptian sundial dating to the first half of the sixth century also shows the seven planetary gods (MacCoull, Leslie S.B., 'Philoponus and the London sundial: some calendrical aspects of the De opificio mundi', *Byzantinische Zeitschrift* 82 (1989), pp. 19–21, p. 19 f.).
75 Cf. M.D. Goodman, A.J. Holladay: 'Religious scruples in ancient warfare', *CQ* 36 (12986), pp. 151–171, here pp. 160–2.

NOTES

Chapter VII

1. McGuire, Meredith, *Lived Religion* (Chicago, 2008).
2. Certeau, Michel de, *Arts de faire* (Paris, 2007).
3. See for example D'Ambra, Eve, 'A Myth for a Smith: A Meleager Sarcophagus from a Tomb in Ostia', *AJA 92* (1988), pp. 85–99, for the study of a sarcophagus.
4. For the analysis of funerary practices of the Ancient Near East Porter, see for example Porter, Anne, 'Evocative topography: experience, time and politics in a landscape of death', in *Sepolti tra i Vivi – Buried among the Living: Atti del Convegno Internazionale* (Roma, 2008), pp. 195–214.
5. Ammerman, Nancy Tatom, *Everyday Religion: Observing Modern Religious Lives* (Oxford [u.a.], 2007).
6. For the later period see Rebillard, Eric, *The Care of the Dead in Late Antiquity* (Ithaca, 2009).
7. The following sections are an enlarged version of Rüpke, Jörg, *Der Tod als Ende der Sterblichkeit: Cultus – (Im)mortalitas: Zur Religion und Kultur – Von den biologischen Grundlagen bis zu Jenseitsvorstellungen* (Rahden/Westf., 2012). I am grateful to Elisabeth Begemann for the translation of that paper.
8. See Feldmann, Klaus and Werner Fuchs-Heinritz (eds), *Der Tod ist ein Problem der Lebenden: Beiträge zur Soziologie des Todes* (Frankfurt a. M., 1995).
9. An overview in Bremer, J. M., Th P. Hout and R. Peters (eds), *Hidden Futures: Death and Immortality in Ancient Egypt, Anatolia, the Classical, Biblical and Arabic-Islamic World* (Amsterdam, 1994); Bremmer, Jan N., 'The soul, death and the afterlife in early and classical Greece', in J.M. Bremer, T.P. Hout and R. Peters (eds), *Hidden Futures: Death and Immortality in Ancient Egypt, Anatolia, the Classical, Biblical and Arabic-Islamic World* (Amsterdam, 1994), pp. 91–106; Edwards, Catharine, *Death in Ancient Rome* (New Haven and London, 2007); Fine, Steven, 'Death, Burial, and Afterlife', in *The Oxford Handbook of Jewish Daily Life in Roman Palestine* (Oxford, 2010), pp. 440–63; Garland, Robert S., *The Greek Way of Death* (Ithaca, NY, 1985); Morris, Ian, *Death-Ritual and Social Structure in Classical Antiquity* (Cambridge, 1992); Rife, Joseph L, 'Toynbee, Death and Burial in the Roman World', *BMCR 1997* (1997), pp. 1–21; Samellas, Antigone, *Death in the Eastern Mediterranean (50–600 A.D.) The Christianization of the East: An Interpretation*, Studien und Texte zu Antike und Christentum 12 (Tübingen, 2002). For the modern period see Cannadine, David, 'War and death, grief and mourning in modern Britain', in J. Whaley (ed.), *Mirrors of Mortality: Studies in the Social History of Death* (London, 1981), pp. 187–242; Douglas, J. Davies, *Death, Ritual and Belief: The Rhetoric of Funerary Rites* (London, 1997); Humphreys, S. C., *The Family, Women and Death: Comparative Studies* (London, 1982); Segal, Alan F., *Life After Death: A History of the Afterlife in the Religions of the West* (New York [u.a.], 2004); Whaley, Joachim (ed.), *Mirrors of Mortality: Studies in the Social History of Death*, Europa social history of human experience 3 (London, 1981).

10 Gallone, Anna, 'Sepolti tra le mura della prima Roma: Il caso delle tombe sulla pendice Palatina', in *Sepolti tra i Vivi – Buried among the Living: Atti del Convegno Internazionale* (Roma, 2008), pp. 653–66, espec. 663 referring to Plut. *Pobl.* 23.

11 On the term, see Schrumpf, Stefan, *Bestattung und Bestattungswesen im Römischen Reich: Ablauf, soziale Dimension und ökonomische Bedeutung der Totenfürsorge im lateinischen Westen* (Bonn, 2006), p. 78 n. 210.

12 Thus Johanson, Christopher, 'A Walk with the Dead', in *A Companion to Families in the Greek and Roman Worlds* (Chicester, 2011), pp. 408–30, 421 following Keith Hopkins.

13 See Rawson, Beryl, 'The express route to hades', in P. McKechnie (ed.), *Thinking like a Lawyer: Essays on Legal History and General History for John Crook on his Eightieth Birthday*, Mnemosyne Suppl. 231 (Leiden, 2002), pp. 271–88.

14 See Rüpke, Jörg, *Religion of the Romans* (Cambridge, 2007), p. 232; *Année Epigraphique* 1971, 88, col. II; Hinard, François (ed.), *La mort, les morts et l'au-delà dans le monde romain Actes du colloque de Caen 20-22 novembre 1985* (Caen, 1987). The text now *Libitina e dintorni: Libitina e luci sepolcrali; le leges libitinariae campane; Iura sepulcrorum; vecchie e nuove iscrizioni; atti dell'XI Rencontre Franco-Italienne sur l'Epigraphie*, Libitina 3 (Roma, 2004), pp. 47–51.

15 Livy 40.19.3; Horatius, *Epistulae* 1.7.6–7; Seneca, *De beneficiis* 6.38.4.

16 See the exemplary study of Graham, Emma-Jayne, 'Becoming persons, becoming ancestors: Personhood, memory and the corpse in Roman rituals of social remembrance', *Archaeological Dialogues* 16 (2009), pp. 51–74 on the senator M. Nonius Balbus.

17 Seneca, *Dialogi* 4.19.1.

18 Mielsch, Harald, *Überlegungen zum Wandel der Bestattungsformen in der römischen Kaiserzeit* (Paderborn, 2009), followed (without quoting him) by Davies, Glenys, 'Before Sarcophagi', in *Life, Death and Representation: Some New Work on Roman Sarcophagi*, Millennium-Studien 29 (Berlin, 2011), pp. 21–54, 47. 50f.

19 See Newby, Zahra, 'In the guise of gods and heroes', in *Life, Death and Representation: Some New Work on Roman Sarcophagi*, Millennium-Studien 29 (Berlin, 2011), pp. 189–228.

20 Nielsen, Marjatta, 'United in death: the changing image of Etruscan couples', in *Gender Identities in Italy in the first Millennium BC* (Oxford, 2009), pp. 79–95.

21 Graf, Fritz, 'Victimology: or, how to deal with untimely death', in *Women and Gender in Ancient Religions: Interdisciplinary Approaches* (Tübingen, 2010), pp. 227–40.

22 Davies, Glenys, 'Before Sarcophagi', in *Life, Death and Representation: Some New Work on Roman Sarcophagi*, Millennium-Studien 29 (Berlin, 2011), pp. 21–54.

23 As formulated by Jan Willem Tellegen at a conference in Tilburg in December 2008.

NOTES

24 See Tsouna, Voula, *The Ethics of Philodemus* (Oxford, 2007), 261 f. on the importance accorded by Philodemus to wills in fighting the fear of death.
25 Servius, *In Aeneidem* 12.603.
26 Tac. *ann.* 3.1–5; Versnel 1980.
27 Meuli, Karl, *Gesammelte Schriften* (Basel, 1975).
28 On the following see Schrumpf, *Bestattung*, 2006, who reconstructs burial procedures by mainly following literary sources.
29 Ibid., 172; Varro fr. 105 ff. Riposati.
30 *XIItab* 10.3; Cic. *leg.* 2.59.
31 Dyck, Andrew R., *A Commentary on Cicero, De legibus* (Ann Arbor, 2004), *ad loc.*
32 Aug. *CD.* 6.9 = fr. 162 Cardauns.
33 Varro, *De vita populi Romani* fr. 111.
34 Kierdorf, Wilhelm, *Laudatio funebris: Interpretationen und Untersuchungen zur Entwicklung der römischen Leichenrede,* Beiträge zur Klassischen Philologie 106 (Meisenheim a. Glan, 1980); dating: Rüpke, Jörg, *Religion in Republican Rome: Rationalization and Ritual Change* (Philadelphia, 2012).
35 Varro, fr. 109 Riposati; Serv. *Aen.* 12.142–3.
36 For Rome, see Grossi, Maria Cristina; Mellace, Valeria Silvia, 'Roma, via Portuense: la necropoli di Vigna Pia', in A. u. a. H. Faber (ed.), *Körpergräber des 1.-3. Jahrhunderts in der römischen Welt,* Schriften des Archäologischen Museums Frankfurt 21 (Frankfurt a. M., 2007), pp. 185–200; for the provinces further papers in Faber, Andrea *et al.* (eds), *Körpergräber des 1.-3. Jahrhunderts in der römischen Welt – internationales Kolloquium Frankfurt am Main 19.–20. November 2004* Schriften des Archäologischen Museum Frankfurt, Bd. 21 (Frankfurt am Main, 2007) and Scheid, John (ed.), *Pour une archéologie du rite: nouvelles perspectives de l'archéologie funéraire* (Rome, 2008).
37 Concerning the sacrifice, see Fest. 296.37-298.4L.
38 Cic. *leg.* 2.57.
39 Ceres: Gell. 4.6, Fest. 242,11-18L; Scheid, *Archéologie du rite,* p. 138.
40 Bodel, John, 'The Organization of the funerary trade at Puteoli and Cumae', in *Libitina e dintorni : Libitina e luci sepolcrali; le leges libitinariae campane; Iura sepulcrorum; vecchie e nuove iscrizioni; atti dell'XI Rencontre Franco-Italienne sur l'Epigraphie,* Libitina 3 (Roma, 2004), pp. 147–72, espec. 157. For the following Cic. *leg.* 2.60 with the commentary of Dyck.
41 Varro, fr. 111 Riposati; Tac. *ann.* 3.2.2. Bones: Buccellato, Anna; Catalano, Paola; Musco, Stefano, 'Alcuni aspetti rituali evidenziati nel corso dello scavo della necropoli Collatina (Roma)', in J. Scheid (ed.), *Pour une archéologie du rite: nouvelles perspectives de l'archéologie funéraire,* Collection de l'École française de Rome 407 (Rome, 2008), pp. 59–88, here p. 86.
42 Picuti, Maria Romana, 'Il contributo dell'epigrafia latina allo scavo delle necropoli antiche', in ibid., pp. 43–58, here p. 57.
43 Bel, Valérie, 'Evolution des pratiques funéraires à Nîmes entre le IIe siècle av. J.-C. et le IIIe siècle ap. J.-C.', in J. Rüpke and J. Scheid (eds), *Bestattungsrituale und Totenkult in der römischen Kaiserzeit/Rites funéraires et culte des morts*

aux temps impériales Potsdamer altertumswissenschaftliche Beiträge 27 (Stuttgart, 2010), pp. 93–112.

44 Martin-Kilcher, Stefanie, 'Römische Gräber: Spiegel der Bestattungs – und Grabsitten', in J. Scheid (ed.), *Pour une archéologie du rite: nouvelles perspectives de l'archéologie funéraire*, Collection de l'École francaise de Rome 407 (Rome, 2008), pp. 9–27, here p. 19; see also Witteyer, Marion, 'Spurensuche: mikrotopografische Befundbeobachtungen an Gräbern aus Mainz und Umgebung', ibid.), pp. 189.

45 Martin-Kilcher: 'Römische Gräber', 21.

46 Details in Braune, Sarah, *Convivium funebre: Gestaltung und Funktion römischer Grabtriklinien als Räume für sepulkrale Bankettfeiern*, Spudasmata 121 (Hildesheim, 2008).

47 Suetonius, *Divius Iulius* 12.2.

48 Verg. *Aen.* 3.64; cf. Cic. *leg.* 2.55. *Everriator:* Paul Fest. 68.9–13L.

49 Scheid, John, "Contraria facere': Renversements et déplacements dans les rites funéraires', *Annali dell'Istituto Universitario Orientale, Archeologia e storia antica* 6 (1984), pp. 117–39.

50 Ulpian, *Digestae* 11.7.1.

51 Borg, Barbara and Christian Witschel, 'Veränderungen im Repräsentationsverhalten der römischen Eliten während des 3. Jhs. n. Chr', in G. Alföldy and S. Panciera (eds), *Inschriftliche Denkmäler als Medien der Selbstdarstellung in der römischen Welt* (Stuttgart, 2001), pp. 47–120.

52 Zanker, Paul and Björn Ewald, *Living with Myths: The Imagery of the Roman Sarcophagi* (New York, 2012).

53 *Digestae* 11.7.6.1 and 11.7.2. esp. 7–9.

54 Ulp. *dig.* 11.8.4.

55 Thus Ov. *fast.* 5.419–446.

56 Cic. *Leg.* 2.22 – and I follow Andrew Dyck's reconstruction of the text.

57 Plin. *NH* 35.160.

58 For example, Graf, Fritz and Sarah Iles Johnston, *Ritual Texts for the Afterlife: Orpheus and the Bacchic Gold Tablets* (New York, 2007), no. 9.

59 Rebenich, Stefan, 'Garten, Gräber und Gedächtnis: Villenkultur und Bestattungspraxis in der römischen Kaiserzeit', in H. Börm, N. Ehrhardt and J. Wiesehöfer (eds), *Monumentum et instrumentum inscriptum: Beschriftete Objekte aus Kaiserzeit und Spätantike als historische Zeugnisse. Festschrift Peter Weiß zum 65. Geburtstag* (Stuttgart, 2008), pp. 187–201, 197; *CIL* 6.17992.

60 Petronius, *Satyricon* 71.5–12; Petersen, Lauren Hackworth, 'The baker, his tomb, his wife, and her breadbasket: the monument of Eurysaces in Rome', *The Art Bulletin* 85, 2 (2003), pp. 230–57.

61 Kolb, Anne and Joachim Fugmann, *Tod in Rom: Grabinschriften als Spiegel römischen Lebens* (Mainz, 2008), 122.

62 As interpreted by Petersen, 'Baker', pp. 245–7.

63 Kolb and Fugman: *Tod*, 123 f.

64 Neiske, Franz, 'Rotuli und andere frühe Quellen zum Totengedenken (bis ca.

NOTES

800)', in U. Ludwig, T. Schilp and D. Geuenich (eds), *Nomen et Fraternitas: Festschrift für Dieter Geuenich zum 65. Geburtstag*, Ergänzungsbände zum Reallexikon der Germanischen Altertumskunde 62 (Berlin 2008), pp. 203-20, 203. For the Jewish reception see summarily Fine, Steven, 'Death, burial, and afterlife', in *The Oxford Handbook of Jewish Daily Life in Roman Palestine* (Oxford, 2010), pp. 440-63, 456.
65 Petersen: 'Baker', p. 234.
66 Hesberg, Henner von, *Römische Grabbauten* (Darmstadt, 1992), Meadows, Andrew and Jonathan Williams, 'Moneta and the monuments: coinage and politics in republican Rome', *JRS 91* (2001), pp. 27-49.
67 See Rüpke, Jörg, *Religion in Republican Rome* (Philadelphia, 2012), pp. 62-81.
68 Stewart, Peter, *Statues in Roman Society: Representation and Response* (Oxford, 2003).
69 Cicero, *De re publica* 6.10.
70 Petersen: 'Baker', p. 251.
71 Rüpke, Jörg, 'Apokalyptische Salzberge: Zum sozialen Ort und zur literarischen Strategie des 'Hirten des Hermas'', *Archiv für Religiongeschichte 1* (1999), pp. 148-60.

INDEX

Acilius Glabrio, M'. 41
Actium 91
aedes Vestae 103
Aelius Aristides 33
Aemilius Lepidus, M. 40, 45
Aeneas 16, 131
aesthetics and religion 60
aetiology 98
afterlife 6, 135, 139
Alexander the Great 33
Allah 62
Allia 103
altar 128
ancestors 129
animus 131
Apollinaria (festival) 88
appropriation 119
ara 128
Arval Brethren (priesthood) 67, 91
astrology 9–10, 33, 98, 108–111, 117, 138
atheism 58
Atistia (wife of Eurysaces) 132–133
atomism 133
Augustus 68, 72, 85, 108, 111
Augustus pontifex maximus 73
augurs 9–11, 18
Aurelian 28
auspices 10–11, 109
Axial age 2, 23–24

Babylonia 110
Bacchanalia 8, 15
banquet 90
black days 102
bones, findings of 127
Breviarium Romanum 97
burial 121, 124–129, 138

Caecilius Metellus, L. 39
Caesar, Gaius Julius 49, 68, 91, 114, 120, 124
calendar 4, 15, 18–19, 41–43, 46, 48, 80, 91, 98, 109, 138 (*see also fasti*)

calendarium historicum 98
calendarium universale or *calendarium ecclesiae universae* 97
Catholic 95–97
ecclesiastical 99
festival 92, 94
Gregorian 80, 95–100, 110
Julian 5–6, 19, 80, 85, 87, 93–95, 99, 114
liturgical 97
local 94–95
lunisolar 85, 87
marble 91–93
Numaic 145[37]
Palestinian 87
pin 116
Protestant 96–97
Campania 81, 88, 92
Campus Martius 13
canonization 34–35
'carpenters procession' 54
Casa dei Vettii 54
catarchontomancy 109, 113
Catholic 62
Cato the Elder, M. Porcius 14, 49, 90
cella 60
cemetery 135–136
cena novemdialis 128
cenotaph 129, 135
Ceres 126
Chalcidium 128
Christianity 1, 5, 7, 27, 29, 135
Chronograph or Chronicle of 354 93, 116
church 2
Cicero, M. Tullius 7–8, 25–27, 50, 53, 55, 58–59, 61, 109, 120, 125–127, 130
Circus Maximus 13
Clemens Romanus 65–66, 76–77
Codex Theodosianus 27
coins 61, 69
collegium Capitolinorum 145[30]
collegium mercatorum 145[30]
Colosseum 70

RELIGION: ANTIQVITY AND ITS LEGACY

comitia 83
communication 4, 9, 20, 28, 33, 35, 55, 101, 118–119, 122–123, 128, 138
conclamatio 134
confessionalism 34, 100
consecration 126
consolation 130–131
Constitution's day 105
Cornelius Scipio Africanus, P. 60, 134
Coruncanius, Ti. 40
cosmic order 9
Cotta, C. Aurelius 55, 61
council of Constance 95
  of Nicaea 87, 95
  of Trent 95–96
cremation 121, 125–130
Cremera 103–104
cubiculum 135
cults 13–14, 26, 32, 52, 71
  ancestor 128–129
  imperial 71–72, 94
cultural accommodation 77
Cybele 61–62

day (status) 83, 102–103, 105–107, 111
Dea Dia 91–92
dea Nenia 125
death 6, 120–122, 135
decemviri sacris faciundis 18
dedication days 42
de-individualization 130, 137
deisidaimonia 57–58
deities, protective 54
deposition 127–128, 133
destruction of the temple (Jerusalem) 66
Diana 88
dies aegyptiaci 107
  Alliensis 104
  atri (black days) 102, 106–108, 112–113
  comitiales 102
  communes 107
  inominales 106, 113
  natales (birth days) 83, 106
  natales templorum 41–42, 44, 84
  postriduani 102, 104–106
  proeliares 102
  puri 102
  religiosi 102, 104
  vitiosus 102
Dio, Cassius 66, 112–115
Diocletian 28
disciplina 27–28
divi filius 91
divination 6, 8–9, 40, 108–110, 115–117
divinization 5, 128–130, 135

dominus et deus 76
Domitian 66–67, 69–72, 76
Domus Aurea 70
dramatic performances 16
Dura Europos 86, 88

Easter 87
Eber, Paul 98–99
Egypt 111
elite 8, 16, 20, 40
embalmment 122
Enlightenment 34
Ennius, Q. 16, 42–43, 46
entertainment 48
epic 16, 49
Epicureanism 55, 133
epigraphy 93
Epistle to the Hebrews 5, 63–64–65, 74–78
Epona 88
eponym 41
Epulo, C. Cestius 131
epulum 18
Equirria 12
Etruria 81, 92
Euhemerism 42
Eurysaces, M. Vergilius 32, 132–133
eusebeia 58
evocare deos 20
evocatio 16
Exodus 65, 75
exsequiae 125
extispicy 109

fabula praetexta 16
fas 83, 105
fasti 4, 19, 41–42, 44, 84, 86, 90–92, 101, 105, 116 (*see also* calendar)
  decemviral reform 107, 113
  Fasti antiates maìores 83, 91
  Fasti Guidizzolenses 81, 88
  Fasti Praenestini 84, 93
  Fasti Sabini 87
  Fasti Tauromenitani 81
  fasti triumphales 98
  fasti triumphales Barberiniani 12
  Fulvian *fasti* 43, 46
feriae 19, 83, 103, 106, 112
  denicales 128
Feriale Cumanum 88
festivals 84, 88, 90, 92
  imperial 89, 91
fides 27
Flaccus, Verrius 84, 93
Flamen Dialis 17–18, 69–70, 78, 103
Floralia 46

172

INDEX

Fortuna 54
Forum Transitorium 70
Friday the thirteenth 111
Fulvius Nobilior, M. 19, 40–41, 50
funeral 121–122
  cortege 121, 125
funestus (funesta) 128
funus acerbum 122

games 12–13, 46, 70, 72, 84
  gladiatorial 124, 128
genealogies 2, 22–23, 25, 47, 50–51
Genius 14
geomancy 9
Germanicus 124
Goltwurm, Caspar 99
grave monuments 32, 129–135
Gregory XIII 95
grief 124–130
  'violent' 124

hairesis 26
haruspices 9, 20, 40, 109
healing cults 13–14
Hellenistic empire 24
hemerai apophrades 110
hemerologia 85
Herodotus 36
historical knowledge 2
historiography 4, 35–40, 48, 51
history of religion 2, 22, 35
holocaust 121, 128
horoscope 111
horse races 12
house altar 15

iconography 7, 62, 115
identity 38–39, 49–50, 59, 90, 93, 99–100, 105, 135, 147[25]
Ides (in the calendar) 83, 90, 94, 106
idolatry 52–53, 62
Iesus Dei filius 67, 76
image 3, 40, 57, 67, 133
  divine (anthropomorphic) 4, 45, 52–55, 58–59, 61–62
imagination 4, 52
immortality 135
incineration 127–129
independence day 105
individuality 30–31, 33
individualization 2, 29, 33, 130, 132, 137, 147[25]
inhumation 121, 123, 126
inscriptions 39, 69–70, 86, 91
  funerary 39, 116, 121–122, 129–130, 133

intercalation 81, 85, 95–96, 112–115
interpretatio Romana 49
Islam 1
Islamic Salafism 78

Jerusalem 66
Jesuology 65, 67, 75–76
Judaism 1
Judas 50
Julian (emperor) 68
Jupiter 9, 55
  Capitoline 60

kairos 108
kalendae Ianuariae 15
kalends 83, 90, 94, 106

lamentation 125
Lares (household gods) 14, 58, 128
Latium 81, 92
laudatio funebris 39, 43, 125
Law of the Twelve Tables 120, 124–127
leges Aeliae et Fufiae 10
legislation 17, 28
Lemuria 103, 130
Lex Acilia 145[36]
  curiata de imperio 104
  Irnitana 89
  Libitinae Puteolana 124–126, 128
  municipii 89
  Ursonensis 89, 120
liber linteus 85
Liberty 58–59
Libitina 121
Licinius (emperor) 27
Licinius Lucullus, L. 45
list of bishops 98
  of consuls 41, 44, 92
  of magistrates 42, 86, 93, 98
  of martyrs 98
literature 17
litterae nundinales 81
Livius Andronicus 16
Livy (T. Livius) 40, 69, 104
locus religiosus 129
Lucus Libitinae 121
ludi 12–13, 46, 70, 72, 84 (*see also* games)
  Capitolini 12
Lunaria 116

Macrobius 93, 112–113, 115
mafurtium 124
magic 33
Mantuanus, Iohannes Baptista 98
marriage 121

martyrology 99
media 24, 28, 71, 92, 108, 119, 138
mediterranean cultures 1, 3
Melchizedek 65, 75
memory 3, 36–39, 44, 50, 63, 105, 130, 133
Mercury 54–55
Mesopotamia 111
Minerva 54
Minucius Felix 26
Missale Romanum 97
mobility 32, 60
modernization 100
monumentalization 53, 132
Muhammad 35
mundus 103
munera 128
municipia 84
museum 40
Mycenae 110
mythical narratives 4, 7, 37–38, 52, 119
mythological framework 16, 119

necropolis 126
nefas 83
Neptunalia 88
Nero 104
Nerva 73
New Testament 5, 63–64, 78
New Year festivals 89–90
nones (in the calendar) 83, 90, 106, 113–114
Numa 15, 41, 43, 50
Numeri 65
nundinae 82, 90–91, 106–107, 112–115

October equus 12
oikumene 16
omen 104, 110
orientation 2, 36–38, 105–107, 112–113, 116–117
Orphic circles 15, 131
ossa legere 127

panarium 134
pantheon 17, 32
parapegmata 94
pater familias 121
pater patriae 74
pax deorum 144[20]
Penates 58, 128
Pentateuch 75
persecution 66
Petronius 132
Philo 65
philosophy 17, 48

physical preservation 122
piety 34, 58, 72
planetary gods 115
Plato 130
Plautus 10
Pliny the Elder 45–46, 66
Pliny the Younger 73–74, 75–76
Plutarch 57–58, 69
poetry 48
Polemius Silvius 107
polytheism 1, 4, 17, 32, 42, 52, 61
Pompeii 61–62
pontifex maximus 5, 18–19, 40, 64, 68–70, 72–73
pontiffs 17
popular culture 138
porca praesentanea 126, 128
Postumius Albinus, L. 40
practical coherence 120
presence 60–62, 71, 123
prestige 11, 18
Priapus 54
priests 5, 17, 64 (*see also* Arval Brethren; augurs; pontiffs; *Septemviri Epulones*; Sodales; *Vestals*)
privatization of religion 2
procession 11–12
'to Cybele' 61
prodigy 11
propaganda 92
property 19–20, 53
prophets 10
proskynesis 58
prosopography 17
protective deities 54
Punic Wars 16
purity 69, 128
Puteoli 121
pyramid 130–131
pyre 126–127, 129

Quellenforschung 65
Quindecemviri sacris faciundis 67, 72
Quinquatrus 106
Qumran 91
Qur'an 35, 65

ratio 27
reception 119
recognition 133–134
reflection 3–5, 8, 52
Reformation (Protestant) 34, 62
religio 7–8, 25–26, 28, 49
religion (religious) 2, 37, 117
    ancient and modern 137

INDEX

'civic' 14, 25
contextualization 5, 7
diversity 16
exchange 7, 24
formation 3, 34
historicization 3-4, 43
history 2, 22, 35
image and self-image 3
individuality 3
individualization 2, 3
as institution 49
internet 101
'invisible' 14
'lived' 118, 139
locative 25, 29, 48
pluralism 6, 8
'polis' 14, 25
practices 3, 5, 8, 11, 13-14, 63, 72
privatization 2, 14
system 4, 8, 14
tradition 3, 5, 9, 17, 47
transformation 3
'world' 23
'religionization' or 'religionification' 28, 33
representation 4-5, 52, 60-62, 97-98, 118-119, 122
ricinium 124
ritual 4, 5, 8, 11-12, 14-15, 20, 37, 52, 138
grief 124-129
participation 15
Robigalia 46
Roman citizenship 47
Roman Empire 3, 7, 24, 100
Roman Republic 35
Rome 4, 15-17, 25-26, 46, 66, 109, 111-112
Romulus 111
Rottweil 116

sacra et auspicia 7-8
sacralization 53
sacrifice 2, 63, 126-128
sanctuary 57-58
sarcophagi 122, 129, 135
Saturnalia 15, 88-90
scripture 35
secta 26, 28
secularization 2, 136
Seneca 57, 122, 131
Septimontium 88-89
Septimviri Epulones 67
Septizodium 116
Septuagint 63, 65, 74
Shinto 50
Sibylline books 20, 67
silicernium 128

social capital 6, 120, 122, 125, 136
presence 122-123, 133-135
Sodales Flaviales 70, 71
sollemnes 102
Somnium Scipionis 134
Spagnoli, Giovanni Battista 98
spirituality 2
Stalin 99
statue 4, 42, 53, 58-61, 123, 132-133
Suetonius 68-70, 74, 85, 93
superstition 57-58
supplications 12

Taormina 86
Tarquinius, Sextus (Roman king) 50
Tatius, Titus 43-44
temple 4, 20, 37, 42, 53, 60, 97
aedes Vestae 103
destruction of the temple (Jerusalem) 66
of Hercules 40-41, 44, 46
Tenakh 67, 75
Terminalia 112
Tertullian 47, 89
testamentum 123, 132
theatre 13, 48
theology 17
thermae of Trajan 116
thiasoi (Dionysian) 131
Thukydides 36, 38
time 6
Titus 66-68, 71-72, 76
toga praetexta 68
tomb *see* grave monuments
tomb of Eurysaces 32, 132-133
tradition 14, 16-17, 35, 64
Trajan 73-75
transcendent 1
Trauerwut 124
Treves 116
Trimalchio 132
tripudium 10
triumph 11, 15, 48
Trojan War 16
tunica 124-125

uncertainty 101, 108-109
universality 46, 49, 80
unlucky collision of days 112-113, 115
unlucky days 103, 107, 110, 112
urn 121, 127
Usard of Saint-Germain-des-Près 99
ustrinum 120, 127-128

Valerius Flaccus, C. 69

Varro, Marcus Terentius 4, 17, 43-44, 46-48, 50-51, 53, 55, 93, 124-126, 131, 149[19]
vates 10
Vatican Council, Second 78, 97
Velleius 61
Vespasianus 66-67, 71
Vestales (Vestal Virgins) 17-18, 69
Virgil 16, 128, 131
vision 4
vitulatio 106
Volkanalia 88
votives 13, 33, 101

vows 13
Vulso, Manlius 40

week 81, 90, 99-100
  nundinal 106
  planetary 83, 91, 113, 115
  Roman 83
witchcraft 122
world order 1

xoana 54

zodiac 116

INDEX OF MODERN RESEARCHERS

Aberson, Michel 145[38]
Abramenko, Andrik 154[23]
Ageron, Charles-Robert 149[6]
Aitken, Ellen Bradshaw 153[8]
Alföldy, Géza 168[51]
Ammermann, Nancy Tatom 119, 165[5]
Ando, Clifford 27, 146[18], 146[22], 151[27]
Annus, A. 162[49]
Arnason, Johann P. 143[3], 146[5], 146[6], 146[8], 146[9], 146[10]
Athanassiadi, Polymnia 148[38]
Attridge, Harold W. 153[3], 153[9], 153[10]

Baecker, Dirk 162[42]
Bakker, Jan T. 144[27]
Balch, David L. 150[8]
Banton, M. 152[29]
Barchiesi, Alessandro 146[15]
Barton, Tamsyn 144[12]
Bassani, Maddalena 144[27]
Baumann, Richard A. 160[23]
Beard, Mary 143[7], 151[18], 154[17]
Bel, Valérie 167[43]
Belayche, Nicole 148[36]
Belfiore, Valentina 156[5]
Bellah, Robert N. 147[26]
Bendlin, Andreas 147[30], 148[36]
Berlin, Brent 161[35]
Bernstein, Frank 144[17]
Bispham, Edward 150[4]
Bochinger, Christoph 158[39]
Bodel, John 159[1], 167[40]
Borg, Barbara 168[51]
Bouché-Leclercq, Auguste 162[44]
Bowersock, G.W. 143[2]
Bowes, Kim 147[33]
Bowring, Richard John 150[29]
Boyle, A.J. 154[38]

Braune, Sarah 168[46]
Bremer, J.M. 165[9]
Bremmer, Jan N. 141, 165[9]
Brownlee, John S. 150[29]
Bruce, Freerick Fyvie 155[55]
Buccellato, Anna 167[41]

Campion, Nicholas 162[41], 163[54]
Cancik, Hubert 145[39], 147[30], 149[12], 151[22], 155[45]
Candillo, Daniela 155[41]
Cannadine, David 165[9]
Cardauns, Burkhart 150[19], 150[3]
Catalano, Paola 167[41]
Certeau, Michael de 119, 164[2]
Chadwick, John 163[50]
Clark, Anna J. 151[13], 151[14]
Clarke, John R. 54-55, 150[8], 151[10], 151[11]
Clauss, Manfred 154[16], 155[41]
Coleman, Kathleen M. 155[45]
Coyne, George V. 158[37]
Cramer, Fredrick H. 162[44]
Crang, Mike 151[15]
Crawford, Michael 157[24]
Curry, Patrick 162[41]

D'Ambra, Eve 165[3]
Davies, Glenys 166[18], 166[22]
Davies, Jason P. 149[11]
Dawson, Lorne L. 143[5]
Degrassi, Attilio 156[1], 160[8]
DeSilva, David A. 156[59], 156[60]
Dominik, J.W. 154[38]
Donald, Merlin 23
Donohue, Alice A. 152[35]
Douglas, J. Davies 165[9]
Dunand, F.O. 141
Duval, Paul-Marie 163[67]

INDEX

Dyck, Andrew R. 167[31], 167[40], 168[56]
Eber, Paul 158[46]
Edmonds, Radcliffe G. 145[29]
Edwards, Catharine 165[9]
Eidinow, Esther 144[25]
Eisenstadt, Shmuel N. 23, 143[3], 146[3], 146[5], 146[7]
Elias, Norbert 162[46]
Ellingworth, Paul 156[59], 156[60]
Ellrod, Jacob 158[38]
Engler, Steven 142
Eriksson, Sven 162[48], 164[71] 164[72], 164[73]
Ernout, Alfred 161[32]
Erskine, Andrew 145[32]
Estienne, Sylvie 151[26]
Ewald, Björn 168[52]

Feeney, Denis 149[15]
Fejfer, Jane 151[14], 151[17]
Feldmann, Klaus 165[8]
Ferri, Giorgio 145[41]
Fine, Steven 165[9], 168[64]
Fink, R.O. 157[13]
Fishwick, Duncan 155[40]
Flint, V. 148[39]
Flower, Harriet I. 143[9]
Forsén, Björn 144[23]
Fredrick, David 154[38]
Frey, J. 151[27], 158[39]
Fuchs-Heinritz, Werner 165[8]
Fugmann, Joachim 168[61], 168[63]

Gadamer, Hans-Georg 60
Gager, John G. 162[43]
Gallone, Anna 165[9]
Garland, Robert S. 165[9]
Gebauer, J. 152[33]
Geertz, Clifford 152[29]
Gelardini, G. 153[8], 155[58]
Georgoudi, Stella 162[40]
González, Julián 157[24]
Goodman, M. D. 164[75]
Gordon, Richard L. 143[6], 144[23], 148[39], 151[25], 152[30], 154[17]
Graf, Fritz 166[21], 168[58]
Grafton, Anthony T. 160[19]
Graham, Emma-Jayne 166[16]
Gräßer, Erich 155[51]
Graulich, Michel 162[47]
Gray, Patrick 155[57], 156[62]
Grethlein, Jonas 149[4]
Greyerz, Kaspar von 148[40]
Grossi, Maria Christina 167[36]
Grotefend, Hermann 158[35]

Gsell, Stéphane 154[32]
Gustaffson, Gabriella 145[41]
Guthrie, W.K. 145[29]

Haeperen, Françoise van 154[20], 154[16]
Hagner, Donald A. 155[57]
Hahn, Alois 147[27]
Halbwachs, Maurice 149[6]
Halman, Loek 147[28]
Hardie, Philip 154[33]
Harries, Byron 160[13]
Harris, William V. 147[35]
Harskamp, A. van 147[25], 147[28]
Hennig, John 159[49]
Herz, Peter 157[30]
Hesberg, Henner von 151[23], 151[24], 152[33], 169[66]
Heyberger, Bernard 152[36]
Hinard, Francois 166[14]
Hodges, Richard 143[1]
Hoesen, Henry B. van 163[55]
Hoey, A. 157[13]
Holladay, A. J. 164[75]
Holmes, Brooke 147[35]
Hölscher, Lucian 148[42]
Hopkins, Keith 166[12]
Hoskin, Michael A. 158[37]
Hout, Th. P. 165[9]
Hubbeling, Hubertus G. 152[31]
Hughes, Philip Edgcumbe 155[51]
Huizinga, Johan 163[56]
Humphreys, S. C. 165[9]
Hurst, Lincoln Douglas 153[7]

Isaacs, Marie E. 156[62]
Izzet, Vedia 150[4]

Janowitz, Naomi 148[38]
Jaspers, Karl 23, 146[2]
Joas, Hans 146[3]
Johanson, Christopher 166[12]
Johnston, Sarah Iles 161[40], 168[58]
Jones, Brian W. 154[32], 154[33], 154[37]
Jong, I. de 163[55]
Jounel, Pierre 159[49]

Kajava, Mika 159[1]
Kantiréa, Maria 155[40]
Käsemann, Ernst 156[61]
Kastenmeier, Pia 150[9]
Kaufmann, Thomas 158[39]
Kay, Paul 161[35]
Kierdorf, Wilhelm 167[34]
Kindt, Julia 144[25]
Kippenberg, Hans G. 142, 143[5]
Klein, Kerwin Lee 149[9]

Knoblauch, Hubert 159[1]
Koch-Piettre, Renée 162[40]
Koester, Craig R. 153[3], 153[7], 155[50], 155[52], 155[54]
Kolb, Anne 168[61], 168[63]
Krech, Volkhart 159[1]
Kühne, Heinrich 158[45]

Labat, René 162[47]
Laffi, Umberto 157[9]
Langdon, Stephen 163[51]
Leberl, Jens 153[14], 153[15]
Lehoux, Daryn 164[72]
Leitz, Christian 162[47], 163[51]
Levene, David S. 155[46], 155[47], 155[48]
Lianeri, Alexandra 149[4]
Lieburg, Fred van 148[40]
Lieu, Judith 146[16]
Lincoln, Andrew 153[5]
Linderski, Jerzy 143[10]
Loader, William R.G. 153[6]
Lubtchansky, Natacha 151[26]
Luckmann, Thomas 144[24]

Maass, Ernst 164[70]
MacBain, Bruce 145[42]
MacCoull, Leslie S.B. 164[74]
Maier, Harry O. 154[36]
Malik, Jamal 159[1]
Marchand, Suzanne L. 143[4]
Martin, Dale B. 151[19]
Martin-Kilcher, Stefanie 167[44], 168[45]
Masel, Katharina 158[36]
Mason, Eric Farrel 153[5]
McGuire, Meredith B. 118–120, 147[34], 164[1]
Meadows, Andrew 169[66]
Meillet, Antoine 161[32]
Mellace, Valeria Silvia 167[36]
Merlin, Donald 146[4]
Meuli, Karl 124, 167[27]
Michels, Agnes Kirsopp 163[62]
Mielsch, Harald 122, 166[18]
Mikalson, Jon D. 163[50]
Miles, Suzanna W. 162[47]
Mitchell, W.J. Thomas 151[20]
Molthagen, Joachim 153[11]
Morley, Neville 143[4]
Morris, Ian 165[9]
Mossman, J. 147[35]
Muchembled, Robert 148[40]
Mulsow, Martin 148[41]
Musco, Stefano 167[41]
Musschenga, Albert W. 147[25], 147[28]
Mylonopoulos, Joannis 150[6]

Naef, Silvia 152[36]

Naiden, Fred S. 144[21]
Nauta, Ruurd R. 153[15], 155[49]
Neiske, Franz 168[64]
Neugebauer, Otto 163[55]
Neuwirth, Angelika 149[2]
Newby, Zahra 166[19]
Nielsen, Marjatta 166[20]
Noll, Mark A. 148[42]
Nora, Pierre 149[6]
North, John A. 141, 143[7], 146[16], 147[29], 151[18], 154[17]

Orlin, Eric M. 145[38]
Ornan, Tallay 150[5]
Osiander, Lucas 158[40]
Osten, Dorothee Elm von der 148[36]
Östenberg, Ida 144[18]
Ouwerkerk, Coenraad A.J. van 152[29]

Pailler, Jean-Marie 144[28]
Palazzo, Eric 159[48], 159[48]
Panciera, Silvio 168[51]
Parker, Robert 141, 143[6], 154[27]
Peters, R. 165[9]
Petersen, Lauren Hackworth 168[60], 168[62], 169[65], 169[70]
Petsalis-Diomidis, Alexia 147[35]
Picuti, Maria Romana 167[42]
Plas, D. van der 152[29], 152[34]
Popkin, Richard Henry 148[41]
Porter, Anne 165[4]
Pouzadoux, Claude 151[26]
Price, Simon 143[7]
Pritchett, W. Kendrick 160[5]

Radke, Gerhard 161[35], 161[36]
Rajak, Tessa 146[16]
Rawson, Beryl 166[13]
Rebenich, Stefan 168[59]
Rebillard, Eric 165[6]
Reeves, M. Barbara 157[18]
Rehm, Albert 164[72]
Reynolds, Gabriel Said 149[2]
Richardson, David M. 145[36], 156[2]
Ricoeur, Paul 37
Rife, Joseph L. 165[9]
Rissi, Matthias 155[53]
Rochberg, Francesca 162[49]
Rohls, J. 151–152[27]
Rolfe, J.C. 154[24]
Rosenberger, Veit 144[15], 145[42]
Rosenstein, Nathan 160[20]
Ruck, Brigitte 157[11]
Rüpke, Jörg 141, 143[6], 144[14], 144[17], 144[18], 144[19], 144[22], 144[23], 145[33], 145[34], 145[35],

INDEX

145[36], 145[40], 146[15], 147[30], 147[31], 148[36], 149[3], 149[7], 149[8], 149[10], 149[15], 149[16], 149[17], 149[18], 150[24], 150[27]150[28], 151[22], 151[25], 152[1], 154[18], 154[19], 154[22], 154[25], 156[63], 156[64], 156[1], 156[2], 156[3], 156[4], 157[10], 157[11], 157[14], 157[25], 157[26], 157[27], 157[32], 158[33], 159[47], 159[1], 161[24], 161[40], 163[66], 165[7], 166[14], 167[34], 167[43], 169[67], 169[71]
Rüpke, Ulrike 149[8]
Rüsen, Jörn 149[5]

Salzman, Michèle Renée 157[31], 164[68]
Samellas, Antigone 165[9]
Saxer, Victor 157[22]
Scheer, Tanja S. 145[32], 152[35]
Scheid, John 167[36], 167[39], 167[41], 167[43], 167[44], 168[49]
Scheidel, Walter 146[15]
Schilling, Heinz 148[40]
Schipper, Kristofer 163[53]
Schmid, Alfred 162[44]
Schmidt, Francis 150[1], 162[40], 163[55]
Scholer, John M. 153[4]
Schörner, Günther 144[23]
Schreiber, Georg 164[68]
Schrumpf, Stefan 166[11], 167[28], 167[29]
Segal, Alan F. 165[9]
Simon, Udou 159[1]
Smith, Christopher J. 150[4]
Smith, Jonathan Z. 28, 143[8], 147[24]
Snyder, Walter F. 157[13], 164[71]
Sorokin, Pitrim Alexandrowitsch 164[68]
Stausberg, Michael 142
Stavrianopoulou, Eftychia 159[1]
Steiner, Deborah Tarn 152[30]
Stepper, Ruth 154[20], 154[29]
Stern, Henri 157[31]
Stern, Sascha 157[10]
Steuernagel, Dirk 151[22]
Stewart, Peter C.N. 151[17], 152[32], 152[33], 169[68]
Stoll, Oliver 157[18]
Strobel, August 163[54]
Stroumsa, Guy G. 152[1], 153[2]
Struck, Peter T. 161[40]
Stuckrad, Kocku von 144[12], 148[37], 156[2]
Sührig, Hartmut 159[50]
Swerdlow, Noel M. 160[19]

Tannenbaum, Nicola 163[52]
Tavenner, Eugene 161[34]
Taylor, Charles 32, 143[8], 147[32]
Taylor, Mark C. 147[24], 159[2]
Tellegen, Jan Willem 166[23]
Thóth, István György 148[40]
Trümpy, Hans 158[44]
Tsouna, Voula 166[24]
Tyrell, Hartmann 159[1]

Unger, Georg Friedrich 163[65]
Urner, Christiana 153[12], 153[13]

Vanhoye, Albert 156[62]
Ventris, Michael 163[49]
Versnel, Hendrik S. 152[34], 166[26]
Veyne, Paul 147[23]
Vinzent, Markus 149[1]
Vries, Hent de 141

Wackernagel, Jacob 161[32], 161[33]
Waldner, Katharina 148[36]
Wallraff, Martin 151[27]
Wang, Hsiu-huei 163[53]
Wayman, Alex 162[41]
Whaley, Joachim 165[9]
Whitehouse, David 143[1]
Whittaker, Gordon 162[47], 163[53], 163[54]
Wiegandt, K. 146[3]
Williams, Jonathan 169[66]
Wiseman, Timothy P. 144[13], 145[31]
Wistrand, Erik 164[71]
Witschel, Christian 168[51]
Witteyer, Marion 168[44]
Wittrock, Björn 23–24, 143[3], 146[5], 146[6], 146[8], 146[9], 146[10]
Wobbe, Theresa 159[1]
Woolf, Greg 24, 146[11]
Worp, K.A. 163[55]
Woudhuizen, Fred 156[5]

Yonge, C.D. 151[21]

Zanker, Paul 168[52]
Zerubavel, Eviatar 159[51], 164[68]
Zimmermann, R. 152[27]
Ziolkowski, Adam 144[16]
Zivie-Coche, C. 141

INDEX LOCORUM

Afranius, *Comidiae (com.)* 163: 161[37]
Ammianus Marcellinus 28.4.24: 164[68]
Année Epigraphique 2001.182: 154[34]
Aristides, Aelius, *Sacred Discourses (Log.)* 33
Asclepius 24: 146[18]
Athenaeus, *Deipnosophistes* 1.20c-d: 146[17]
Augustine, *The City of God (civ.)* 6.4, p.
   251.13–16: 150[23]
 -6.9: 167[32]
 -6.10: 151[18]
 -7.17, p. 295.22: 150[25]
Ausonius, *Opuscula* 16.12.12 Prete.: 143[11]

Caesar, *Commentaries on the Gallic War
  (Gall.)* 6.17.1: 150[26]
Cassius Dio 40.47.1: 163[60]
 -43.45: 152[28]
 -48.33.4: 163[64]
 -60.24,7: 163[58]
 -67.3.3f.: 154[31]
Cato, *On agriculture (agr.)*: 14
 -143: 157[28]
Censorinus, *De die natali* 2.1. 161[§&]
 -17.8: 150[22]
Cicero, *On Divination (div.)*: 109
 -1.28: 143[11]
 -*On his house (dom.)* 51: 150[2]
 -108–112: 151[21]
 -*On the laws (leg.)*:130
 -2.22: 168[56]
 -2.55: 168[48]
 -2.57: 167[38]
 -2.58: 120
 -2.59: 167[30]
 -2.60: 127, 167[40]
 -*On the Nature of the Gods (nat.)*: 50, 55,
   61
 -1.6–84: 151[12]
 -1.28: 162[45]
 -1.81: 151[12]
 -1.83: 151[11]
 -1.84: 151[16]
 -2.8: 146[13]
 -3.5: 7
 -3.39: 146[13]
 -3.42: 146[13]
 -3.48: 146[13]
 -3.54–59: 146[13]
 -*On the Republic*: 131
 -6.10: 169[69]
 -*Philippica (Phil.)* 14.22: 144[21]
 -*Pro Flacco (Flacc.)* 69: 146[14]
1 Clemens (1 Clem): 76
 -13.24: 65

 -36.1: 76
 -36.2–6: 65
 -37: 76
 -61.3: 76
*Coins of the Roman Empire in the British
  Museum (CREBM)* 2,300ff. 7A ff.:
  154[30]
 -2.419–438: 154[36]
 -*1 Collossans (1 Coll)* 1.18: 155[56]
Corpus inscriptionum latinarum (CIL) 1, p.
  594: 157[23]
 -3.12218: 154[19]
 -4.5202: 164[69]
 -4.6779: 164[69]
 -6.826: 154[34]
 -6.17992: 168[59]
 -6.30837a-c: 154[34]
 -6.31294: 154[18]
 -6.40453: 154[18]
 -9.4955: 154[19]
 -10.1605: 164[71]

Ennius, *Euhemerus*: 42–43
 -*Annales (ann.)*: 42–43
Exodus (Ex) 28: 75

Festus 144.14–146.2 L: 160[8]
 -242.11–18 L: 167[39]
 -296.12–14 L: 160[10]
 -296.37–298.4 L: 167[37]
 -304.33–306.8 L: 161[31]
 -316.18–20 L: 143[11]
 -348.22–30 L: 160[4]
Firmicus Maternus, *De errore profanarum
  religionum (err.)* 7: 146[12]

Gaius, *The Institutes (inst.)* 2.3–9: 19
Gellius, *Attic Nights* 2.24.14: 157[29]
 -4.6: 167[39]
 -4.6.10: 160[23]
 -4.9.5–6: 159[3,] 159[4]
 -5.17.1–2: 160[21]
 -5.17.2: 160[12]
 -5.17.3–5: 161[30]
 -5.17.5: 160[19]
 -6.1.6: 151[25]

Hebrews (Hebr): 5, 63–64–65, 67, 74–78
 -1.4: 74
 -1.6: 76
 -2.11–18: 76
 -2.3–4: 76
 -4.14: 74
 -4.15: 76

180

INDEX

-5.4–5: 74
-7.11–19: 75
-7.22: 75
-8.1: 77
-8.2: 75
-10.20: 75
Horatius, *Carmina (Carm.)* 4.14.34–18: 160[16]
-*Epistulae (epist.)* 1.7.6–7: 166[15]

Inscriptiones Graecae (IG) 14.429: 157[12]
Inscriptiones Italiae (Inscr. It.) 13.2: 156[1]
   -13.2.15: 160[12]
   -13.2.56–59: 156[2]
   -13.2.52–53: 157[15]
   -13.2.189: 163[57]
   -13.2.191: 160[16]
   -13.2.208: 160[14]
   -13.2.215: 161[28]
   -13.2.235: 157[20]
   -13.2.249: 161[27]
   -13.2.279: 157[19]
   -13.2.283: 157[17]
   -13.2.301: 164[71]
   -13.2.305: 164[69], 164[70]
   -13.2.307: 164[71]
   -13.2.309: 164[71]
   -13.2.313: 164[71]
Inscriptiones Latinae liberae rei publicae 508: 156[7]
   -589: 156[6]
Inscriptiones latinae selectee (ILS) 258: 154[18]
   -267: 154[19]
   -4914: 154[34]
   -6087: 157[23]
Isidorus, *De natura rerum (nat.)* 1.4: 161[38]

Josephus, *Bellum Judaicum* 2.8.1: 146[20]
Juvenal 6.569–576: 164[68]

Lactantius, *De mortibus persecutorum (mort. pers.)* 34: 146[21]
Livy 2.27.5: 145[30]
   -4.2.5: 143[11]
   -5.50.4: 145[30]
   -6.1.1–2: 160[12]
   -6.1.11f.: 160[14], 160[21]
   -9.38.15–16: 160[17]
   -10.47.6–7: 144[26]
   -26.19.5: 151[25]
   -27.8.4–10: 154[25]
   -31.8–9: 144[20]
   -37.50: 149[13]
   -38.1–11: 149[13]
   -39.5.14 ff.: 149[14]
   -39.13: 8
   -40.19.3: 166[15]

   -41.17.3: 144[21]
Lucan 7.409: 160[12]
Lydus, *De mensibus (mens.)* 4.65: 161[27]
   -4.168: 161[27]

Macrobius, *Saturnalia (Sat.)* 1.13.16–19: 163[59]
   -1.15.21: 160[9]
   -1.16.15–18: 160[5]
   -1.16.18: 160[8]
   -1.16.21: 160[7], 161[38]
   -1.16.21–24: 160[12]
   -1.16.23: 160[14]
   -1.16.24: 160[6]
   -1.16.24–25: 160[23]
   -1.16.26: 161[30]
   -1.16.27: 159[3]
   -1.16.28: 160[6]
Martial 4.66.3: 157[29]
   -9.25.5: 161[36]
Minucius Felix, *Octavius* 6.1: 146[17]
   -20.6: , 146[19]

Notizie degli Scavi (NS) 1879.44: 164[69]
   -1899.64: 154[19]
   -1901.330: 164[69]

Ovid, *Amores* 3.8.23: 154[26]
   -*Fasti (fast.)*: 93–94, 98
   -1.295: 158[34]
   -2.193–6: 160[13]
   -3.393–8: 160[11]
   -4.731–4: 154[28]
   -5.419–446: 168[55]
   -5.485–490: 160[8]
   -6.225–234: 154[28], 160[11]
   -6.563–8: 160[15]
   -6.763–8: 160[19]
   -*Love's Remedy (rem.)* 219f.: 160[12]
   -*Metamorphoses (met.)* 15.622–744: 144[26]
   -*Tristia* 2.549f.: 158[33]

Paulus ex Festo 68.9–13 Lindsay: 168[48]
   -253.12–14 L: 160[5]
   -293,8–9 L: 154[26]
Petronius 30.4: 161[24]
   -*Satyricon* 71.5–12: 168[60]
Plautus, *Miles gloriosus (Mil.)*: 10
   -*Rudens (Rud.)*: 10
Pliny the Elder, *Natural History (NH)*: 161[34]
   -8.206: 154[26]
   -18.285: 150[21]
   -34.15f.: 152[237]
   -36.185: 151[23]
   -35.160: 168[57]

Pliny the Younger, *Panegyric (paneg.)*: 73
 -39–40: 75
 -52.1: 155[44]
 -52.2: 152[28]
 -64.2: 155[47]
 -83.5: 73
 -94: 73
Plutarch, *Caesar (Caes.)* 56: 160[16]
 -*Camillus (Cam.)* 19.1: 160[14]
 -*Moralia (mor.)* 269e: 161[29]
 -*On superstition (superst.)*: 57
 -3c-d: 58
 -4a: 58
 -6b: 58
 -7d: 58
 -9b: 58
 -11: 58
 -10a-12: 58
 -13: 58
 -14: 58
 -*Publicola (Publ.)* 23: 165[10]
 -*Roman Questions (q. R.)*: 69
 -25: 160[21], 161[25], 161[29]
Propertius, *Elegies* 2.11.4: 161[37]
 -4.7: 127

Roman imperial coinage (RIC) 2, Domitian 11–23: 154[30]
Romans 8.29: 155[56]

Seneca, *Consolations*: 122, 131
 -*De beneficiis (benef.)* 6.38.4: 166[15]
 -*Dialogi (dial.)* 4.19.1: 166[17]
 -7.25.3: 161[37]
 -*On superstition (superst.)*: 57
 -fr. 36 Haase = fr. 69 Vottero: 151[18]
Servius, *In Aeneidem (Aen.)* 12.142–3: 167[35]
 -12.603: 166[25]
Servius auctus, *In Aeneidem* 1.505: 150[3]
Shepherd of Hermas (Herm.): 134
Statius, *Silvae (silv.)*: 69
 -1.1.62: 155[43]
 -1.1.74: 155[44], 155[42]
 -5.1.189–191: 155[44]
 -5.138: 155[42]
Suetonius, *Augustus (Aug.)* 59: 157[8]
 -92.2: 157[27], 161[39], 163[63]
 -*Domitianus (Domit.)* 1.2: 155[39]
 -4.4: 154[35]
 -5: 154[37]
 -8.3–4: 154[31]
 -9.1: 155[39]
 -12.2: 75
 -13.2: 155[43]
 -*Iulius (Iul.)* 12.2: 168[47]
 -*Titus* 9.1: 154[24]

Tacitus, *Annals (ann.)* 3.1–5: 166[26]
 -3.2.2: 167[41]
 -15.41.2: 160[18]
Tertullian, *Ad nationes (nat.)* 1.13: 163[67]
 -*On idolatry (idol.)* 10: 163[67]
 -10.3: 157[21]

Ulpian, *Digestae (dig.)* 11.7.1: 168[50]
 -11.7.2: 168[53]
 -11.7.6.1: 168[53]
 -11.8.4: 168[54]

Valerius Maximus 6.9.3: 154[25]
Varro, *De re rustica (rust.)* 1.1.6: 150[21]
 -2.1.20: 154[26]
 -*de vita populi Romani (vit. pop. Rom.)*: 124
 -fr. 105ff. Riposati: 167[29]
 -fr. 109 Riposati: 167[35]
 -fr. 111 Riposati: 167[33], 167[41]
 -*Divine Antiquities (ant. rer. div.)*: 4, 17, 43, 46, 50, 55
 -fr. 3: 47
 -fr. 9: 48
 -fr. 11: 48
 -fr. 12: 44, 47, 93
 -fr. 13–15: 47
 -fr. 16: 47
 -fr. 17: 47
 -fr. 18: 45, 48, 150[3]
 -fr. 19: 47
 -fr. 22: 57
 -fr. 31: 48
 -fr. 32: 47
 -fr. 33: 47
 -fr. 35–39: 43
 -fr. 38: 150[3], 150[7]
 -fr. 42: 45
 -fr. 43–44: 45
 -fr.45: 45
 -fr. 46a: 45
 -fr. 49–50: 48
 -fr. 192: 55
 -fr. 200: 47
 -fr. 214–221: 44
 -fr. 225: 55–56
 -fr. 228: 55, 150[25]
 -fr. 262: 47
 -fr. 271: 47
 -*On Latin Language (ling.)*, 5.74: 150[20]
 -6.14: 161[31]
 -6.29: 160[22]
Virgil, *Aeneid (Aen.)*: 131
 -3.64: 168[48]
 -6.429: 161[37]
 -*Georgics (georg.)*: 161[34]